MW00413405

EDUCATION, POLITICS, AND PUBLIC LIFE

Series Editors:
Henry A. Giroux, McMaster University
Susan Searls Giroux, McMaster University

Within the last three decades, education as a political, moral, and ideological practice has become central to rethinking not only the role of public and higher education, but also the emergence of pedagogical sites outside of the schools—which include but are not limited to the Internet, television, film, magazines, and the media of print culture. Education as both a form of schooling and public pedagogy reaches into every aspect of political, economic, and social life. What is particularly important in this highly interdisciplinary and politically nuanced view of education are a number of issues that now connect learning to social change, the operations of democratic public life, and the formation of critically engaged individual and social agents. At the center of this series will be questions regarding what young people, adults, academics, artists, and cultural workers need to know to be able to live in an inclusive and just democracy and what it would mean to develop institutional capacities to reintroduce politics and public commitment into everyday life. Books in this series aim to play a vital role in rethinking the entire project of the related themes of politics, democratic struggles, and critical education within the global public sphere.

SERIES EDITORS

HENRY A. GIROUX holds the Global TV Network Chair in English and Cultural Studies at McMaster University in Canada. He is on the editorial and advisory boards of numerous national and international scholarly journals. Professor Giroux was selected as a Kappa Delta Pi Laureate in 1998 and was the recipient of a Getty Research Institute Visiting Scholar Award in 1999. He was the recipient of the Hooker Distinguished Professor Award for 2001. He received an Honorary Doctorate of Letters from Memorial University of Newfoundland in 2005. His most recent books include *Take Back Higher Education* (co-authored with Susan Searls Giroux, 2006); *America on the Edge* (2006); *Beyond the Spectacle of Terrorism* (2006), *Stormy Weather: Katrina and the Politics of Disposability* (2006), *The University in Chains: Confronting the Military-Industrial-Academic Complex* (2007), and *Against the Terror of Neoliberalism: Politics Beyond the Age of Greed* (2008).

SUSAN SEARLS GIROUX is Associate Professor of English and Cultural Studies at McMaster University. Her most recent books include *The Theory Toolbox* (co-authored with Jeff Nealon, 2004) and *Take Back Higher Education* (co-authored with Henry A. Giroux, 2006). Professor Giroux is also the Managing Editor of *The Review of Education, Pedagogy, and Cultural Studies*.

Critical Pedagogy in Uncertain Times: Hope and Possibilities
Edited by Sheila L. Macrine

The Gift of Education: Public Education and Venture Philanthropy
Kenneth J. Saltman

*Feminist Theory in Pursuit of the Public: Women and
the "Re-Privatization" of Labor*
Robin Truth Goodman

*Hollywood's Exploited: Public Pedagogy, Corporate Movies, and
Cultural Crisis*
Edited by Benjamin Frymer, Tony Kashani, Anthony J. Nocella, II, and
Rich Van Heertum; with a Foreword by Lawrence Grossberg

*Education out of Bounds: Reimagining Cultural Studies for
a Posthuman Age*
Tyson E. Lewis and Richard Kahn

Academic Freedom in the Post-9/11 Era
Edited by Edward J. Carvalho and David B. Downing

*Rituals and Student Identity in Education: Ritual Critique for
a New Pedagogy*
Richard A. Quantz with Terry O'Connor and
Peter Magolda (forthcoming)

Educating Youth for a World beyond Violence
H. Svi Shapiro (forthcoming)

America According to Colbert: Satire as Public Pedagogy post-9/11
Sophia A. McClennen (forthcoming)

Citizen Youth: Culture, Activism, and Agency in a Neoliberal Era
Jacqueline Joan Kennelly (forthcoming)

HOLLYWOOD'S EXPLOITED

PUBLIC PEDAGOGY, CORPORATE MOVIES, AND CULTURAL CRISIS

Edited by
Benjamin Frymer, Tony Kashani,
Anthony J. Nocella II, and
Rich Van Heertum

Foreword by
Lawrence Grossberg

HOLLYWOOD'S EXPLOITED
Copyright © Benjamin Frymer, Tony Kashani, Anthony J. Nocella II, and
Rich Van Heertum, 2010.

All rights reserved.

First published in 2010 by
PALGRAVE MACMILLAN®
in the United States—a division of St. Martin's Press LLC,
175 Fifth Avenue, New York, NY 10010.

Where this book is distributed in the UK, Europe and the rest of the world,
this is by Palgrave Macmillan, a division of Macmillan Publishers Limited,
registered in England, company number 785998, of Houndmills,
Basingstoke, Hampshire RG21 6XS.

Palgrave Macmillan is the global academic imprint of the above companies
and has companies and representatives throughout the world.

Palgrave® and Macmillan® are registered trademarks in the United States,
the United Kingdom, Europe and other countries.

ISBN: 978–0–230–62199–2

Library of Congress Cataloging-in-Publication Data

Hollywood's exploited : public pedagogy, corporate movies, and cultural
crisis / edited by Anthony J. Nocella, II ... [et al.] ; foreword by Lawrence
Grossberg.
        p. cm.—(Education, politics, and public life)
        ISBN 978–0–230–62199–2
        1. Motion pictures—Social aspects—United States. I. Nocella,
Anthony J.

PN1995.9.SS6H65 2010
302.23'4—dc22   2010018914

A catalogue record of the book is available from the British Library.

Design by Newgen Imaging Systems (P) Ltd., Chennai, India.

First edition: December 2010

10 9 8 7 6 5 4 3 2 1

Printed in the United States of America.

For those plants, animals, humans, and elements on this planet that have been exploited.

CONTENTS

Praise for Hollywood's Exploited   ix

Foreword   xiii
Lawrence Grossberg

Preface   xv
Toby Miller

Acknowledgments   xxi

Introduction   1
Benjamin Frymer, Tony Kashani,
Anthony J. Nocella II, and Richard Van Heertum

Part 1   Hollywood & Ideology

1 The Imperial System in Media Culture   13
   Carl Boggs

2 Hollywood and the Working-Class Hero:
   Diamonds in the Mean Streets of Boston   29
   Richard Van Heertum

3 Hollywood's Missionary Agenda:
   Christonormativity and Audience Baptism   45
   Shirley R. Steinberg

4 Hollywood Incarcerated and on Death Row: Bjork,
   Schwarzenegger, and the Pedagogy of Retribution   65
   Richard Van Heertum

Part 2   Hollywood Represents the Other

5 From Ms. J. to Ms. G.: Analyzing Racial Microaggressions
   in Hollywood's Urban School Genre   85
   Tara J. Yosso and David Gumaro García

6   Hollywood's Cinema of Ableism: A Disability
    Studies Perspective on the Hollywood
    Industrial Complex   105
    Tony Kashani and Anthony J. Nocella II

7   International Citizenry in the Age of the Spectacle   115
    Shoba Sharad Rajgopal

8   LGBT-Themed Hollywood Cinema
    after *Brokeback Mountain*: Renegotiating
    Hegemonic Representations of Gay Men   131
    Michael A. Raffanti

Part 3   Hollywood Ages

9   Modes of Youth Exploitation in the
    Cinema of Larry Clark   153
    Douglas Kellner

10 Sixteen and Pregnant: Media Mommy Tracking and
    Hollywood's Exploitation of Teen Pregnancy   171
    Caroline K. Kaltefleiter

11 *About Schmidt* and About the Hollywood
    Image of an Aging Actor   189
    Karen E. Riggs

Part 4   Hollywood Beyond the Human

12 Ecological Connections and Contradictions:
    Penguins, Robots, and Humans in
    Hollywood's "Nature" Films   203
    Salma Monani and Andrew Hageman

13 Hollywood and Nonhuman Animals:
    Problematic Ethics of Corporate Cinema   219
    Tony Kashani

List of Contributors   235

Index   243

PRAISE FOR HOLLYWOOD'S EXPLOITED

"*Hollywood's Exploited* is a much needed text in today's media saturated society. The editors have included a collection of top contributors to comment on the representations that emerge from Hollywood. This book is timely and is definitely appropriate for any course that needs a critical evaluation of popular media representations." —Abraham P. DeLeon, University of Texas at San Antonio

"This compendium on Hollywood film and how it constructs and manipulates the prisms through which we see Others under the bourgeois order is a superb springboard for scholars across the planet, and especially in the Global South, to forge ahead with similar studies of film and its representations in their own cultures, Bollywood, Nollywood and much much beyond. The sharp in-depth focus solely on Hollywood here invites analysts to build a comparative critical cinematology that looks at film industries, their political economy and ideologies in contexts as diverse as the old 'socialist' bloc, the PRC, Cuba, Indonesia, Palestine and elsewhere. Doors are opened to envisioning what a non-capitalist, non-exploitative and radically egalitarian people's cinema might aspire to be, while learning to read films from American Leviathan against their very grain." —Bill Templer, University of Malaya, Malaysia

"*Hollywood's Exploited* is a book that every consumer of media and entertainment needs to read. The contributors to this volume leave no area unexamined as they provide readers with the tools we need to engage with products of the entertainment industry appropriately: with a critical perspective oriented toward uncovering oppression, discrimination, and the exercise of power. Bravo!" —Matthew Walton, composer of *Sundance*, an opera about Native American political prisoner Leonard Peltier

"Hollywood has tremendous power in our society. For anyone chipping away at conventional thought or behavior, a critical analysis of Hollywood would seem essential." —Dr. Lisa Kemmerer, author of *In Search of Consistency: Ethics and Animals*

"This book not only helps us understand the hidden assumptions and the constricted world view contained in Hollywood movies, but also helps us show how those very movies can be used in the classroom for a critical understanding of society." —Dr. Ali Zaidi, SUNY Canton

"This collection of provocative essays provides ample fuel to fire heated public conversation on role of Hollywood and the media at-large in shaping the social imagination regarding the identity we assign others. The authors explore Hollywood's role in shaping the social imagination on race, class, gender, animals, disability, youth, religion and other matters is bound to renew tensions in the culture wars." —Dr. David Gabbard, East Carolina University

"An outstanding critical analysis of the Hollywood Industrial Complex. A book that shows what Hollywood is all about, exploitation and propaganda. A must read for anyone interested in understanding the value of media as a form of public pedagogy." —Nick Cooney, The Humane League of Philadelphia

"We live in a society where public worldviews are shaped significantly by visual media, and decreasingly by traditional forms of print and news media. In this context, it becomes necessary to critically examine and unpackage the hegemonic (and potentially counter-hegemonic) effects of mainstream film. This book is a first step in deconstructing the more oppressive aspects of popular visual media, while recognizing its revolutionary potentials." —Dr. William T. Armaline, Justice Studies Department, San José State University

"We challenge future educators to change the world, but rarely offer them the tools to make it happen; this book is a 'power tool' for transformative pedagogy." —Dr. Judy K. C. Bentley, Editor-in-Chief, *Social Advocacy and Systems Change*

"An outstanding book to unchain the many violent constructed images by the media of those that are oppressed and marginalized.

Too often media does not take responsibility for youth and people of color that are wrongly convicted because of their constant propagandizing of youth being 'deviant' and people of color being 'criminals.' This book uncovers the truth about corporate Hollywood." —Joshua Calkins, co-founder and director, Save the Kids (STK)

"As youth employ more forms of media to gather information, teachers must critically examine and utilize films as a vital tool for education. *Hollywood's Exploited* breaks new ground in higher education by providing space to challenge non-academic media, and arguing that film can be a useful educational tool comparable to that of the traditional 'required textbook.'" —Sarat Colling, founder and director, *Political Media Review* (PMR)

"Media powerfully shape people's perceptions of themselves and the world around them. For people of color who struggle with a legacy of oppression, it is clear that such imagery can profoundly impact how youth especially see their potential. So, *Hollywood's Exposed* openly addressing media misinformation comes at a crucial time, where mainstream media's dominant narrative of post-racialism swims against the reality people of color live daily." —Ernesto Aguilar, Pacifica Radio

"In a world in which social oppressions become embedded in the collective consciousness of global citizens, it leaves people wondering: 'How does the elite do it so well?' A short answer might say: 'Well, they have an entire complex of entertainment at their disposal in Hollywood, sold to the highest bidder!' In order to begin unraveling how we've come to accept this stifling status quo, we need critical voices analyzing media entertainment from a variety of social justice perspectives. This book is the place for exactly that. Frymer, Kashani, Nocella, and Van Heertum adeptly collect the critiques. Changing the world is up to us!" —Deric Shannon, TransformativeRadio.org

"Ever been struck by how Hollywood uncritically reproduces simplistic and hierarchical notions of difference, even when it attempts to go beyond these? Noticed the recent commoditization of your politics in recent blockbusters? *Hollywood's Exploited* helps you fight back, equipping you with the necessary tools for critical thinking and re-imagining better media." —Dr. Richard Twine, author of

Animals as Biotechnology—Ethics, Sustainability and Critical Animal Studies

"Using the tools of 'critical pedagogy' the authors engage with the hegemonic behemoth of Hollywood, alternatively symbolized as the handmaiden of the U.S. military industrial complex or as a lead culprit in the New International Division of Labor. With counter hegemonic fervor, the authors take apart the neat images of pristine nature, heroic white teachers, and paternalistic gazes and thus unearth cinematic microaggressions which reinforce Euro-American frontier narratives, 'white man's burden,' sexist, homophobic, ableist, racist, ageist voyeurism, especially in a post 9/11 world. Students of film will come away with a keen sense of media literacy and will be trained to ask critical questions about slickly packaged films. —Mechthild Nagel, Professor of Philosophy, SUNY Cortland

FOREWORD

Lawrence Grossberg

"Hollywood"—the name is as resonant as any in the increasingly multilingual vocabularies that circulate around the world and across populations. Its powers—not only economic and cultural, but also political—have haunted critics and intellectuals for at least a century. It has been appropriated, blamed, and even occasionally celebrated by arguments that range across the entire spectrum of political positions. In the academy, we have tried to teach "Hollywood" as skills, as technology, as art, as economics, as ideology. *Hollywood's Exploited* attempts to teach Hollywood as our favorite—or at least most popular—teacher. A pedagogy of the pedagogical.

Pedagogy is the beginning, maybe even the process, of political struggle and social change in a democratic society. Critical pedagogy wants to move people into places where they can "see" that the world does not have to be the way it is, that it can be something different in the future, and that what we do matters in shaping which future is actualized.

But if critical pedagogy is to move people, and society, in productive ways, it must start where people already are, where they live their lives; it must work on, in both senses, the popular. The fact is, at least in my opinion, that critical pedagogy has not been very successful, to some extent, because it has not faced its own monsters (definitely not of the Hollywood type).

It has to look under its own bed, inside its own closets, in its own mirrors, if it is to understand the mundane and everyday heroisms that are at the heart of the pedagogical. It is worth identifying some of those monsters that haunt progressive critical work. The first, vanguardism, assumes that we already know the answers and it is our job to "educate" others so that they gleefully "choose" to follow the path we lay out for them. The second, let's call it "apocalypsism," ensures that every generation has the same nightmare, in which they are finally confronting power that has—whether through qualitative or quantitative changes, and under a variety of names (commodification, real subsumption, etc.)—finally successfully colonized the entirety of the world and of people's lives. There is, paradoxically, little sense of historical specificity and even less modesty (for it demands of us an impossible heroism). The nightmare can only end if we are willing to embrace the political complexity that results from acknowledging that people are not cultural dopes but active agents who sometimes use Hollywood's messages in creative ways, that Hollywood produces complex and contradictory messages both within and across individual texts, and finally, that Hollywood's lessons are ultimately lived only in the complex web of relations that constitute people's lived reality.

The third monster involves the love/hate relationship, within critical and progressive intellectual work, between theory and politics. Theory is rarely treated modestly, as a tool that may well give one a bit more insight, a bit more purchase, in one's attempt to understand what's going on. Instead, it is too often taken as the Law, defining what we allow ourselves to see, sometimes blinding us to things that are obvious to others. So if the latest, sexiest theory tells us that representation (and even ideology) is no longer the primary form of power, then with the single sweep of a simple historical brush, theory has blinded us to what may be obvious to others. On the other hand, theory is too often ignored in practice but never in name, dissolving the line between pedagogy and political diatribe, ethical proselytizing, and moral certitude.

There are other monsters: for example, the inevitable need to present, and the unintended ease with which people can be overwhelmed by a seemingly endless list of the forms of power and the sites of oppression. Yet, the criticism of identity politics and its proliferation can end up in the demand for return to a more simple politics of capitalism and class, one that reduces the complexity of power relations, and the multiplicity of processes and positions of subordination and of the ways of living them.

All of these questions are tangled up in the efforts of contemporary critical pedagogy—and in the efforts of the editors and authors of *Hollywood's Exploited*. Here is an attempt to define a pedagogy of Hollywood, one that faces its monsters even as it seeks ways to face the many monsters of Hollywood (where not all monsters are equally bad and some may even be good). Teach on!

Preface

Why Do First-World Academics Think Cultural Imperialism Doesn't Matter When So Many Other People Disagree?

Toby Miller

In 1820, the noted essayist Sydney Smith asked: "In the four quarters of the globe, who reads an American book? Or goes to an American play? Or looks at an American picture or statue?" (1844: p. 141). Due to the imbalance of its textual trade, notably with Britain, the United States quickly became an early-modern exponent of anticultural imperialist, pro-nation-building sentiment. Herman Melville, for example, opposed the literary establishment's devotion to all things English, questioning the compatibility of an Eurocentrically cringing import culture with efforts to "carry Republicanism into literature" (Newcomb 1996: p. 94). These arguments influenced domestic and foreign policies alike. When the first international copyright treaties were being negotiated on the European continent in the nineteenth century, the United States refused to protect foreign literary works—a belligerent stance that it would denounce today as piratical. But then the country was a net importer of books and seeking to develop a national literary patrimony of its own. Washington, D.C. was not interested in extending protection to foreign works that might hinder its own printers, publishers, or authors from making a profit.

Distance and culture have always preoccupied the U.S. media. For example, in the nineteenth century, Charles Knight, an important figure in the development of the book industry and the popular press, spoke of the train, the telegraph, and the photograph as "a victory over time and space." And in the 1920s, Nobel Prize-winner William Shockley, inventor of the transistor, referred to the advent of a mechanical age, characterized by the capacity to travel, speak, and kill—long-distance (Briggs & Burke, 2002). These elements remain foundational to U.S. culture—mobility, militarism, and communication. Extensive work over many decades has applied this history to the success of Hollywood overseas as an amalgam of state and corporate collusion and exploitation of the New International Division of Cultural Labor (Miller et al., 2005).

Inspite of this, twenty-five years ago, it became fashionable in First-World academia to downplay Hollywood's importance, both domestically and internationally, to argue that U.S. influence over popular culture was waning in a numerical sense, and never mattered much anyway in terms of its impact. This argument was a cultural correlative of neoliberalism—the fiction of the ratiocinative, calculating consumer who could make or break film and television drama thanks to the whimsical power of individual interpretation and cultural locale. The fiction was mobilized to caricature theories of cultural imperialism as a self-hating First-World guilt trip that condescended to the Third World.

However, the cultural-imperialism thesis was developed during the 1950s in the Global South, alongside *dependencia* theories of the global economy. Cultural *dependistas* in Latin America argued that the United States was transferring its dominant value system to others. There was said to be a corresponding diminution in the vitality and standing of national and regional identities. This position associated U.S. political, military, and economic hegemony with dominance over news agencies, advertising, market research, public opinion, screen trade, technology, propaganda, and telecommunications. It was exemplified in the symbolic weight of Hollywood. Furthermore, the long history of U.S. participation in Latin American politics and then its involvement in Southeast Asian wars during the 1960s encouraged critics to draw links between the military-industrial complex and the media. They pointed out that communications and cultural exports bolstered U.S. foreign policy and military strategy, enabling the expansion of multinational corporations.

From the early 1970s, most notably via the United Nations; Educational, Scientific, and Cultural Organization; and the Non-Aligned Movement, this critique took a global-policy form to add to its much earlier national incarnations. Third-World countries lobbied for what was variously termed a New International Information Order or New World Information and Communication Order (the NWICO), mirroring calls for a New International Economic Order and a revised North-South dialogue that had begun with the Group of 77 and the United Nations Conference on Trade and Development. But within a decade, NWICO was brought down by, *inter alia*, the insistence of the United States on the free flow of communications, the loss of budgetary support for UNESCO under Thatcher and Reagan, the collapse of state socialism, and the rise of neoliberal-trained political and media elites in the Global South.

Nevertheless, the discourse of cultural imperialism continues, despite the Kool-Aid of neoliberal empowerment. This book is a testament to the ongoing importance of Hollywood's representational power, the way that its accounts of subjectivity, of humanness, of life itself, weigh heavily on how we imagine ourselves and our past and future. I want to devote the remainder of this short preface to some numbers that contextualize those analyses in a global frame. I'm especially concerned here with the place where most people watch Hollywood, which is on television. I want to argue against the claims that Hollywood no longer matters due to the choice provided by deregulated media systems and new technologies.

In 1983, the United States was estimated to have 60 percent of global TV drama sales. By 1999, that U.S. figure had grown to 68 percent , including 81 percent of TV movies. In 1995, 89 percent of films screened on Brazil's cable channels were U.S. imports and 61 percent of time dedicated to cinema on Mexican TV as well. Cable and satellite opened up the Middle East across the 1990s. U.S. film channels and a special Arab-dedicated Disney service, respectively, were strikingly successful—by 1999, Disney was making US$100 million a month in the Middle East. Three years later, Showtime debuted ten new channels through Nilesat. Since its earliest days in the 1960s, Malaysian television has relied on U.S. films for content, which dominate prime time. The same is true in Sri Lanka and the Philippines, where local films are rarely seen on television. Eurodata TV's analysis of films on television finds that Hollywood pictures drew the highest audiences in twenty-seven nations across all continents (Miller, 2010).

The Soviet Union was a major exporter of screen drama to East Germany and Bulgaria. When state socialism was succeeded by authoritarian capitalism, the picture changed dramatically. By 1997, the United States had displaced Soviet sales to Eastern and Central Europe. The de-Sovietization process of privatizing TV stations also decimated the screening of local films—previously the most significant genre in terms of time on the schedule— in favor of imported drama, from you know where (Miller et al., 2005).

Although prime time on broadcast TV worldwide is usually occupied by local shows, in the largest wealthy market, Western Europe, the dominant drama series in 2007 were *CSI: Miami, Desperate Housewives, Lost, Without a Trace,* and *The Simpsons.* In Asia, 25 million fans watch *CSI* on Sony's AXN satellite network. And young people's drama? An astounding 80 percent of programming for children outside the white-settler colonies and China comes from Hollywood. Nickelodeon is available in well over 150 countries. So young people across Ghana, Kenya, Nigeria, and South Africa are familiar with *SpongeBob SquarePants* (Miller, 2010).

Aren't the newer media supposed to have decimated U.S. influence, relegating Hollywood to one more participant in a growing global ecumene, exemplified by YouTube? Far from undermining the mainstream media, YouTube videos are the greatest boon imaginable to Hollywood. Rather than substituting for film and TV drama, these excerpts and commentaries promote it, promising new business opportunities. While amateur material forms the majority of content on YouTube, it is barely watched in comparison to the vastly more popular texts that come from the culture industries: Fifteen of the site's top-twenty search terms are for Hollywood texts (Miller, 2009).

This matters in terms of both text and industry. Jacques Attali (2008) explains that a new "mercantile order forms wherever a creative class masters a key innovation from navigation to accounting or, in our own time, where services are most efficiently mass produced, thus generating enormous wealth." The Global North, China, and India recognize that their economic futures lie in copyright and finance rather than agriculture and manufacturing. In other words, they seek revenue from innovation and intellectual property, not minerals and masses. Hence, former U.S. Secretary of State and master of the dark art of international relations Henry Kissinger's consulting firm advises that the United States must "win the battle of the world's information flows, dominating the airwaves as Great Britain once ruled the seas" (Rothkopf 1997: pp. 38, 47).

Hollywood continues to be a key player in that struggle for dominance, both textually and economically. Its messages about the good life and the bad life, and its balance of trade, make the mythic "American way of life" simultaneously a false tonic and a depressing draught for people all over the world. One way we can counteract that influence is by taking its representational protocols seriously, as the book you hold in your hands does, and recalling the critique of cultural imperialism as we do so.

REFERENCES

Attali, Jacques. (2008, Spring). "This is not America's final crisis." *New Perspectives Quarterly*: 3133.

Briggs, Asa and Peter Burke. (2002). *A social history of the media: From Gutenberg to the Internet*. Cambridge: Polity Press.

Miller, Toby, Nitin Govil, John McMurria, Richard Maxwell, and Ting Wang. (2005). *Global Hollywood 2*. London: British Film Institute.

Miller, Toby. (2009). "Cybertarians of the world unite: You have nothing to lose but your tubes!" *The YouTube Reader*. Ed. Pelle Snickars and Patrick Vondereau. Stockholm: National Library of Sweden. 424–440.

Miller, Toby. (2010). *Television studies: The basics*. London: Routledge.

Newcomb, Horace. (1996). "Other people's fictions: Cultural appropriation, cultural integrity, and international media strategies." *Mass Media and Free Trade: NAFTA and the Cultural Industries*. Ed. Emile G. McAnany and Kenton T. Wilkinson. Austin: University of Texas Press. 92–109.

Rothkopf, David. (1997). "In praise of cultural imperialism." *Foreign Policy* 107: 38–53.

Smith, Sydney. (1844). *The works of the Rev. Sydney Smith*. Philadelphia: Carey and Hart.

ACKNOWLEDGMENTS

First and foremost we would like to thank Susan Searls Giroux and Henry A. Giroux for their remarkable and long-lasting commitment to public critical pedagogy, working tirelessly toward social justice. We are grateful that they have accepted *Hollywood's Exploited* as part of their book series with Palgrave Macmillan. We would also like to thank Richard Kahn for bringing us together and congratulate him on his new book *Critical Pedagogy, Ecoliteracy, & Planetary Crisis: The Ecopedagogy Movement*, a must-read for anyone concerned about the future of this planet. We have been fortunate to have in this book an excellent preface and an outstanding foreword by two of the finest thinkers in humanities today, Toby Miller and Lawrence Grossberg. They took the time, and, with their writing, have shared generously their thought-provoking insights. Our families, faculty colleagues, and students have been sources of inspiration and support. We wish to thank our erudite contributors, providing cutting-edge discussions in every chapter of this book. We want to thank them all. Samantha Hasey at Palgrave Macmillan deserves our special thanks. She has been an outstanding representative working with us to complete all facets of the project in a timely manner.

We wish to thank our colleagues who have patiently reviewed the manuscript and articulated their superb words of reflections. Thank you, Abraham P. DeLeon, Bill Templer, Michael Parenti, Peter McLaren, Ali Zaidi, David Gabbard, Nick Cooney, William T. Armaline, Judy K. C. Bentley, Joshua Calkins, Sarat Colling, Lisa Kemmerer, Matthew Walton, Ernesto Aguilar, Deric Shannon, and Norman Solomon.

Ben would like to thank Richard Kahn for inviting me to be a part of this book and his fellow editors for their critical intellectual spirit and truly collaborative efforts.

Rich wants to thank all the people over the years who have helped strengthen my writing and analysis of media, including my advisor

Doug Kellner and so many others; to single out Jeff Menne, who offered wonderful comments and edits on my class chapter; Ben on my death penalty chapter; and my fellow editors generally for their hard work and dedication to the project.

Tony wants to acknowledge the patience and support of the love of my life Aida Dargahi, an outstanding academic and artist in her own right. My brother Ali, my father Reza, and my mother Shirin have always been instrumental in my success as an academic and a person in search of wisdom and balance. I also want to thank Norman Solomon and Doug Morris, who graciously took the time out of their extremely busy schedules, reviewing the book manuscript, and in turn offering their excellent reflections.

Anthony thanks Sarat Colling with Political Media Review and my very dear friend who has supported me through this project; Elana Levy, Kevin, Joshua Calkins, Brittani, Brittany, Jackie, Jamie, Terell, Colette, Danielle, Jay, Jeremy, Brian, Jared, Owen Hoppe, Bister, Jennifer, Liat, Matt, Andrew, Abe DeLeon, Luis Fernandez, Deric Shannon, Nick Cooney, Bill Martin, Pattrice Jones, Ramsey Kaanan, Charles Patterson, Stephen Clark, Steve Wise, Will Potter, Justin Hand, Tom Regan, Carol Gigliotti, Jim Mason, John Feldman, Sarah Kramer, Julie Andrzejewski, Annie Potts, Richard White with the *Journal for Critical Animal Studies*, Richard Twine, Jason Bayless, John Alessio, Adam Wilson with Downbound, Anastasia Yarbrough, Karen Davis, Uri Gordon, Kaltefleiter, Vasile Stanescu, John Sorenson, Lauren Corman, Maxwell Schnurer, Shannon Keith, Rik Scarce, Helena Pedersen, Roger Yates, Leesa Fawcett, Amie Breeze Harper, Charlotte Laws, David Nibert, Constance Russell, Anuj Shah, Patrick Hoyt, Alma Williams, Nicola Taylor, Cary Wolfe, Amy Fitzgerald, Nicole R. Pallotta, Sherryl Vint, Mark Rowlands, Lindgren Johnson, Veda Stram, Carrie Smith, Corey Lewis, Jodey Castricano, Ward Churchill, Piers Beirne, Richard Loder, Peter Castro, Carl Boggs; Charles Weigl Zach, Lorna, and Kate with AK Press; Sviatoslav Voloshin, Ali Zaidi, John Asimakopoulos from Transformative Studies Institute; Elana Levy, with great respect to all of SHAC 7 in and out of prison, Daniel McGowan and Jenny, Dave (with Hugs for Puppies), Maury Harris, John Burke, John Taylor, Steve Best, Richard Kahn, Barron Boyd, Nancy Piscitell, Cliff Donn, Jeff Chin, Robert A. Rubinstein, Lisa Mignacca, Micere Githae Mugo, Bill Skipper, Richard Kendrick, Mecke Nagel, Andrew Fitz-Gibbon, Caroline Tauxe, Caroline Kaltefleiter, Herb Haines, and Peter McLaren; Ben, Kevin, and Jimmy; everyone at the Program on the Analysis and Resolution of Conflicts; 03–04 PARC

Crew—Marco, Jason, Heather, Matt, Jamie, Micah, Mike, Megumi, Trish, Michelle, Amy, Sandra, Egle, Amber, Monique, Diane, Holly, Angie, and Naomi; Syracuse Bicycle: Paul, Christian, Brian Dan, Bobcat Brian, Hoag, Chris, Turbo, and the rest of the crew; everyone with New York Alternatives to Violence Program inside and outside especially at Auburn Prison, American Friends Service Committee in Syracuse—Linda, Chrissie, and Twiggy; Outdoor Empowerment; Transformative Studies Institute; Institute for Critical Animal Studies; Save the Kids, Green Theory and Praxis; Central New York Peace Studies Consortium; Peace Studies Journal, of course all of my wonderful students at Le Moyne College, Hillbrook, SUNY Cortland and Syracuse University; and all of the hardworking staff at Hillbrook Youth Detention Facility.

Finally, we hope this anthology will stimulate dialogue not only in academic settings, but also in public spheres outside the academy.

Introduction

Benjamin Frymer, Tony Kashani, Anthony J. Nocella II, and Richard Van Heertum

> I went into the business for the money, and the art grew out of it. If people are disillusioned by that remark, I can't help it. It's the truth.
>
> Charlie Chaplin

This anthology is an invitation to think and talk about Hollywood in new ways. We invite readers to consider Hollywood as a powerful, yet contested industry that serves as a global transmitter of cultural pedagogy and purveyor of images and messages, which may or may not be in the best interests of diverse marginalized and exploited groups across the world. Today, the influence of Hollywood continues to spread outward across the social and political landscape, altering the very dynamics of how we live and perceive the world around us. Hollywood films thus play a profound role in the shaping of today's worldviews, individual identities, and audiences' perception of themselves and others. We maintain this to be true, especially when one recognizes the iconographic role Hollywood films play in spreading enticing images of American consumerism. Hollywood has always had global ambitions, and the neoliberal project of globalization has given it the muscle to extend its reach, transcending its epicenter in Los Angeles to capture the heart of the capitalist entertainment market across the planet.

Hollywood is one instrument in the neoliberal project of rearticulating citizenship as consumption, and the authors of this anthology collectively argue that it has been quite successful toward this end.[1] But that is not the whole story, for we maintain that many filmmakers, following in the footsteps of visionaries like Charlie Chaplin, Lillian Gish, Abel Gance, Maya Deren, Orson Welles, and Fritz Lang are creating the kind of cinema that is enlightening audiences about the human condition, and in turn, providing compelling images of social transformation (Kashani, 2009). Thus, while films, television, and new media often indirectly serve the global aims of capitalist society, reproducing hegemonic norms, values, and beliefs and promoting a form of cultural politics that naturalizes the surrounding world and its sociopolitical structure (namely, neoliberal globalization), they also serve as potent sources for progressive politics, democratization, and avenues for empowerment and social justice.

We argue that Hollywood cinema, and media culture in general, play a pivotal role previously relegated predominantly to other elements of civil society, including the family, the church, and formal educational institutions (Gramsci, 1972), creating a type of curricular offering that the critical theorist Henry Giroux has labeled "public pedagogy" (Giroux, 2001). Public pedagogy describes the learning that occurs in and through cinema and media culture that "bridge[s] the gap between private and public discourses, while simultaneously putting into play particular ideologies and values that resonate with broader public conversations regarding how society views itself and the world of power, events, and politics" (Giroux, 2001). Like the hidden curriculum in schools, Giroux argues that screen culture, which includes TV, cinema, and advertisements, is the handmaiden of neoliberalism.

As cultural theorist Lawrence Grossberg (1992, 1997, 2005) and many of the authors of this volume suggest, audiences are increasingly sophisticated in their encounters with media and are not the passive receptors of messages that the Frankfurt School once proposed (Adorno & Horkheimer, 2002; Marcuse, 1964). Instead, we believe cynicism, apathy, and a general embrace of consumer and spectacle culture (even with ironic distance) define the ways that Hollywood influences beliefs, values, and attitudes (Frymer, 2009). Hollywood movies, then, serve as a significant educational force toward the construction of social and political identities, the growth of popular opinion, and the establishment of official knowledge in an increasingly global society, though in both predictable and unpredictable ways.

Grossberg and other critical theorists of popular culture increasingly acknowledge and embrace the audiences' ability to have their own interpretations and in turn intervene to create their own cultural spheres (Grossberg, 2005; Hall, 1996). While we agree that media culture does provide these spaces of empowerment and celebration of diversity, as well as the opportunity to play with identity, we are more interested here in critically interrogating the ways in which cinema creates and disseminates particular ideological positions. To this end, this volume analyzes the thematic, ideological, and exploitative thrust of Hollywood cinema in general, as well as the particular exploitation of marginalized groups. (Our contention is that Hollywood is often actively engaged in supporting the dominant ideological positions of our epoch, including sexism, racism, xenophobia, American exceptionalism, and militarism. However, the potential of cinema can and must be developed in ways exemplified by the book's diverse range of essays if it is to be a progressive civic institution that supports democratic life and cultural diversity.

Transgression does occur within Hollywood. Counterhegemonic messages exist not only on the margins, but also in the mainstream films of Hollywood cinema. Few films are purely supportive of, or invested in, the status quo, instead existing in the nebulous hues of gray where contradictory messages coexist. Cinema ruptures while it confirms, critiques while it transcends, and reinforces as it recants. Film is a teaching machine (Giroux, 2002), a medium of communication, and also a complex art form (Kashani, 2009). We posit this art form's radical potential lies in its ability to step outside the dominant discourse, rationality, and sensibility, and offer alternative realities that both critique and transgress social reproduction. As Marcuse (1978) argues in *The Aesthetic Dimension*, this occurs more in the form than in the content-indicating the limits of ideology critique itself. This resonates with an age where form often trumps content and the line between truth and fiction continues to blur.

As Fredrick Jameson (1991) has long argued, media reinforces the historical amnesia of late capitalist society through nostalgia films and television that turn history into a pastiche of mere style and fashion, erasing it in lieu of a falsified aesthetic and naïve reification that also reflects our general inability to re-present our culture. Hollywood goes further though to re-present not only history, but contemporary society as well. It does this by producing representations of the acceptable, the cool, and the desirable in its movies, advertisements, and through a wide variety of commodity paraphernalia designed to support the films, and indirectly consumer culture itself. Again, in these activities, Hollywood should be understood as an institution working to sustain the larger consumer culture and the role free-market capitalism has in defining our needs, wants, and desires to perpetuate a system of political economy that has increasingly moved towards the propagation of reactionary forms of identity. Yet it does this while often openly and covertly challenging that very system—as can be seen perhaps most clearly in dystopian and sci-fi films like *Avatar*, *The Road* and *The Book of Eli* that openly critique capitalism and nefarious corporate leaders.

As Giroux wrote in his book *Breaking In to the Movies: Film and the Culture of Politics* (2002), cinema is a crucial site for evaluating the workings of public pedagogy as it links private and public discourses/experiences, and because Hollywood is a powerful social institution that encodes normative attributes of identity, civic value, and cultural meaning that delineate political ideals and possibilities. This book attempts to provide a fresh and lively contribution toward this end. We argue that interpretations of individual films must be dialectically tethered to an analysis of the political economy of film as a whole. As critical social theorists have long argued, Hollywood film is a manifestation of what the Frankfurt School called "the culture industry" (Adorno & Horkheimer, 2002). The culture industry helps frame and refract the lenses through which we view our experiences of the world and increasingly mediates the social contexts of our lives. In fact, one could argue that Hollywood and media culture in general create an environment where mediation is the defining characteristic of reality itself. It seems in the new millennia, truth and reality are harder to find amidst the miasma of competing voices and images. Nothing is true until it goes through the feed loop of media culture, solidifying and reifying reality to its perspectives and ideological biases. By providing representations of personal identity for popular consumption, as well as a dramatic structure for normative codes of behavior, Hollywood works to define not only the form of social life, but much of its content as well. Increasingly, audiences appear to identify themselves within market-constructed stereotypes and modes of behavior that influence their fashion, hairstyle, artistic tastes, social interaction, and views of gender, race, class, age, sexuality, nonhuman life forms, and the environment.

In the bigger picture, however, it is important to explore the potentially positive effects of media alongside critique. The Internet has certainly opened up new spaces for dialogue, social interaction, contestation, and action. Blogs, social networking sites, alternative media sources, and political action sites all have the potential to establish new public spheres from the vestiges of the past. Students are meeting, interacting, and performing cultural exchanges on the Internet, expanding the diversity of interactions with divergent beliefs, opinions, and cultures. They are using the Internet to gain alternative perspectives on key political issues, to discuss and debate those issues, and to organize action to challenge them. And cinema opens up space to step outside the dominant rationality and social order, and contemplate alternative modes of social organization together with documentaries, counterhegemonic and publically produced films and shorts that challenge the status quo and current order of things.

Hollywood's Exploited, then, is an interdisciplinary and collaborative anthology that offers a compelling analysis of contemporary Hollywood films (and the larger industry and society to which they are dialectically related) in light of Giroux's ideas about public pedagogy, looking to use analysis and deconstruction to forge critical media literacy that can awaken new forms of audience agency.[2] The book brings together a talented collection of prestigious and emergent scholars chosen to provide a critical multiperspectival and intersectional lens on the production, distribution, and interpretation of mainstream film and its relationship to the politics of otherness. In particular, *Hollywood's Exploited* illuminates the manner in which Hollywood and society co-construct exploitative forms of identity—as defined across a range of categories such as race, gender, sexuality, disability, nationality, species, naturalness, and age—toward the production of a dehumanizing and antidemocratic form of public pedagogy. *Hollywood's Exploited* aims to help readers better understand the way in which marginal groups are stereotyped, objectified, and appropriated in formulaic narratives for commodity consumption instead of democratic deliberation.

BOOK SECTIONS AND CHAPTER OUTLINES

We have organized the chapters of this collection into four sections. First, *Hollywood & Ideology* includes four essays on the ways Hollywood cinema reconstructs and affirms dominant ideologies. In his provocative essay **The Imperial System in Media Culture**, Carl Boggs analyzes the role of Hollywood cinema in perpetuating the increased militarism of American culture today. Exploring a number of films, including *Rambo* and *Charlie Wilson's War*, Boggs argues that Hollywood films tend to support the imperialist aims of recent administrations and recent American military action in places like Afghanistan and Iraq.

Next, in his essay **Hollywood and the Working-Class Hero: Diamonds in the Mean Streets of Boston**, Richard Van Heertum deconstructs representation of the working class in a series of recent films, including *Gone Baby Gone*, *Good Will Hunting*, and *Mystic River*. He argues that the working class tends to be juxtaposed against an Other that is shown as implicitly superior, providing images and narratives of characters that are violent, destructive, and unredeemable, and that corrupt all those mired within their midst—particularly youth.

Shirley Steinberg follows with her essay **Hollywood's Missionary Agenda: Christonormativity and Audience Baptism**, arguing

that "North American audiences have become Christonormativized
by Hollywood productions of mainstream films and television programs, which create the ambience that everyone is Christian."
Steinberg breaks down the complex interconnectivity of Hollywood,
television, and institutional Christianity, revealing an ideological
juggernaut that reinforces Christianity as the normative belief of all
Americans. Richard Van Heertum then concludes the section with
his essay **Hollywood Incarcerated and on Death Row: Bjork,
Schwarzenegger, and the Pedagogy of Retribution.** He posits
that the death penalty serves as the legitimizing vehicle for our entire
prison industrial complex and that capital punishment is itself partially legitimized through popular film, where justice is enacted predominantly through the destruction of evil. He then deconstructs a
series of films related to the death penalty to explore their underlying
messages and how they can be used by educators to help students
more critically analyze the justice system in America today.

The second section of the book, *Hollywood Re-presents the Other*,
examines representations of difference by race, class, disability, and
sexuality. In the first chapter of the section, **From Ms. J. to Ms. G.:
Analyzing Racial Microaggressions in Hollywood's Urban
School Genre,** Tara Yosso and David Garcia provide a fascinating
exploration of the ways Latino/a culture is exploited in Hollywood
urban ghetto films like *Freedom Writers* and *Dangerous Minds*. They
argue that these films tend to reproduce negative images of youth of
color and troubling racial myths, including portraying them as dangerous, sexually promiscuous *cholos* with bad parents and no motiva-
tion to succeed. By analyzing the deficit thinking and ideologies in
these purportedly uplifting tales, they challenge us to look deeper
than the surface of films that otherwise seem to provide positive
messages.

Tony Kashani and Anthony Nocella II follow by asking
whether Hollywood exploits people with disabilities in their essay
**Hollywood's Implicit Ableism: A Disability Studies Perspective
on the Hollywood Industrial Complex.** They examine a number
of films, including *Rain Man* (1988) and *Tiptoes* (2003) in relation to Hollywood's thematic exploitation of people with mental
and physical disabilities, as well as the way it employs its star power
to represent them in formula-based films. Next, in **International
Citizenry in the Age of the Spectacle,** Shoba Sharad Rajgopal
examines Hollywood's Eurocentrism. Rajgopal deconstructs the ways
in which Hollywood manufactures, through its spectacle cinema,
certain rigid representations of the "non-American" citizens of the

globe. She asks and responds to the question of whether Hollywood perpetuates the "colonial gaze," yielding whiteness as a standardized norm.

Michael A. Raffanti concludes the section with **LGBT-Themed Hollywood Cinema after** *Brokeback Mountain*: **Renegotiating Hegemonic Representations of Gay Men.** Here he examines the dynamics of Hollywood as a system that maintains cultural hegemony in the United States and across the globe. Raffanti analyzes Ang Lee's love story *Brokeback Mountain* in addition to *I Now Pronounce You Chuck and Larry* (2007), *Milk* (2008), and *Brüno* (2009). Employing a critical theory lens, Raffanti maintains that "Hollywood's hegemonic forces seem to be negotiating a cinema of tolerance that nonetheless maintains Hollywood's control and exploitation of gay visibility and images."

The third section of the book, *Hollywood Ages*, focuses on representations of age and aging, with two chapters on youth and one on the elderly. Douglas Kellner, in **Modes of Youth Exploitation in the Cinema of Larry Clark**, analyzes treatment of youth culture in Hollywood in general and the films of provocative director Larry Clark in particular. He argues that Hollywood films tend to provide negative stereotypical views of youth as dangerous to themselves and the larger society. Looking at Clark's oeuvre, he sees the director exploiting teen bodies as objects of voyeurism and sexual fetishism, providing a panorama of highly prejudicial images of youth as hypersexual alcohol and drug abusers that are generally passive victims of circumstance. Next, in **Sixteen and Pregnant: Media Mommy Tracking and Hollywood's Exploitation of Teen Pregnancy,** Caroline K. Kaltefleiter analyzes the films *Juno* and *The Education of Shelby Knox* to examine the exploitation of teen sexuality and pregnancy in both cinema and on television. Using her own experiences as a teenage girl in the Texas Panhandle, Kaltefleiter uncovers the central class, race, and gender dynamics typically hidden in Hollywood narratives of teen pregnancy.

Karen E. Riggs concludes the section with *About Schmidt* **and About the Hollywood Image of an Aging Actor,** focusing on representations of aging in Hollywood through the film *About Schmidt*. She looks at the extensive online commentary on the film, Jack Nicholson's aging character, and general issues of age and aging on the IMDB.com website, providing a fascinating window into a vivid Hollywood portrayal of aging and audience responses to that portrayal. She poses the question, "What does it mean to be old?" and explores how today's Baby Boomers are redefining its meaning.

The final section of the book, *Hollywood Beyond the Human*, examines discourses and representations of nature, machines/technology, and nonhuman animals. Salma Monani and Andrew Hageman use the recent Hollywood hits *March of the Penguins* and *Wall·E* to illuminate the complexities and contradictions, as well as the pedagogical potentials, inherent in many cinematic representations of nature in their essay **Ecological Connections and Contradictions: Penguins, Robots, and Humans in Hollywood's Nature Films**. They assert that "analysis of the representations of nonhuman animal, machine, and human in each film serves to emphasize how these generic films are useful illustrations of what many Hollywood films offer as prescriptive environmental pedagogy." In the midst of our ecological crisis, they propose a "methodology of ecocinema critique" to foster critical readings of these films and the complex interrelationships between humans, machines, and nature they portray.

Finally, in his interdisciplinary article, **Hollywood and Nonhuman Animals: Problematic Ethics of Corporate Cinema**, Tony Kashani challenges readers to examine their ethics in relation to Hollywood's regarding representations of nonhuman animals. His creative inquiry looks at Hollywood's speciesism in relation to our learned speciesism, while looking at films that come out of the system but paradoxically contain "critical narratives in support of nonhuman animals." Kashani's ethical argument points the way to the possibility of the kind of cinema that can teach humanity a morality that transcends humanist limitations.

OUR OBJECTIVE

As these sections and chapters indicate, the overarching goal of *Hollywood's Exploited* is to demonstrate how critical pedagogy can be enacted as a form of cultural studies that can work to critically interpret Hollywood films in new ways that can serve as potent vehicles of a reconstructed public pedagogy capable of broadening the public sphere of democratic debate and civic exchange. *Hollywood's Exploited* seeks to augment the literature of critical pedagogy and cultural studies, and appeal to a broad spectrum of readers interested in questioning the meaning of many of today's most popular texts, as well as the way in which their form and content "make meaning" for us all. We believe that just as too many progressive voices are absent from the media and political debates, so, too, is real cultural criticism outside academia. With this collection, we offer our own form of engagement with this problem, attempting to transcend the sometimes arcane world of academia to bring these debates into the mainstream.

NOTES

1. Like many, we see neoliberalism as the dominant global paradigm today, founded as a project of market liberation, government retrenchment, and dismantling of the social safety net. Its defining principle is that the market has the power to efficiently and effectively mediate the production and allocation of economic and social goods, from consumer products to governance to medical care, energy, retirement funding, and education. Toward this end, it calls for privatization, market liberation (domestically and abroad), diminished government oversight, lower marginal personal and corporate taxation, and, really, establishment of market ethics and rationality across economic, political, and social institutions (Giroux, 2004; Macedo, Dendrinos, & Gounari, 2003; Stiglitz, 2002).
2. See Kellner and Share and Van Heertum and Share for further explanation of what critical media literacy entails and its project of creating critical media consumers that can deconstruct ideology, become cognizant of the political economy and production of film, and create their own counterhegemonic texts (Kellner & Share, 2007; Van Heertum & Share, 2006).

REFERENCES

Adorno, T. W., & Horkheimer, M. (2002). *Dialectic of enlightenment.* New York: Continuum.

Frymer, B. (2009). The media spectacle of Columbine: Alienated youth as an object of fear. *American Behavioral Scientist, 52* (10), 1387–1404.

Giroux, H. (2001). Private satisfactions and public disorders: Fight Club, patriarchy, and the politics of masculine violence. *JAC: A Journal of Composition Theory, 21*(1), 1–31.

Giroux, H. (2002). *Breaking in to the movies: Film and the culture of politics.* New York: Blackwell.

Giroux, H. (2004). *The terror of neoliberalism: Authoritarianism & the eclipse of democracy.* London: Paradigm Publishers.

Gramsci, A. (1972). *Selections from the prison notebooks.* New York: International Publishers.

Grossberg, Lawrence (1992). *We gotta get out of this place: Popular conservatism and postmodern culture.* New York: Routledge.

Grossberg, Lawrence (1997). *Dancing in spite of myself: Essays on popular culture.* Durham: Duke University Press.

Grossberg, Lawrence (2005). *Caught in the crossfire: Kids, politics, and America's future.* Boulder: Paradigm Publishers.

Hall, S. (1996). *Questions of cultural identity*. Thousand Oaks, CA: SAGE Publications.

Jameson, F. (1991). *Postmodernism or, the cultural logic of late capitalism*. Durham, NC: Duke University Press.

Kashani, T. (2009). *Deconstructing the mystique: An introduction to cinema*. Dubuque, IA: Kendall/Hunt.

Kellner, D., & Share, J. (2007). Critical media literacy is not an option. *Learning Inquiry, 1*(1), 59–69.

Macedo, D., Dendrinos, B., & Gounari, P. (2003). *The hegemony of English*. Boulder, Colo.: Paradigm Publishers.

Marcuse, H. (1964). *One-dimensional man: Studies in the ideology of advanced industrial society*. Boston: Beacon Press.

Marcuse, H. (1978). *The aesthetic dimension: Toward a critique of Marxist aesthetics*. Boston: Beacon Press.

Stiglitz, J. (2002). *Globalization & its discontents*. New York: W.W. Norton & Company.

Van Heertum, R., & Share, J. (2006). Connecting power, voice and critique: A new direction for multiple literacy education. *McGill Journal of Education, 41*(3).

1

HOLLYWOOD & IDEOLOGY

1

THE IMPERIAL SYSTEM IN MEDIA CULTURE

Carl Boggs

One of the remarkable features of the contemporary American landscape is the extent to which Hollywood studios turn warfare into stunning media spectacles—a phenomenon shared with TV and video games, which, like movies, are the beneficiaries of much of the same high-tech spectacle. Violence and bloodshed, the inevitable product of extreme military encounters, have become the artistic and technological stuff of modern cinematic overkill, whether at the hands of Tony Scott or Oliver Stone, Edward Zwick or Stanley Kubrick, Michael Bay or Steven Spielberg. It is Spielberg's work that probably best exemplifies the war spectacle, for he is the master not only of the combat genre but of related fare like action/adventure movies. If scenarios of death and destruction wind up as the inescapable fruits of Empire, they are simultaneously the stock-in-trade of Hollywood blockbusters, both mirroring and contributing to the irrepressible culture of militarism.

Aside from intensifying economic crises and social decay, the Bush years spurred an elevated militarization of both the political and popular culture, marked by escalating incidents of civic violence, rapid expansion of the Pentagon war machine, an aggressively imperial foreign policy, and a media increasingly saturated with images and narratives of violence. The trends Tom Pollard and I explored in our book *The Hollywood War Machine* have only deepened and show no signs of receding (Boggs and Pollard, 2006). The markers are rather difficult to miss: two continuous, bloody wars of occupation in Iraq and Afghanistan; a stepped-up "war on terrorism"; threats to Iran; nuclear buildup; and growing security-state power at a time of recurrent domestic mass killings, sustained high levels of crime, accelerating hate crimes, and a sprawling prison-industrial complex. By 2009 the United States was spending nearly $1 trillion yearly to feed its military colossus, not counting hundreds of billions (possibly trillions) more on the Iraq debacle—expenditures reaching nearly *three-fifths* of the world total and dwarfing such competitors as Russia (all of $25 billion), China ($85 billion), and North Korea (a menacing $6 billion). To maintain U.S. global supremacy, the Pentagon has established ten unified command structures covering most of the planet. No country or empire in world history has even approached this scope of military power, so it would be astonishing if ideological networks did not operate nonstop to invest that power with maximum domestic popular support, in the absence of which the burdensome risks and costs of war (and preparation for war) would surely be rejected by the general population. In the absence of a genuine state propaganda machine in the United States, these ideological functions inevitably become the province of the corporate media and popular culture. As might be expected, therefore, the militarized culture Pollard and I analyzed in *The Hollywood War Machine* is today even more deeply entrenched in the social order.

The steady growth of a militarized society in the United States cannot be understood apart from the expanded role of media culture in its different forms: TV, radio, Internet, publishing, video games, and film. An unsurpassed source of information, opinion, and entertainment, the corporate media have become the main linchpin of ideological hegemony in the United States, a repository of values, attitudes, and myths that shape public opinion on a daily basis. Transnational media empires like Disney, Time-Warner, Viacom, News Corporation, and General Electric, bulwarks of privilege and power, routinely celebrate the blessings of a "free market" economy, the virtues of personal consumption, the wonders of a political system built on freedom and democracy, a benevolent and peace-loving U.S. foreign policy, the need for a globalized permanent war system to protect against imminent foreign threats, and, of course, old-fashioned patriotism. A wide panorama of militaristic images and discourse infuse media culture today, probably nowhere more so than in Hollywood cinema, helping legitimize record Pentagon budgets and U.S. armed interventions abroad. Elements of the mass media can be viewed as propagandistic, but we are talking about something entirely different—the extension of already deeply ingrained traditions within the popular and political cultures that by the 1990s had come to permeate every corner of American life.

The deepening militarization of American society corresponds to global realities of the current period: U.S. imperial power, measured in economic, political, cultural, and military terms, now reaches every corner of the globe, dwarfing the scope of all previous empires. Of course, ruling elites want the public to believe this power is being wielded for entirely noble ends, for universal principles of freedom, democracy, and human rights, in accordance with the long-held myth of Manifest Destiny—a sense of imperial entitlement—but the historical actuality has always clashed with this convenient self-image. From its beginnings, the United States moved inexorably along the path of colonialism, racism, and militarism, first waging the Indian Wars and conquering vast areas of Mexico, and then, following the settlement of North America, pushing outward into Latin America and Asia at the end of the Spanish-American War. For most of the twentieth century, the United States either was at war or preparing for war across two World Wars, Korea, Vietnam, Central America, the Balkans, Afghanistan, and Iraq, with no end in sight at the end of the first decade of the twenty-first century. World War II established the permanent war economy, later bringing with it a security state of epic proportions—the kind of military-industrial complex that President Dwight Eisenhower warned about at the end of his presidency. By the 1990s the United States had firmly established itself as an unchallenged superpower, backed by the largest war machine ever, with bases in 130 nations, massive surveillance and intelligence capacity, a planned military presence in space, and consumption of more resources than all other major armed forces in the world combined.

With expanding U.S. imperial power, the always-vital mechanisms of legitimation take on new meaning. All power structures need systematic ideological and cultural supports, or "hegemony" along the lines theorized by Italian cultural theorist Antonio Gramsci, but the imperatives of Empire give new meaning to these ordinary requirements. Empire, a bloated war economy, constant armed interventions—all must be made to appear "natural," routine, and desirable if not noble. Themes of national exceptionalism, super-patriotism, the glories of high-tech warfare, and the demands of a (global) civilizing mission help satisfy this legitimation function, as does the impenetrable hubris associated with economic, technological, and military supremacy. To translate such an ideological matrix into popular language, to fully incorporate it into the political culture, is the task not so much of a classical propaganda apparatus but of an educational system and media culture appropriate to advanced capitalism. In the United States today, media culture is an extension of megacorporations that comprise the largest and most influential media-entertainment complex ever developed. And Hollywood film-making has become increasingly central to this complex, and thus a crucial instrument for legitimating Empire.

The U.S. pursuit of global supremacy brings with it a growing concentration of corporate, government, and military power surrounded by a refined law enforcement and surveillance apparatus that, while in some ways indispensable, cannot by itself furnish legitimation. That is the function of media culture. Hollywood filmmaking contributes admirably to this function, despite the release of pictures here and there that run counter to the dominant paradigm. Legitimation occurs not primarily by means of censorship or outright propaganda (though both surely exist), but through ordinary canons and formulas of studio productions, where "conspiracies" are scarcely necessary to enforce hegemonic codes. The repetitive fantasies, illusions, myths, images, and story lines of Hollywood movies can be expected to influence mass audiences in predictable ways, much in the fashion of advertising or public relations. One popular response to the flood of violent combat, action/adventure, sci-fi, and horror films is a stronger readiness to support U.S. military operations that, in a patriotically charged milieu, require little justification. This aspect of legitimation is unique to American foreign policy, the only nation in the world with a sprawling network of military bases around the world.

To be sure, complex societies like the United States have many agencies of politicization, but none today rival the power of media culture. As Douglas Kellner points out, "Media culture spectacles demonstrate who has power and who is powerless, who is allowed to exercise force and violence, and who is not. They dramatize and legitimate the power of the forces that be and demonstrate to the powerless that if they fail to conform, they risk incarceration or death" (Kellner, 1995: p. 11). It is a culture that includes film, TV, video games, and music overwhelmingly geared toward young people, whose social views are in their formative stage and thus highly impressionable. That such views might be partial, uneven, or lacking in coherence hardly detracts from their intensity, which often achieves its peak around issues of patriotism and use of military force. The corporate media routinely translates U.S. imperial agendas into deeply felt popular beliefs and attitudes about the world and the U.S. role in it, usually validating something akin to the motif of national exceptionalism. Despite its liberal image and reputation, therefore, Hollywood tends to produce expensive, high-tech, entertaining movies that, directly or indirectly, help satisfy the ideological requirements for Empire. One might go further: owing to powerful tendencies within the general culture, the once-prevailing liberal tradition itself appears to have lost its significant hold on public opinion as it collapses into an increasingly conservative paradigm.

The Hollywood war machine has itself moved into full gear over the past several years, capitalizing on the post-9/11 American sense of a wounded, vengeful, but still very imperialistic nation prepared to set the world straight. A few cinematic examples will suffice here. Irwin Winkler's *Home of the Brave* (2007) tells the story of four courageous American soldiers at the end of their Iraq tours of duty, sent on one final humanitarian mission to a remote Iraqi village. The unit is ambushed, taking heavy losses—part of a narrative showing how well-intentioned U.S. troops are suddenly torn from good deeds by a scheming, ruthless enemy. In Peter Berg's *The Kingdom* (2007), we encounter a team of U.S. government agents sent to investigate the terrorist bombing of an American facility in Riyadh, Saudi Arabia, where frenzied attempts are made to locate and flush out Arab madmen from their underground cells. In a final battle between good guys and bad guys at the entrance to a hideout, it is the good guys (led by FBI agents) who prevail against difficult odds. Jesse Johnson's *The Last Sentinel* (2007) depicts a group of super-soldiers, highly skilled warriors assigned to protect "civilization" against swarms of devious villains, although in this saga, the heroes must depend on electronic advantages to ensure success. In *Terminator*-style action, the good warriors learn to think and behave like machines for what will be the epic struggle to save the human race. In Henry Crum's *Crash Point* (2006), a strike force team faces off against terrorists who have stolen a ground control encoder that allows someone to hijack a plane by remote control. The terrorists, who are not surprisingly Muslim, plan to crash a jetliner into a secret U.S. military intelligence base in Southeast Asia. The strike force unit must locate and destroy the encoder to foil the terrorists and, in the process, avert a new world war. They manage to succeed. Peter Travis' box-office hit *Vantage Point* (2008) depicts the assassination of a U.S. president attending (what else?) a global war on terrorism summit in Spain. With the evildoers mercilessly attacking the very citadel of American power, the crowd goes into shock and panic as the drama unfolds repeatedly from different angles. This Manicheistic narrative was heavily promoted as a cinematic message alerting the American people to new threats against the global order by seemingly omnipresent evil forces. In *Live Free or Die Hard* (2007), Len Wiseman brings to screen a reprise of the *Die Hard* pictures starring Bruce

Willis as New York City police detective John McClane, here taking on (and defeating) a group of sinister high-tech terrorists ready to hack into and bring down U.S. computer systems.

In the popular film *Transformers* (2007), Michael Bay revisits his fascination with technowar in a movie depicting combat between opposing robotic forces, the noble and heroic Autobots versus the evil Decepticons, the latter repelled as they assault a U.S. military base in Qatar. A big, loud, violent film that grossed $700 million in American theaters, *Transformers* quickly found its way into another profitable combat video game. The same year, *Rescue Dawn* was released as Werner Herzog's cinematic tribute to U.S. fighter pilots shot down on a mission over Laos during the Vietnam War—a recycling of *Behind Enemy Lines*, where the narrative centers on brave U.S. military personnel taken prisoner by an enemy, in this case, the faceless and brutal Vietnamese. Similarly, Tony Bill's *Flyboys* (2006) traces the adventures of American fighter pilots (the first in history) as they align with the French military to defeat the Germans during World War I. While these pictures often deal only peripherally with military combat, they embellish familiar militaristic themes: male heroism, battlefield camaraderie, superpatriotism, violent struggle of good against evil, noble U.S. objectives, and glorification of high-tech warfare.

Two films of the period deserve special attention for their embrace of strong pro-military themes and their capacity to reach large audiences with messages celebrating U.S. imperial power: *Rambo IV* (2008), referred to simply as *Rambo*, directed by the iconic Sylvester Stallone himself, and *Charlie Wilson's War* (2007), directed by the stalwart Mike Nichols. Revisiting the three original *Rambo* pictures (1982, 1985, 1988), it would be hard to find a warrior hero better exemplifying the virtues of American military action, superseding even the legendary John Wayne. Rambo-inspired films are designed to evoke pride in and identification with the U.S. military, blaming defeat (in the case of Vietnam) on a series of bureaucratic obstacles and leadership mistakes, singling out liberals, antiwar protesters, an unpatriotic media, and civilian decision makers as sources of failure and even betrayal. A valiant armed intervention against evil Communists robbed America of a victory we had every right to win. Within the framework of the "Vietnam Syndrome," the idea that U.S. defeat could result from a powerful movement of nationalists defending their homeland was (and still is) apparently unthinkable. A central ideological function of the Rambo phenomenon has been to perpetuate this peculiar American mythology.

The original *Rambo* tagline read "STALLONE: This time he's fighting for his life." Ted Kotchef adapted David Morrell's popular novel about Vietnam veteran John Rambo (Sylvester Stallone), an elite Green Beret fighter and Congressional Medal of Honor recipient who turns into a killing machine never able to adjust to postwar civilian life. Unable to hold a job, a depressed Rambo drifts from place to place, eventually winding up at the town of Hope, Washington, where he meets a hard-ass sheriff who hates Rambo's scruffy appearance and forces him out of town, whereupon Rambo returns and is quickly arrested. Angered by horrible jail treatment that includes beatings, Rambo escapes to the mountains where he further hones survival and warrior skills. At this point, the vengeful former soldier sets out to prove the accuracy of a prediction by his commanding officer in Vietnam, Col. Samuel Trautman (Richard Crenna): that Rambo will develop the capacity to destroy any and all forces standing in his way. Rambo disables cops and even a National Guard detachment sent to apprehend him, one by one, using the same guerrilla tactics employed by the Vietnamese. Within this cinematic discourse, Rambo emerges both as a forgotten national hero and as the mythical misunderstood vet who turns fate around by relying on lessons taken from the hated enemy.

Turning to the 2008 version of *Rambo*, the battlefield scene is again Vietnam ("Burma" representing an obvious stand-in), which the film strives to embellish as a "good war" that audiences will realize as a perfect opportunity to finally roll back the Communist menace. Rambo returns to Hollywood after a long hiatus, still ready to take on all enemies as he maneuvers through a minefield of bureaucrats, liberals, and weak patriots needing a lesson in masculine warrior politics. The renovated Rambo works to rescue Burmese medical personnel in the midst of civil war, taking on villains so barbaric that nothing less than all-out ruthless violence will suffice. Rambo is more than up to the task, killing with relentless and often creative brutality. A more cartoonish figure than ever, Rambo retains his cinematic status as mythological hero, American to the core, whose efficacy (and appeal) requires that he bring continuous death and destruction to foreign evildoers.

The cinematic tagline of the 2008 *Rambo* reads "Heroes never die…They just reload." Here Rambo, still in peaceful Thailand, rents his jungle boat to a group of Christian missionaries led by Michael Burnett (Paul Schutze) and Sarah Miller (Julie Benz) planning to assist the Karen people of Burma (Myanmar), whom the film incorrectly portrays as uniformly Christian (they are equally devoted to Buddhism and animism as well as Christianity). River pirates commandeer the boat and demand that Rambo hand over Sarah for their sexual pleasure; of course, Rambo refuses, killing the pirates and then justifying his actions by explaining that they would have raped Sarah fifty times and beheaded everyone afterward. Once the missionaries arrive at their destination, they are raided by the Burmese military, with sadistic Major Pa Tee Tint (Maung Maung Khin) ordering his soldiers to pillage and burn everything in sight and murder the inhabitants, sparing just a few missionaries to be later tortured. Thai officials hire mercenaries to rescue the Americans, persuading Rambo to ferry them to the site, where he is able to put his awesome military expertise to work—much needed, of course, given the heinous character of the Burmese troops. The situation is so fraught with horrific violence that *New York Times* critic A. O. Scott is moved to write that these villains "make the Vietcong in the second *Rambo* movie look like paintball-slinging weekend warriors" (*New York Times:* Jan. 25, 2008). The bloodbath that follows is predicable and formulaic enough.

The fourth *Rambo* film enjoyed stupendous box office success, especially among young males often heard cheering every blood-soaked scene. In his review of the movie, critic Peter Rainer writes: "I saw the film on its opening night in a mostly filled theater where every splatter was greeted with whoops...When his [Stallone's] scowl hit the screen, the audiences went wild, knowing that carnage could not be very far away" (*Los Angeles Times:* Feb. 17, 2008). The audiences had plenty of opportunities. No fewer than 236 human beings were brutally killed in this *Rambo* (or 2.59 per minute of footage), compared with measly totals of 69 and 132 for episodes two and three. In one of the greatest movie celebrations of militarized violence ever, human beings are bombed, blasted, stabbed, shot, blown up by grenades, incinerated by fire or flamethrowers, bludgeoned, stomped, beaten, beheaded, and tossed out of aircraft. Rambo alone kills eighty-three of the bad guys, perhaps short of a record but surely enough to uphold his reputation as "the beast." Some cynical observers have commented that Rambo might well have returned in the nick of time, calculating that he is the one warrior persona able to deliver victory out of defeat in the latest catastrophic American imperial venture, Iraq.

Given the huge budgets needed to make high-profile mainstream films, the odds against projects with distinctly antiwar themes, or with narratives focusing on Pentagon misconduct, strategic blunders, misuse of funds, or botched war planning—not to mention atrocities or war crimes committed by U.S. forces—have risen dramatically.

Such *critical* motifs are restricted to lower-budget documentaries like Errol Morris's *The Fog of War* (2006), Eugene Jarecki's *Why We Fight* (2007), and Robert Greenwald's *Iraq for Sale* (2005), or modest indie movies viewed by much smaller art house audiences. After World War I, a few Hollywood pictures appeared questioning the warrior mentality and conventional ways of thinking about combat—for example, King Vidor's *The Big Parade* (1925) and Lewis Milestone's *All Quiet on the Western Front* (1930), both of which reached mass audiences. Such films presented images and narratives of warfare that featured the "war is hell" motif, thus exculpating individuals of acts of military aggression. Few such films accompanied or followed World War II, the quintessential "good war" pitting democratic, free-dom-loving Allies against the hated fascists. A cycle of antiwar films did follow the intensely unpopular Vietnam War, however, including Michael Cimino's *The Deer Hunter* (1978), Hal Ashby's *Coming Home* (1978), Francis Ford Coppola's *Apocalypse Now* (1979), Oliver Stone's *Platoon* (1986) and *Born on the Fourth of July* (1989), and Stanley Kubrick's *Full Metal Jacket* (1988). These films, powerful as they were, focused almost entirely on the *home front* or dramatized the ordeal of *American* forces while largely ignoring the impact of war on the Vietnamese. None of these films held up U.S. foreign and military policies to sustained critical scrutiny.

By the 1990s, even this truncated antiwar cinema would be more difficult to find, aside from documentaries such as those mentioned earlier. Two major films that shifted critical focus to the first Iraq war, David O. Russell's *Three Kings* (1999) and Edward Zwick's *Courage Under Fire* (1996), again dwelled extensively on American battle-field experiences and horrors, leaving the Iraqi side essentially silent. A later, much-acclaimed film dealing with the second Iraq war and occupation, Paul Haggis's *In the Valley of Elah* (2007), concentrated entirely on the war's horrific impact on the home front. Yet another critically lauded film, Terrence Malick's *The Thin Red Line* (1998), offered one of the few "war-is-hell" renderings of a World War II engagement, in this case, the 1943 Battle of Guadalcanal—offering a rare glimpse into *Japanese* battlefield experiences. After 9/11, with the re-election of George W. Bush, the war on terrorism, and U.S. military interventions in Afghanistan and Iraq, the political atmo-sphere shifted markedly rightward, with heightened media attention devoted to patriotism, war, and American engagement of foreign enemies—hardly an atmosphere, in Hollywood or elsewhere in the United States, conducive to big-budget films that might challenge basic premises of U.S. foreign and military policies.

One noteworthy post-9/11 movie appealing to mass audiences with
a reputedly antiwar theme was Mike Nichols's *Charlie Wilson's War*
(2007). In fact, the film offered a somewhat more nuanced, though
still unmistakable, rendering of well-intentioned U.S. global ambitions in another strategic area—this time Afghanistan, where in the
1980s the CIA gave massive aid to Mujahideen rebels fighting Soviet
troops. Based roughly on true events, Nichols's film depicts a maverick
Texas congressman, Wilson, as he boldly flaunts political and bureaucratic obstacles to provide covert support for the "freedom fighters."
In this saga, Wilson (Tom Hanks) works diligently and resourcefully
to boost secret Mujahideen funding from $5 million to $500 million
mostly by trading favors with key congressmen. (The actual funding was closer to $5 billion). Wilson is depicted as a cocaine-sniffing
Houston socialite inspired by patriotic frenzy and obsession with roll-
ing back the Soviet presence in Afghanistan. *Charlie Wilson's War*
presents the Mujahideen as idealistic fighters for all that is good and
just in the world, as saviors of human freedom, when in fact it was
these same fighters—forerunners of the Taliban and Al Qaeda—who
upheld, then as now, a virulent jihadist fascism. The Mujahideen were
championed by the United States for no other reason than that they
opposed Communist power. The problem is that the film obscures
this troubling historical connection, while the presumed beacons of
liberty are shown as childlike in their innocence and helplessness (only
to be rescued by U.S. largesse). Nichols frames his story, entirely consistent with Pentagon and CIA mythology, around the fiction that
U.S. interventions serve admirably to "liberate" backward peoples
looking for just the right political tutelage and economic aid. And we
see American personnel in the field working for humanitarian goals,
while the brutal Soviets are shown deliberately blowing away retreat-
ing Afghan civilians. The operation naturally depends on the tenacity
of a few good Americans working, almost Rambo-style, to overcome
one hurdle after another in the fight to dispose of the Soviet villains.
The legacy of "Charlie Wilson's War," however, has turned rather
sour, as Afghanistan today remains occupied by another power (the
United States) and has degenerated into a cauldron of warlordism,
chaos, drug trafficking, and violence—a sequel totally ignored by
Nichols's film.

In exploring the impact of corporate media culture, a pressing
question is not whether but rather *how* and *to what extent* the content
of motion pictures and other media influence mass publics. Contrary
to the simplistic view put forth by apologists of the media, influence
generally moves along quite diverse paths—for example, people might

actively engage in violent behavior, they might participate as followers, they might lend their support in some fashion, or they might simply go along with violent or militaristic agendas out of indifference.
Whatever the case, it is surely true that mass publics have become
increasingly desensitized to the constant flow of violent images.
There are no mechanistic causes and effects underlying any of these
complex outcomes. *The Hollywood War Machine* explores dozens of
mainstream films—many of them blockbusters—that celebrated some
aspect of militarism: extreme and repetitive acts of violence, male
warrior heroes, gallant U.S. battlefield exploits, technological warfare, superpatriotism tied to noble American pursuits, the targeting
of demonic enemies, and so forth. These motifs define not only combat films but other genres as well, such as action/adventure pictures,
sci-fi movies, Westerns, and historical dramas, deeply influencing the
larger culture, society, and foreign policy—an argument that today,
after eight years of Bush and the neocons, should draw little controversy. Of course, some might choose to ignore this dreadful state of
affairs, or perhaps are little troubled by it, even as the culture industry
and U.S. global behavior follow almost identical patterns. While no
one yet possesses the tools to accurately measure media influence on
popular consciousness (just as consciousness itself remains difficult to
measure), the contention that media culture exerts little or no impact
on public attitudes and behavior would hardly follow.

A deeper problem is the growing media and popular engagement
in the militarization of American society, as orgies of media violence develop into just another American pastime, like baseball and
hunting—practices now fully taken for granted. The parade of ultraviolent war movies, action/adventure films, and combat video games
might be viewed as just a little harmless diversion, with few consequences for general civic and political behavior. Others, however,
have been less sanguine about images of violence and warfare in the
media. President Richard Nixon, managing the Vietnam carnage, was
known to have said he relished seeing *Patton* again and again, moved
by that and similar uplifting combat films, while President Ronald
Reagan could not hide his enthusiasm for the 1980s *Rambo* series,
repeating the warrior's famous utterance (about Vietnam) that "we
get to win this time." In his book *Ronald Reagan the Movie*, Michael
Rogin quotes Reagan as saying: "Boy, I saw *Rambo* last night. Now I
know what to do the next time this happens" (Rogin, 1987: p. 7). Of
course, Reagan could do little about Vietnam, but he could (and did)
preside over a series of proxy wars in Central America costing tens of
thousands of lives. It was ultimately left to the first President Bush

to finally kick the "Vietnam Syndrome" (or so he boasted) with his momentous Desert Storm victory over the powerful Iraqi military. As for the second President Bush, his inspiration reportedly came from watching *Black Hawk Down* (2002), worth several viewings in the buildup to the *real* war against Iraq where, presumably, "we get to win this time" (finishing the job his father started in 1991).

In the case of Vietnam, it is often forgotten that Hollywood produced an endless stream of patriotic, prowar movies about the United States in Indochina, with *The Green Berets* (1967) only the first in a long cycle of films justifying intervention, many fixated on postwar fantasies of reversing the original experience of defeat and humiliation. The original *Rambo* trilogy, as we have seen, transformed Sylvester Stallone into an American warrior icon whose popularity derived from heroic efforts to reverse the "Vietnam Syndrome" in the field of cinema. Few Hollywood films—at least before the 2008 recycling of *Rambo*—so powerfully fused warrior myths of male heroism, patriotism, and stab-in-the-back revenge fantasies with epic struggles against demonic enemies. In an absurd twist intelligible only in the context of U.S. imperial arrogance, it is the Americans—not the Vietnamese—shown here fighting for liberation. *Rambo: First Blood Part II*, like others of its genre, could rewrite history in such a way as to excuse widespread American atrocities against the Vietnamese. Such precursors to later ultrapatriotic, militaristic Hollywood films would have far greater resonance among mass audiences than all of the purportedly "antiwar" Vietnam pictures combined.

As a mythic figure in American popular culture, Rambo, as we have seen, had come to exemplify the super-warrior with roots in the Western frontier, reappropriated for the Vietnam and especially post-Vietnam eras. As Bruce Franklin writes, he "incorporates one of America's most distinctive cultural products, the comic-book hero who may seem to be an ordinary human being but really possesses superhuman powers that allow him to fight, like Superman, for truth, justice, and the American way, and to personify national fantasies ... No wonder Rambo can stand invulnerable against the thousands of bullets fired at him, many from point-blank range, by America's enemies" (Franklin, 2000: p. 194). The *Rambo* movies packed theaters, with viewers cheering wildly at every slaying of a Vietnamese or Russian—repeated two decades later with the new and improved Rambo. During the 1980s the nation was inundated with Rambo warrior goods, such action dolls, walkie-talkies, water guns, pinball machines, and sportswear, not to mention TV cartoons and video games. A *Rambo* TV cartoon special, designed by Family

Home Entertainment for ages 5–12, transformed Rambo into "liberty's champion," a skilled warrior engaged in global struggles against evil. There were even "adult" video spin-offs featuring pornographic images of Rambo (Franklin, 2000: p. 195).

As the 2008 version of the series proves, the *Rambo* spectacle remains a larger-than-life force in American popular culture, good for patriotic rebirthing as well as corporate profit making at a time when we were told the society was immobilized by the "Vietnam Syndrome." The formulaic motif of rescuing POWs from evil Vietnamese Communists became almost standard Hollywood fare, beginning with such crude embellishments of U.S. militarism as *Uncommon Valor* (1983) and *Missing in Action* (1984)—both vehicles of cartoonish heroism set in Indochina. Advertisements for *Missing in Action* trumpeted: "The War's Not Over Until the Last Man Comes Home." Other pictures included *P.O.W.: The Escape* (1986) and *Operation Nam* (1987), produced abroad but featuring American actors, along with a series of mass-marketed POW rescue novels written by Jack Buchanan, the first appearing in 1985 as *M.I.A. Hunter.* The central protagonist of these novels was former Green Beret Mark Stone, who "has only one activity that gives meaning to his life— finding America's forgotten fighting men, the POWs...and bringing them back from their hell on earth" (Franklin, 2000: p. 195). Yet another component of this inverted narrative was the mass slaughter carried out in Cambodia after the U.S. exodus, depicted in macabre detail by the popular movie *The Killing Fields* (1984), where the carnage is presented as if years of U.S. armed intervention had nothing to do with the Khmer Rouge bloodbaths that followed. Other mainstream pictures—far too numerous to explore here—served in varying degrees to glorify or justify U.S. intervention, many listed in Jeremy Devine's *Vietnam at 24 Frames a Second* (Devine, 1995: pp. 371–4). These include *Hanoi Hilton* (1987), another sympathetic depiction of the mythical POW saga replete with diatribes against Jane Fonda, *Swimming to Cambodia* (1987), a takeoff on *The Killing Fields* horrors, *Platoon Leader* (1988), *The Expendables* (1988), *Crossfire* (1988), *Hard Rain—The Tet* (1989), and *Air America* (1990), a Mel Gibson vehicle glorifying the work of CIA pilots in Laos during the Vietnam War. A later Hollywood movie, *We Were Soldiers* (2004), dramatizes American heroism in a critical 1965 battle against North Vietnamese forces in the bloody Valley of Death, an overdone combat saga that almost perfectly fits the paradigm of Hollywood militarism, another in a long history of formulaic war movies adhering to every rule and cliché.

Hollywood filmmaking, like American political culture in general, managed to steamroll over Vietnamese history and politics, then as now. A close scrutiny of reputedly "antiwar" pictures reveals a distinctive flaw: None challenge the reckless use of U.S. imperial and military power, none question the legitimacy of U.S. intervention spanning an agonizing fourteen years, and none accurately depict the horrors experienced by the Vietnamese. To be sure, one can identify plenty of "mistakes" and "excesses" in Washington, D.C. and on the battlefield that hindered U.S. capacity to "win" the war, and the costs (that is, American) turned out to be far too burdensome relative to feasible ends. And enough bad deeds can be attributed to U.S. troops that, under battlefield pressure, sometimes lost control of their senses. As for the imperial agenda itself, well, it was well intentioned if not always expertly planned or managed by the Kennedy liberals and their successors. Most American viewers will simply come away from these films thinking that the Vietnam War was a great, costly tragedy filled with missteps that future, wiser U.S. leaders ought to avoid as they undertake new foreign ventures. Few Hollywood films dealing with Vietnam—*Born on the Fourth of July* is one that comes to mind— have ever transcended these narrow limits. The final destruction of a seemingly durable European colonial system was an epic moment of modern history, but that reality never surfaces in *any* Hollywood film on the Vietnam War, even the most "progressive" of them. To ward off that defeat, the United States conducted a brutal war of attrition, a barbaric project that even the most "antiwar" mainstream pictures have managed to obscure.

On the basis of the previous conclusions, it might be argued that a militarized media culture, having come to fruition during the age of Empire, operates largely as a *propaganda* apparatus that sends out crude messages to gullible mass audiences on the model of early authoritarian regimes. The solidity of popular consensus behind U.S. militarism might well be viewed as evidence supporting the propaganda model. David Robb, in his book *Operation Hollywood*, argues this point of view, suggesting that the film industry has become a full-blown propaganda vehicle, one of the most powerful opinion-forming mechanisms ever. We know that "propaganda" is supposed to be alien to the American experience, but Robb convincingly describes a process that is largely unseen by the public, where blatant political messages in support of the Pentagon are regularly and brazenly transmitted to viewers fully convinced they are getting nothing but "entertainment." Thus: "... the military propaganda that is inserted into our television programs in the form of films and TV shows is done so subtly the American people don't even know it's there" (Robb, 2004). The undeniable fact that the United States has grown more warlike over the past fifty years is cited by Robb as validation of a sophisticated propaganda model.

Robb is surely correct to emphasize the growth of efforts at ideological manipulation in American society over the past few decades, a trend accelerated by the 9/11 events, not to mention the expansion of media culture discussed earlier. He is also on the mark when he points to increased public readiness to endorse U.S. military ventures. At the same time, whether the film medium as such can be described as a propaganda outlet is yet another matter. While some pictures might well fit this model, and many clearly bear the imprint of Pentagon influence, the larger problem is that most filmmakers are already immersed in the political culture and the canons of patriotism, thus typically needing no formal government censorship or controls as they produce movies that fit the contours of U.S. foreign and military policies. In fact, heavy-handed brainwashing techniques can only run counter to entertainment values as well as box office prospects. For producers like Jerry Bruckheimer and directors like Michael Bay, patriotic war spectacles are merely business as usual at the Hollywood studios. Moreover, the expanded role of propaganda *outside* Hollywood cinema actually ends up reinforcing the capacity of motion pictures to help ideologically bolster Empire and the war system. Among other developments, growing corporate power has given rise to a political system that increasingly operates as little more than an organized machine in the service of narrow elite interests. The operation relies heavily on ideological manipulation while combining the input of diverse sectors: party elites, corporations, media, the government, lobbies, and an assortment of think tanks and foundations. In this highly corporatist milieu, what has historically been called "propaganda" extends across the entire social and political landscape, often in subtle ways. In polls conducted during and after the Bush post-911 buildup to the Iraq war, for example, a strong majority of Americans was shown to believe the repeated outlandish lies and obfuscations behind the invasion and occupation. In fact, the whole stratagem of "regime change" and "preemptive war" was stage-managed by the government and military, with nearly total media complicity.

In the provocative 2005 documentary *Why We Fight*, Eugene Jarecki builds his indictment of the U.S. war system on President Eisenhower's warnings about the military-industrial complex, which nearly a half-century later comes across as rather understated. Neither

28 CARL BOGGS

Eisenhower nor Jarecki, however, call attention to a crucial pillar of the system—a militarized popular culture that seems to deepen with each passing year. If this culture does not fully constitute a modern propaganda apparatus, its role in the legitimation process no doubt equals or even *surpasses* that of any such apparatus in history, since its spectacular images and narratives, produced and marketed as "entertainment" or even "news," probably turn out to be more effective than any crude attempts at media censorship and control. Meanwhile, the big studio productions, part of a thriving cinematic culture, have become integral to the very state-corporate order that underlies both the film industry and Eisenhower's nightmare of a military-industrial complex.

REFERENCES

Boggs, Carl and Tom Pollard. *The Hollywood War Machine* (Lanham, MD.: Rowman and Littlefield, 2006).

Devine, Jeremy M. *Vietnam at 24 Frames a Second* (Austin: University of Texas Press, 1995).

Franklin, H. Bruce. *Vietnam and Other Fantasies* (Amherst: Univ. of Massachusetts Press, 2000).

Kellner, Douglas. *Media Culture* (New York: Routledge, 1995).

Robb, David L. *Operation Hollywood* (Amherst: Prometheus Books, 2004).

Rogin, Michael. *Ronald Reagan the Movie* (Berkeley: Univ. of California Press, 1987).

2

HOLLYWOOD AND THE
WORKING-CLASS HERO: DIAMONDS IN
THE MEAN STREETS OF BOSTON

Richard Van Heertum

OVERVIEW

From its early days, Hollywood has had a complex relationship with the working class, both in the production of film and its depiction of their lives. Dwight MacDonald once said that for the movie industry, working-class life was like the dark side of the moon. Early silent films often dealt with working-class heroes, and this continued in the early days of its rise. Ross (1998), in fact, argues that silent films before World War I often portrayed working-class life in sympathetic terms, including addressing organized labor's struggles and even promoting the labor movement. Since then, Ross argues (along with many others), that we have moved to largely negative images of the working class that, often in the guise of gritty realism or naturalism, depict violent, base, unredeemable characters that struggle for meaning and happiness against the powerful with little success. There are, of course, notable exceptions like *Norma Rae* (1979), *Salt of the Earth* (1954), *Rocky* (1976), and *On the Waterfront* (1954), but the dominant image of the working class has been largely negative from the moment characters began to speak.

   In this essay, I will look at three contemporary films that explore Hollywood's treatment of the working class in one of the quintessential American working-class cities, Boston. The three films, *Mystic River* (2003), *Gone Baby Gone* (2007), and *Good Will Hunting* (1997), offer an entryway into a broader exploration of how Hollywood represents the working class and the heroic redeemer. In all three films, I argue that the working class is juxtaposed against an other that is shown as superior by comparison.

A BRIEF HISTORY OF HOLLYWOOD AND THE WORKING CLASS

When studying the history of class and Hollywood, the most surprising thing is how little has been written about it.[1] Linda Dittmars argues that this is partially based on the response of film studies to the allure of post-structuralism and "identity politics" coupled with an "unvoiced recoil from Marxist criticism, as if it is necessarily mired in an outmoded predilection for thematic readings and at odds with the cutting edge discourses of ideology and refracted meanings elaborated by Althusser, Foucault, Machery, Jameson, Bakhtin and others" (Ditmar, 1995, p. 39). Zavarzadeh (1991) argues that the self-absorbed pleasures of contemporary theory redefine ideology, hegemony, and power in ways that make them detached abstractions from materialist analysis of class or oppression in general. The move toward dematerialized forms of alienation and exploitation seems to complement the underlying critique of critical theory from feminists, critical race theorists, postcolonialists, and those doing purely formal media analysis.

And yet class is as important a line of demarcation today as it ever was, and this huge lacuna in recent work, with a few exceptions, fits with America's general penchant to pretend that we are a "classless" society. One could then argue that the working class is to be feared in much the same way as youth of color—they are the embodiment of a deep-seated anxiety of proximity—a fear of falling out of the middle class and into the violent, saturnine world of poverty and alienation. Class anxiety is articulated in horror films from the 1980s forward (Kellner, 2001), and maybe in Hollywood treatment of the working class in general, as the failed promise of the American Dream. In both film studies and film itself, this fear of proximity seems to play out through exclusion and negative portrayals marked as a movement outside the normative peace and comfort of middle-class and affluent lifestyles. By rearticulating this in the converse, we restore the legitimacy of the system and our own class position, including privilege against rampant injustice that is otherwise hard to ignore. At the same time, our base treatment of the working class in general relieves our own complicity in the very system of inequality in which we reside (Nystrom, 2004).

As mentioned earlier, the silent film era engaged often and positively with the working class, and this engagement continued into the 1930s and early 1940s. Bodnar (2003) argues that films in this epoch did provide a critique of capital, through "grim antagonisms," including the worker versus capital (*Daily Bread* (1934)) and collective versus individual and family power (*Grapes of Wrath* (1940)). Gangster films do critique the system, but offer little hope of real change and the "rebel," in this sense, is either punished or killed. The alternative is escape, the arc turn of many of these films, with the working-class hero not confronting or improving the surrounding society, but escaping their class positionality to find material or emotional satisfaction—as exemplified in classic Frank Capra films (McBee, 2004), Will Smith in *The Pursuit of Happyness* (2006) or Disney films like *Cinderella* and *Shrek*. (Giroux, 1999)

In the 1940s and early 1950s, unity replaced emotional and social realism as patriotism and the struggle against fascism and then Communism (Cold War) led to the call for equality outside class warfare terms. Post-World War II, we did return to more realistic portrayals of ordinary people, though McBee (2004) argues it is framed in the struggle between democracy and liberalism. A focus on atrocities and the violent nature of men intertwined with exploration of the dehumanizing effects of the development of consumer culture and the mass society (Mills, 1951). Film noir is a perfect example of this shift, creating a politics of a "dark and dangerous illiberalism disinterested in building a better life by either democratic or liberal means" (Bodnar, 2003, p. 116). Films like *The Postman Always Rings Twice* (1946) showed the dangers to women of working-class males, just as Black male virility serves as a powerful source of white male anxiety and racism (hooks, 1996). In the detective noir, the working-class "hero" is often an honorable but emotionally vacant rake, like Philip Marlowe in *The Big Sleep* (1946) or Sam Spade in *The Maltese Falcon* (1941), nobly eschewing sex (sometimes) and love to serve the corrupt and powerful (and ultimately an arguably skewed sense of justice). And two decades later in *The Hustler* (1961), we see another woman sacrificed for a working-class "loser" who even as he wins, loses, as he will never play pool again.

Moving forward, the 1970s marks both a period of profound change in Hollywood production and a change in the nature of treatment of the working class. While the American auteurs De Palma, Coppola, Lucas, and Scorsese traversed the fading power of Hollywood unions and big studios to forever alter the face of moviemaking, they often wrote and directed self-reflective tales that exemplified their struggle as artists and filmmakers. In the 1970s, we see a strong engagement with the working class from the bleak, dusty town of Anarene, Texas, in *The Last Picture Show* (1971), to the heroic antihero Travis Bickle in *Taxi Driver* (1976), to the somber bleak tragedy of *Mean Streets* (1973) to *Rocky* (1976), where an everyman boxer challenges the system of oppression and in some ways wins. But unlike Terry Mallow (Marlon Brando) in *On the Waterfront* (1954), those victories are more personal than collective and are too often based on individual effort and resolve. Nystrom argues that a series of films from the 1970s actually juxtaposes the working class against the professional-managerial class, reproducing capitalist ideology through an inherent antagonism toward the former, that related to the auteur's desire to fashion themselves as artists separated from the old studio system and unions that limited their autonomy and special talents (Nystrom, 2004).

From the 1980s onward, there has been a move away from the working class to engage more with the middle class and the elites, often as victims of their class positionality. Films still existed in this period, including a series of John Hughes teen comedies based on class antagonism, *Pretty in Pink* (1986) and *The Breakfast Club* (1985), where a lower-class ingénue struggles to get the rich other that can then fulfill their romantic dreams—while simultaneously offering a higher social positionality based on the dual images of popularity and wealth. *Pretty in Pink* (1986) may be the archetype of this genre. Andie Walsh, played by Molly Ringwald, is a teenager "from the wrong side of the tracks" who just doesn't fit into the school she attends, hanging out with two other social outcasts, a friend Ducky and an older woman, Iona. She wears an odd collection of clothes that she often makes herself and lives with her unemployed father in a part of town she is embarrassed of (at the end of the first date with her love interest, she starts to cry as he asks to drive her home, telling him "I do not want you to see where I live.") This love interest, Blayne (Andrew McCarthy), is rich and worried that his connection with her will be a challenge to his class position (with both his parents and peers). Their relationship remains hidden from the outside world, exemplified in a mimetic barnyard sex scene, his rich family in the lavish house beyond. While he appears to commit a form of class suicide in the culminating scene, the implicit message is that she takes him back and will be availed with the wealth and status he offers. Her friend Ducky (Jon Cryer) also takes up with one of the rich girls, thus ensuring his route out of social stigmatism as well—and Iona (Annie Potts) moves toward the mainstream by forgoing her iconoclastic style and persona for a yuppie hairdo and white pants suit in pursuit of a new love interest. In finding love in the end, they all simultaneously find access to status and wealth and the happiness they engender as contrast to their prior lives. A related theme emerges in *The Breakfast Club* (1985), where John Bender (Judd Nelson) and Claire Standish (Molly Ringwald) move from an antagonistic relationship to an amorous one. In the final scene, she kisses him in front of her parents, leaving the audience to question whether the rich girl is simply using the poor loser to rebel against her parents, a thought Nelson intimates earlier. Other films in this subgenre include *Some Kind of Wonderful* (1987), even as he picks the poor, unpopular girl over the rich one, a diamond earring becomes the avatar of their love; *Can't Buy Me Love* (1987), where even as the main character appears to fail in buying popularity and love, ends up with it in the end; *Say Anything* (1989); *Summer Catch* (2001); *Here on Earth* (2000); and *Dirty Dancing* (1987). Outside teen movies, we have *Pretty Woman* (1990), *Two Weeks Notice* (2002), *Jerry McGuire* (1996), and *Mr. Deeds* (2002), among many.

At around the same time, youth of color showed up as dangerous antisocial elements to be controlled in films like *Boyz in the Hood* (1991), *Menace to Society* (1993), *New Jack City* (1991), and even the more compelling and complex *Do the Right Thing* (1989) (Giroux, 1996). The point is that the working class has sometimes existed as a heroic figure in Hollywood, but generally as a flawed hero whose only real victory is escape from their class positionality or an honorable sacrifice or death. Even Rocky didn't win the fight until he had crawled out of the gutter in *Rocky II* (the first fight was an unjust draw). In other cases, the working class is to be feared, avoided as a corrupting influence on society, displacing the shifting economic reality and the corruption of corporations and politicians. This leads to the three films I will discuss next.

MYSTIC RIVER

Mystic River (2003) was directed by the indomitable Clint Eastwood with a star studded cast that included Sean Penn, Kevin Bacon, Tim Robbins, Marcia Gay Harden, Laurence Fishburne, and Laura Linney. The film garnered almost universal critical acclaim, was included on innumerable top 10 lists, nominated for six Academy Awards and five Golden Globes (and won both for Penn as Best Actor and Robbins as Best Supporting Actor), and won the Cesar for Best Foreign Film and numerous other awards. It was also a major box office success with over $90 million domestically and another $66.7 million overseas (www.boxofficemojo.com/movies/?id=mysticriver.htm).

The film, based on a novel by Dennis Lehane and adapted for the screen by Brian Helgland, revolves around three men, Dave Boyle (Robbins), Jimmy Markum (Penn), and detective Sean Devine (Bacon) and their struggle to overcome the effects of an abduction when Boyle was a child. The movie opens with an overhead pan of the South Side of Boston in 1975, with two working-class guys chatting about the Red Sox surrounded by gray, impending doom. The dank blue-gray coloring and moody, ominous background music provide the general aesthetic tenor of the entire film—working-class Boston is a sad and dangerous place where characters struggle to survive the many corrupting influences that surround them. There are dysfunctional families with abusive parents (best portrayed by Jenny O'Hara as Esther Harris, an embittered mother abandoned with a deaf son and another she turns on when she learns he was going to secretly elope), alcohol abuse, crime, secrets and lies, and self-destructive individuals. We then meet the three as boys, playing hockey in the street. As they carve their names into a newly paved sidewalk, shot from a low angle that accentuates their innocence and strength simultaneously, a man emerges from a car and admonishes the boys for destroying public property. He then puts the young Boyle in the backseat and drives off. An ominous-looking second man turns around and smiles at Dave, foreshadowing the abduction and molestation to come, right before Dave looks back at his friends in fear, his innocence literally driving away. We then witness him pleading with the men to stop and then escaping into the woods, as if chased by wolves (a theme that reemerges later). As Dave arrives back home, one of the two fathers of the other boys says "looks like damaged goods to me," the leitmotif of the entire film. As with *Gone Baby Gone*, it is the working class itself that has corrupted his innocence and ruined his life—here embodied in the image of two "working-class" thugs who pretend to be cops. This is further exemplified by the shadows that seem to always paint the faces of these three characters, the scars of a past they cannot seem to escape.

The tagline of *Mystic River* is "We bury our sins, we wash them clean." This relates to later events in the film that I will discuss next, but really captures the movie's heart in that sins either caused by others or the main characters seem to flow from their positionality in the world—namely as working-class "Southies." This is backed by its gritty realism, often used as the cover for portraying poor, working-class characters in this light, even as fantasy tales and hyperbolic fiction pervade treatment of the rich. A. O. Scott captures the underlying aesthetic, without mentioning the class dynamics at play, when he argues, "This grim theology is as close as anyone comes to faith, but Mr. Eastwood's understanding of the universe, and of human nature, is if anything even more pessimistic. The evil of murderers and child molesters represents a fundamental imbalance in the order of things that neither the forces of law and order nor the impulse toward vengeance can rectify" (Scott, 2003). In the next scene in the film, David Boyle is now grown up with a wife and a kid, though still wearing the same Red Sox hat from the first scene of the film. He is playing ball with his son when a flashback to the abduction and the words "get in" flash into his memory. As the story unfolds, we see that David has been damaged beyond recognition by this event from his youth and fallen out of touch with his two friends, Markum, who went to prison in his youth and is now married with three daughters (he owns a convenience store), and Devine, who is a detective whose wife left him right before their first child was born.

All seem to carry the weight of this sin, though the other two from afar. Markum's eldest daughter Katie (Emmy Rossum) appears in his store acting oddly and we learn that she is about to elope with neighborhood kid Brendan Harris (Tom Guiry). The next morning she turns up dead and the remainder of the film deals with attempts by Devine and his partner Whitey Powers (Fishburne) and Markhum and his two cohorts to find the killer. Ironically, the same night that Emma is killed, Dave comes home from the bar with blood on his hands, we later find out, from killing a man having sex with a child. In a Shakespearean turn, his wife assumes he is Katie's killer, and little by little the others come to agree. Markum's personal crusade for justice culminates in him killing Boyle before finding out the very next morning from Devine that the murderer was not Boyle but two kids, Brendan's deaf brother and his good friend.

One could argue that *Mystic River* was sold as a tragedy that explored the lasting effects of violence on three men germinating outward to profoundly influence their families, friends, and the whole of their small community. And yet two scenes at the end of the movie seem to largely undermine any counterhegemonic messaging it would have otherwise offered, even as Scott and many other critics believe the film does the opposite. As Markum enters his house after realizing his mistake, his body framed with the cross tattooed across his back, his wife enters the room. He tells her what he has done but instead of admonishing him, she deifies him as a king and god that has restored order to the family and saved them from the evil force that took their daughter. She vilifies Celeste as a bad wife and claims their superiority over all the other "weak" people, with Jimmy as the symbolic doppel-ganger of the complete man—sexy, violent, and strong—before mak-ing love to him. Later, Markum emerges from the house, surrounded by his family and friends. Devine looks over and smiles with reverence, seemingly honoring Sean Penn for having killed an innocent man and restoring order to the community as he playfully points a finger gun at him. Off in the distance, a haggard, frenetic Celeste looks about desperately waving at her son in the parade beyond. Who is the hero of the film? It appears to be Markum, even as he exacted his revenge on the wrong man. Donning his sunglasses and James Dean coif, he responds to Devine's shot with a callous though whimsical gesture of "what can you do" before placing the sunglasses back on. He is the symbolic American renegade, a man of few words, who avenges his daughter's death—the ultimate form of loss in our society. He is the American monomyth reinvented in the guise of an antihero (Jewett & Lawrence, 1977). And so life goes on, violence begets violence and in the background a scene of traditional Americana unfolds, a parade with fire engines, children, and the revelry of the country in its nod to its naïve, hopeful past. The children are honored, the band plays a classic song, and peace is restored.

The semiotic impact of the scene seems to transcend any literal interpretation of the film. Violence and masculinity are the language of the working class here, as in most filmic representations, and the damage wrought by both defines the specter of everyone in the com-munity. Whether Black or white, the working class is to be feared and avoided, as death and misery follow them wherever they go. Crime is rampant, bad parenting almost de rigueur (though Markum and Boyle do appear as relatively caring fathers), and escape for the char-acters the only way out of this tempest of despair. Katie Markham, in her minor role in the film, in fact embodies that very promise of escape and its ultimate failure. In her death, we see the very com-munity she is trying to escape brought to the edge of destruction, yet saved by another act of violence: the killing of the innocent working-class lamb Boyle by the antiheroic redeemer.

GONE BABY GONE

In *Gone Baby Gone* we again see escape derailed, this time by the masculine honor system of the working class, enacted through the hero Patrick Kenzie (Casey Affleck), who rises above the other char-acters through his education and street smarts, intermingled with a toughness culled in his youth and years as a hard-nosed, noirish detective on the mean streets of Boston. The escape in this case is that of a young girl Amanda McCready (Madeline O'Brien) from her drug-addled, alcoholic mother Helene (Amy Ryan) and the corrupting influence of the surrounding community. As Manohla Dargis argues, "Talk about not wanting our love! Ugly in voice and deed, Helene is the underclass mother from hell, a hazard, a druggie, a villain in waiting. [She] is a nightmare, or at least the embodiment of a certain familiar fear: the bad woman (welfare queen) periodically held up as a symptom of some grave social disorder" (Dargis, 2007). The promise of escape is to a middle-class family existing on the bucolic outskirts of town, far away from the base existence of drug dealers and addicts, corrupt cops, ex-cons, bad parents, working-class stiffs, child molesters, and violent thugs that populate almost every scene in the film. Gritty realism is again the aesthetic of the film, with first-time director Ben Affleck providing a gripping and naturalistic image of Boston, including the use of real people from the area—their sadness and despair written on their faces like a history of the unspoken class battles that define America's dark underbelly, the poverty on the other side of our entrepreneurial-inspired material wealth and woebegone promise of equality and democracy (at least for these folks).

The opening line of the film, from Patrick, provides the backdrop for all that is to come: "I always believed it was the things you don't choose that makes you who you are. Your city, your neighborhood, your family. People here take pride in these things, like it was something they'd accomplished. The bodies around their souls, the cities wrapped around those. I lived on this block my whole life; most of these people have...This city can be hard. When I was young, I asked my priest how you could get to heaven and still protect yourself from all the evil in the world. He told me what God said to His children. 'You are sheep among wolves. Be wise as serpents, yet innocent as doves.'" Amanda is the sheep among wolves, damaged by a world she neither chose nor embraced, but one that will corrupt and define her for the rest of her life (or so we are led to believe). The narrative opens with her abduction and the search leveled by the police and Patrick, along with his partner Angie Gennaro (Michelle Monaghan), to find her.

A series of plot twists follow until a dramatic scene at the quarry where Amanda is seemingly lost in a trade between the police, Patrick, and the seedy Jamaican drug dealer Cheese (Edi Gathegi) and his underling. As her doll floats in the dark, murky waters below and the surrounding serene beauty of nature is accentuated with a stunning overhead pan, the image of innocence lost is vividly portrayed through contrast. And this contrast is the unspoken leitmotif of the whole film: children at the edge of the camera's eye or unseen, but defiled or destroyed by the dark, perilous world that surrounds them. Along the way, we meet a cast of increasingly unseemly characters, including a bar full of depressed, violent thugs; several drug dealers; and a broken family led by absentee mother Helene (who spent several nights a week at the local bar drinking and doing coke, stole money from Cheese on a busted drug deal, and once left her daughter in the car during a day at the beach where she was "literally roasted.") After her presumed death, we learn that it was all a plot by a corrupt cop Remy Bressant (played brilliantly by Ed Harris) and Helene's ex-convict brother Lionel (Titus Welliver) to get the stolen money from Helene. But things turned bad, people died, and they ultimately decide to give the girl to honored police captain Jack Doyle (Morgan Freeman) and his white wife—one presumes this choice was made to make the alternative life more palatable to an audience that may be troubled by a Black savior to young white girl (even one as popular to white audiences as Freeman).

Patrick uncovers the plot and after Bressant's death is forced to choose between leaving the girl in the more stable and loving home of Doyle or returning her to Helene. He chooses the latter, thus blocking her escape from the base, corrupting world around her and arguably sealing her fate (or so we are led to believe in the final scene). Affleck captures the full brutality of this world in the seedy bars of the neighborhood, the coarse language of the street, the hypermasculinity of all the main characters, with kids who exist on the periphery of many scenes, skipping rope, playing, or being victimized by the working class and poor. The main narrative is supplemented by another abducted boy, killed by a skinny pedophile Patrick, who later kills himself after he, Bressant, and partner Nick Poole (who dies) break into the home the man is staying in with two cocaine addicts that make the other characters seem exemplary by comparison. Bressant and Doyle have spent their entire careers chasing pedophiles after Doyle lost a child as a younger man. Thus, innocence lost is the underlying message of the film, with that innocence juxtaposed against the debasing influence of the lower class. And while the film is brutal in its realism, many critics revel in the brutality, including *Washington Post*'s Stephen Hunter: "And that's what makes 'Gone Baby Gone' such a pleasure, the absolute fidelity with which it penetrates and makes real the non-Brahmin, unhip parts of that really interesting urban swamp up there, with all its colorful eddies and whorls of hatred, ugliness, hostility and, of course, treachery" (Hunter, 2007).

Gone Baby Gone was another critically acclaimed film, garnering 28 nominations and 9 wins, mainly for director Affleck and actress Amy Ryan. Its tagline is "Everyone Wants The Truth... Until They Find It." This is at the heart of the film, and really all three analyzed here. Below the surface of working-class life in America is an ugly cesspool filled with violence, drugs, sex, lies, and unrequited desires. In an act that he believes defines his commitment to the community, Patrick loses his lover, defames a police officer who spent his life chasing child abductors, and arguably returns a girl to a mother who in the culminating scene appears to be little changed by the events that transpired. As the girl looks blankly forward at the television screen, with Patrick sitting beside her, we recognize that he has probably made the wrong choice and that circumstance really does define us—that anyone with any sense would make the choice to escape the "gritty realism" of the poor and working class in America—and that only a fool could find beauty in this world. Dargis (2007) argues in the same review, "Even so, one of the graces of 'Gone Baby Gone' is its sensitivity to real struggle, to the lived-in spaces and worn-out consciences that can come when despair turns into nihilism. Mr. Affleck doesn't live in these derelict realms, but, for the most part, he earns the right to visit." Maybe that is what these films really offer, an opportunity to check in on the "struggles" and "nihilism" of the poor and working class, then return home to the same confines of our own immeasurably superior lives, derailing any complicity in the suffering of the masses brought on by our collective silence and inaction. We get access to some "truths" but find them as unsavory as the characters in the film do and thus are happy to escape. This leads us to the third film, where a singular exodus is finally realized.

GOOD WILL HUNTING

Good Will Hunting may be the most complex treatment of the working class of the three films. In one sense, the working-class characters are juxtaposed against the elite, intellectual community of Boston and often shown superior. In another, one could see the film as a rendering of the old Rouseauian noble savage discourse. The working class is portrayed as superior in a sense to the vain, sterile elites who have little backbone, use one another, appear alienated and emotionally vacant, and are largely unaware of the privilege that defines their lives. Will Hunting (Matt Damon), the noblest of the savages, is offered the opportunity to transcend his class position through his intelligence. In fact, *New York Times* critic Janet Maslin goes as far as portraying

Will as a "Cinderella at the blackboard," though his golden slipper is his intellect and Massachusetts Institute of Technology (MIT) the castle on the hill (Maslin, 1997). Yet the story revolves around his fear of this opportunity and desire to remain in the safe community he has built versus the allure of the unknown.

Ironically, it is two kids from Boston who offer such a complex treatment, two kids who had spent their acting youth tending to play the opposite—elite boys at elite institutions. The two wrote an extraordinary script that auteur impresario Gus Van Sant carefully crafted to toe the line between a sentimental education film and a nonathletic entry into the long list of American Dream-cum Horatio Alger fairy tales, like *Rocky*, *Rudy* (1993), and *Cinderella Man* (2005). Here intelligence rather than brawn or athletic prowess is the route out of the dour mean streets. The film opens with a series of alternating shots, going back and forth between Will's troubled life (including a street fight they start with some kids in the neighborhood) and the elite world of MIT. This overt juxtaposition continues throughout the film, setting it up as a morality tale where we must decide which is preferable. As the narrative develops, we find Will in court defending himself against assault charges for the fight and losing the case. In the crowd, however, is Professor Gerald Lambeau (Stellan Skarsgård) who realizes that it was Will, the janitor, who solved a complex mathematical proof he had left as a challenge to his graduate students. Jerry steps in to save Will from prison by adopting him as a sort of son, saving him from the "retarded gorilla" he later calls Will's friends, most importantly, Chuckie Sullivan (Affleck). From here, Will and Jerry develop a working relationship, and through the help of Jerry's professor and amateur therapist friend Sean Maguire (Robin Williams), Will starts to contemplate the life he is living versus the life available to him. He meets a girl, Skylar (Minnie Driver) at a Harvard bar, and through her, Jerry, Sean, and Chuckie come to recognize his potential. In the end, he leaves the job he finally accepts after refusing one offer after another, and chases Skylar to Stanford, leaving behind Chuckie and the working-class life he was ready to embrace for the rest of his life.

Ultimately, the question of how to see the working class in relationship to the larger society is hard to fully grasp. Will, Chuckie, and the others clearly have a friendship that transcends the narrow world that surrounds them. Will is smarter than those around him, but also floats through the film with a chip on his shoulder, using his genius to belittle and shame the elite and wealthy around him. He becomes the mentee and, at some level, mentor of Professor Lambeau, who admires him for his genius but builds a level of noblesse oblige as well, ultimately loathing him at some level for confronting his "class" position—defined through his academic accomplishment. More complex is the relationship between Will and the psychologist Sean. Both are working class, and over time a close relationship develops based on their shared cultural history and the markers of that relationship—physical abuse, the Boston Red Sox, and the pain that accompanies growing up poor in America.

The elite structure attempts to co-opt Will for its perpetuation, symbolized most clearly through Jerry but also in Sean, who went through a similar metamorphosis of transformation himself, only to reject it and return to his roots after his wife died of cancer. The two figures, both alumni of MIT, struggle over Will's soul, Sean wanting to free him of the past and Jerry interested in ushering him into elite culture. Three scenes define the framing of the entire film, where we often see the working class juxtaposed against the rich and the rich found wanting. The first occurs in a Harvard bar with Will and his friends. Chuckie approaches Skylar and her friend to try to strike up a conversation, under the false pretenses that he is a fellow Harvard student. A Harvard student steps into the conversation and embarrasses Chuckie, but Will then steps in himself and thoroughly shames the student with his superior intellect. Later he talks briefly with Skylar, gets her number, and then, upon leaving, embarrasses the student again.

A second short scene involves Jerry and Sean Maguire at a local pub. The usual male bonding of the working class is occurring, as Sean tells a joke he had heard from Will about a stewardess and pilot. Lambeau enters and orders a Perrier, and Sean jokes "that's French for soda water." As they sit down and the conversation continues, Lambeau shows himself to be so isolated from the real world he doesn't even know who the Unabomber is. Lambeau then belittles Maguire, arguing about Will's future, to which Maguire responds "you arrogant bastard." This is the general position of the elites, unaware of the world around them and attempting to shape the young Will to their model of normative life, like Judah Loew ben Bezalel molding his Golem to his ultimate destruction.

The third scene involves Will and Chuckie discussing their futures over a beer at the construction site where they both work. As they lean on Chuckie's truck, he admits that he has a dream that one day he will show up at Will's apartment and find it abandoned. Will protests that they will grow old together, but Chuckie responds, "It would be a straight insult for you to be here in 20 years." He then continues, "No you don't owe to yourself, you owe it to me." His point is that

Will's genius is a route out of the world that they spend the film building up and escape would be any sane person's dream, admitting, "I would die to have what you have." In an act of true friendship and sacrifice, Chuckie impels Will to leave the life that is clearly inferior, the life of the working class. While this is understandable at the level of material existence, it again places wealth and privilege as innately superior to that of the noble working man. His talent is not about making the world a better place, it's about rising above one's station in life and moving toward the normative. This is broached earlier in a conversation between Will and Sean, when Sean and he discuss the honor of the working man, and Sean lauds his father for putting him through school before later admitting he was an abusive, alcoholic.

Ultimately, in "stealing Sean's line" Will chooses to chase the embodiment of success in romantic terms, the girl who encompasses rich and elite culture indirectly. Love appears conflated at some level with the larger internal struggle, but as he departs on his journey in the beat-up car his friends bought him for his twenty-first birthday, Will ultimately fulfills the dreams of his friend Chuckie (to escape Boston working-class life), his mentor Sean (to stake a claim in the world based on his gift), and of the underdeveloped love interest, who appears to truly love Will but may embody the desire of the rich to arguably find authenticity in proximity to the nobility of the poor.

One could then argue that his love interest herself is the very embodiment of entryway to elite culture, as she is a rich girl from England that is pre-med at Harvard. As Roger Ebert argues, "Here is a character who has four friends who love and want to help him, and he's threatened by their help because it means abandoning all of his old, sick, dysfunctional defense mechanisms" (Ebert, 1997). Of course, these sick, dysfunctional defense mechanisms partially revolve around Will's faithful dedication to working-class life and his friends, but in escape he joins the normative where critics and the audience are more comfortable. This is at the center of the American conundrum, the celebration of wealth and social mobility confronted by the inherent nobility of hard work and poverty as not a moral failing, but a strength of character that confronts the stark realities of capitalism. In the end, Will chooses escape just as the characters in *Mystic River* and *Gone Baby Gone* would have liked to.

CONCLUSION

In the three films analyzed here, the working class of Boston is deconstructed, generally in a negative light. While *Good Will Hunting* certainly provides a more compelling case for the honor and friend-ship of the main characters, both Will and Sean ultimately chose to escape their class backgrounds and pursue the life that opportunity has provided. Both are also marked by the scars of abusive parental figures (for Will, it is foster parents) and see a light in the elite culture they critique throughout the film. Escape from the milieu portrayed in all three films seems natural, but we are then left to ask broader questions about class in America.

Who is to blame for poverty? Is it the characters themselves, who seem to tacitly embrace their place in the world (as Patrick argues in his opening paean to his city)? Is it the corrupting power of parents who just don't raise their kids right? Or are there deeper structural and cultural issues at play? Those issues are elided in all of these films, and we are led on a natural path to arguably believe that the poor are to blame for their own problems (Giroux, 1996). That idea of poverty as a moral failing goes back to our roots as a country, and has been reinforced by conservatives since Reagan with growing success.

So what positive can we take from these films? Kellner and Share have argued that critical media literacy is partially based on providing students with the skills and knowledge to understand the profound effects of media on their lives and to deconstruct cultural texts from diverse perspectives (Kellner & Share, 2007). Examining these films, or others in this genre, with students provides a powerful starting point to discuss class in America. As Dittmar argues, films like these and others, like *The Grapes of Wrath*, *Norma Rae*, or *Salt of the Earth*, can be used to provide positive images of the working class that can be empowering for youth and teach film from a working-class per-spective (Ditmar, 1995). There should be a reason for showing these films, but SMART board and other technology has certainly made it easy to incorporate some aspect of critical media literacy into the class-room, even with the constricting influence of No Child Left Behind and the "teach to the test" mentality that appears ubiquitous today. Class is too absent from debates inside and outside the classroom today, and we must find ways to bring it back into the conversation, as it continues to define the specter of much suffering and inequality in America (and across the globe) today.

NOTE

1. There are, of course, exceptions, like the articles mentioned earlier and Nystrom, D. (2009). *Hard hats, rednecks, and macho men: Class in 1970s American cinema*. (New York: Oxford University Press).

44   RICHARD VAN HEERTUM

REFERENCES

Bodnar, J. (2003). *Blue-collar Hollywood: Liberalism, democracy, and working people in American film.* Baltimore: The John Hopkins University Press.

Dargis, M. (2007, October 19, 2007). Human frailty and pain on Boston's mean streets. *The New York Times.*

Ditmar, L. (1995). All that Hollywood allows: Film and the working class. *Radical Teacher*(46), 38–45.

Ebert, R. (1997, December 25, 1997). Good Will Hunting. *Chicago Sun Times.*

Giroux, H. (1996). *Fugitive culture: Race, violence and youth.* New York: Routledge.

Giroux, H. (1999). *The mouse that roared: What disney teaches.* Lanham, MD: Rowman and Littlefield.

hooks, b. (1996). *Reel to real: Race, sex, and class at the movies.* New York: Routledge.

Hunter, S. (2007, October 19, 2007). There's something rotten in Beantown. *Washinton Post.*

Jewett, R., & Lawrence, J. (1977). *The American monomyth.* New York: Doubleday.

Kellner, D. (2001). *Media culture: Cultural studies, identity and politics between the modern and the postmodern.* New York: Routledge.

Kellner, D., & Share, J. (2007). Critical media literacy is not an option. *Learning Inquiry, 1*(1), 59–69.

Maslin, J. (1997, December 5, 1997). Logarithms and biorhythms test a young janitor. *The New York Times.*

McBee, R. (2004). Hollywood, the working class, and emotional realism. *Reviews in American History, 32,* 97–104.

Mills, C. W. (1951). *White collar.* Boston: Beacon Press.

Nystrom, D. (2004). Hard hats and movie brats: Auterism and the class politics of the new hollywood. *Cinema Journal, 43*(3), 18–41.

Ross, S. (1998). *Working-class Hollywood: Silent film and the shaping of class in America.* Princeton, NJ: Princeton University Press.

Scott, A. O. (2003, October 3, 2003). Dark parable of violence avenged. *The New York Times.*

Zavarzadeh, M. u. (1991). *Seeing films politically.* Albany, NY: State University of New York Press.

3

HOLLYWOOD'S MISSIONARY AGENDA: CHRISTONORMATIVITY AND AUDIENCE BAPTISM

Shirley R. Steinberg

> Christotainment could have only materialized in this particular his-
> torical moment with its particular social and political characteristics.
> How long this moment will last, I don't know—I'm afraid it's not
> going away very soon.
>
> Joe L. Kincheloe, *Christotainment: Selling Jesus*
> *Through Popular Culture*

INTRODUCTION

The normativization of an ideology involves creating an illusion
of a state of being that *should be*, not one that *is*. I contend that
North American audiences have become Christonormativized by
Hollywood productions of mainstream films and television programs, which create the ambience that everyone is Christian—actually
Protestant in belief, and if they aren't—well, they just don't belong.
Normativization occurs when the dominant culture is hegemon-
ized into *the normal* way of being. In this case, hegemony occurs
in North America because Christianity is assumed to be the dominant culture. North Americans consent to acknowledging this, and,
for example, Jews, Muslims, Hindus, Buddhists, and atheists normativize the December holidays as *Christmas* holidays. Christianity
drives our calendars, our conversations, and is more than the religious culture of North America. Christianity is invisibly dictated.
Hegemony occurs between different individuals and groups who consent to *what* the culture should be. Christianizing is different from

Christonormativizing. When attempts are made to proselytize and convert, the nature of missionary work is apparent—that is an attempt to Christianize. However, when the dominant culture includes themes and messages expected to be acceptable by all citizens, the outcome is not mere missionary zeal (Steinberg and Kincheloe, 2009), it is Christonormativization.

In this chapter, I examine Christotainment on TV and in film. I discuss two types of programming:

- Films that directly represent Christian fundamentalism, created to teach, convert, reaffirm beliefs, and save
- Television shows created for the viewing public, without overt or obvious inscription of Christianity, that is, mainstream TV shows

Both represent the Christonormativized screen. Within these two types of programming, I focus on two themes: *the Rapture*, and *tacit and overt Hollywood Christianity*. In examining Rapture programming, I look at the *Left Behind* films and television series *Revelations*. In analyzing tacit and overt programming, I refer to mainstream television shows and several films. I also examine the use of Christianity to ward away demons as a normalized solution to evil. I discuss the reflected themes and how they inscribe and perpetuate the growing industry that Joe Kincheloe and I have called Christotainment (Steinberg and Kincheloe, 2009).

IT'S THE END OF THE WORLD AS WE KNOW IT

The Apocalypse and the Rapture are central dimensions of twenty-first century Christian fundamentalism. The Book of Revelation in the New Testament is based on the *end of days*, the notion that the Earth will end in a precise way and Jesus Christ will usher in a new era. Such plots are fodder for novels, films, video games, and television shows, which portray horrendous images of Earth's inevitable end. Human beings have always been preoccupied with the end of the world. The arts have contained eschatological (pertaining to the last days) themes depicting man's (sic) greatest fears. Death seems to be the great individual fear; however, a humanist paranoia includes imagining exactly how the entire world will end. When six in ten Americans, according to a *Time/CNN* poll (McAlister 2003), believe that particular fundamentalist interpretations of the Book of Revelation will come to pass, the influence of Christian fundamentalist ideology is not something to dismiss.

Eating Cars with the Man from Mars: Rapture

In the prevailing Christian fundamentalist view of the Apocalypse, Jesus returns to Earth to "deal with" the Antichrist and the billions of people who have rejected the word of God. According to a majority of fundamentalists, Jesus will kill more than two billion people in Israel. Fundamentalist theologians, such as best-selling author Tim LaHaye, contend that this act will create a 200-mile-long river of human blood that is four and a half feet deep. Jesus will return after the Rapture, a condition that occurs within an instant. Those who are worthy of Christ are immediately transported away from Earth, leaving behind those who are not committed to Jesus or who are evil. A battle ensues in which the Antichrist attempts to win all souls still on Earth. After the carnage, Jesus will return to Earth to reign in peace and harmony. The idea that one could be "left behind" to deal with the "wars and rumors of wars" creates unprecedented fear. Today's fundamentalist Christian churches proclaim that the way to avoid the cruel days to come is to receive Jesus Christ as Savior and Lord. Those who aren't saved are doomed, and this ideology of fear is an essential tenet of the North American Christian evangelicals.

LaHaye is the author of the *Left Behind* books and the force behind the feature films based on the series of books. He presents this fundamentalist interpretation of the Book of Revelation as beyond dispute. One of the most influential evangelicals of our time, LaHaye takes a series of unrelated Bible verses and seamlessly places them in a clear narrative that never reflects on the multiple ways that any one of the passages could be interpreted and the narrative constructed. LaHaye and Jerry Jenkins' (the coauthor) narratives are easy to read, simple to comprehend, eminently marketable, and highly influential. At the time of the Rapture, Jesus brings the saved to heaven. The nonbelievers, evildoers, and people from other religious traditions suffer through seven years of war, famine, disease, and pestilence, referred to as the Tribulation. Then Jesus returns to settle age-old scores.

As with any piece of fiction or scripture, the literal interpretation of the Book of Revelation promoted by LaHaye and Jenkins cannot be read outside of the backgrounds of those who have constructed this interpretation. LaHaye, Jenkins, and other Christian novelists are the storm troopers of the cultural wars of the last three decades. In this sociohistorical context, it is not unusual that they might read the Bible and the Book of Revelation through the lens of their present struggle. They want revenge against the hated intellectuals, scientists, liberals/leftists, homosexuals, secularists, abortionists, feminists, Muslims, mainline Christians, Jews, and other enemies who have, in the evangelicals' eyes, worked to destroy true Christians. According to fundamentalist Christians, *those* people have murdered millions and millions of children in their support of abortion and undermined the traditional family by supporting sexual promiscuity, feminism, and the homosexual agenda.

The trilogy of *Left Behind* movies replicates on film what LaHaye and Jenkins originally published in their enormously popular book series. To suggest that the *Left Behind* books are successful would be an understatement at best. Selling nearly 70 million copies of the original book, *Left Behind*, and millions of the succeeding books, the series narrates an eschatological scenario of the looming future of Earth. The films, while extremely popular on DVD, never made much of a mark in theaters; consequently, the revenues earned are even greater than a traditional theater release. The first film, *Left Behind, The Movie* (2000), starred Kirk Cameron, the previous child star of *Growing Pains* and darling of the Christian Right.

Cameron plays Buck Williams, an eager young reporter stationed in Israel investigating a new way to grow food. As he presents an on-camera news update, Syrian armed forces send in an air attack and God destroys the troops, thus replicating the biblical prophecy that God would guard the Promised Land, Israel. Concurrently, airline pilot Rayford Steele (Brad Johnson), a married man with a newly wandering eye, is flying to New York; in an instant, passengers and crew disappear from the flight. Not everyone is gone, but a noticeable selection. Summing up the plot, the Rapture has taken place, and worthy believers have been removed to heaven. Left behind are the nonbelievers, the evil, and the undecided. Buck eventually connects with Rayford, who goes home to find his family missing (they were Raptured) and reads the Bible for solace.

Steele visits a minister in his neighborhood and aligns with him to attempt to understand the Rapture (this clergyman was not faithful enough to have been spirited away). During all of this, the Antichrist is manifest in the persona of Nicolae Carpathia (Gordon Currie). As the film ends, Steele's left-behind daughter accepts Christ, as does Steele, but Buck remains unconvinced. Buck finds his way to the church and is told that Nicolae has proclaimed seven years of peace (as predicted in the Book of Revelation) and that only faith will save them.

The second film, *Left Behind II: Tribulation Force*, debuted in late 2002, and included the same cast as the original film. The third film, *Left Behind: World at War* (2005) stars Lou Gossett Jr. as President Fitzhugh. This film was released to churches as the sites for the premiere in order to create fervor and excitement about the new film. The three films cover the first two books in the series. Following the ushering in of the Rapture, World War III, and the creation of one global community, forces battle with the power of Carpathia. Additional films, eventually covering the entire series, will follow the trilogy.

Following the amazing success of the books, a *Left Behind* young-adult book series was created, as well as *Left Behind: Eternal Forces*, a video game in which players use prayer to increase the strength of fighting forces and attempt to save citizens from evildoers and the Antichrist. Noted by critics as a violent game, *Eternal Forces* is often found in the youth areas of many churches; it is also used by American fighting forces for training, and copies of the game were sent to the Middle East one Christmas to be distributed as gifts for children in Iraq.

Clearly, the fear of losing a place in Heaven and facing the antichrist has moved Christian fundamentalists into fear mode and motivated a voting and politically influential fan base, manifested in the 2004 and 2008 American election results. Revelation-laden political rhetoric has become a common lexicon, and no longer the domain of *The 700 Club* or other Christian broadcast shows. CNN, MSNBC, and network news shows regularly discuss salvation, evildoing, and last days analogies as part of news descriptions. Supported by hegemonic TV and film entertainment, little opposition is named in the dominionist discourse of the last days. Indeed, the selection of Sarah Palin as the vice-presidential nominee in 2008 provided the foundation for normalizing the eschatological discussion as a political platform.

NBC'S *REVELATIONS:* ROSEMARY'S BABY MEETS *THE DA VINCI CODE*

In 2005, NBC created a miniseries (*Revelations*) starring Bill Pullman as Harvard astrophysicist Richard Massey, a grieving father whose only daughter has been savagely murdered by a satanist. After securing the capture of the murderer, Isaiah, the embodiment of evil, Massey returns home a defeated nonbeliever. His company and advice is sought by Sister Josepha Montafiore, a spirited young nun who is dangerously close to excommunication due to her insistence in following signs that she believes will usher in the end of times and the Apocalypse. Sister Josepha is tracing the birth of a male baby to a virgin nun in Greece; she is convinced of the virgin birth and seeks the child, whom she believes to be Christ. The baby has vanished, and the young mother (the virgin nun) has been confined to an institution.

Tortured by Isaiah, Massey is threatened by not only his own destruction but that of all human beings who do not bow to Isaiah. Soon after Massey returns home and meets Sister Josepha, a young Miami girl is struck by lightning and presumed to be brain dead. While evil doctors and hospital administrators argue about the possibility of harvesting her organs, she begins to speak in Latin and to draw and write messages. (The plot segues here to include a Terry Schiavo-esque debate and editorial.) As the nun and astrophysicist try to unravel the tangles of a very confusing plot (which attempts to follow the Book of Revelation quite literally), Massey's daughter's stepbrother/best friend, Hawk (nee Henry), is kidnapped by Isaiah's forces. These armies are led by Isaiah and trained to become "the heir and son" to Isaiah. In order to increase the size of the forces, Isaiah begins to convert convicts to his legions. He escapes prison and starts to build an empire that sports scores of upside-down crosses and followers in black-hooded robes.

Massey and Sister Josepha follow leads all over Europe. They end up in the Middle East after following the directions of the comatose little Miami girl (who is finally murdered by Isaiah's men). The two interpret clues that coincide with the apocalyptic visions of John the Revelator, and eventually save the day by killing Isaiah with a dead exorcist's dagger and rescuing the boy, Hawk. The two separate as friends, Sister Josepha ever faithful and Massey apparently a believer. The series ends with a close-up of the little baby (who was eventually rescued by an excommunicated priest), surrounded by light, and heavenly voices accompany the concluding shots of the boy lying on a carpet in the middle of a desert, guarded by the priest.

Throughout the series, Bible verses separate significant scenes, all dealing with prophecy and the end of days. In addition, interspersed within the six episodes are two beautiful raven-haired women who are only ever seen by Massey. Alternating with the two stunning women are two black cats with gleaming yellow eyes; it is apparent that the bodies are interchangeable. The viewer assumes that the women/cats are closely watching Massey with a satanic interest. The astrophysicist notices the women/cats; he never mentions them, but pauses in confused recognition whenever he spies them.

Revelations was written and created by David Seltzer (*The Omen*), a conservative Jew who insists he had no religious agenda in creating the series. He considers the series a fantasy/drama, and was asked by Gavin Palone to create the series given the current issues plaguing the earth. Palone wanted to address the increasing violence, environmental issues, and wars via the Book of Revelation. In an article in the *New York Times*, Palone stated that "his personal interest in religion and Armageddon stems from a long-ago summer spent at an evangelical Christian camp" *(New York Times* 2005). Seltzer discussed the film with UPI reporter Pat Nason, maintaining that "*Revelations* would not cover the same ground as the *Left Behind* books have—tribulation, followed by the rapture. We are in no way following a fundamentalist track" *(New York Times,* 2005).

Palone told Nason in the same interview that he would not discuss his own personal religious beliefs, but that he showed the pilot

> to friends of mine who are deeply religious and Christian, and wanted to make sure that they felt comfortable with it. And what I got back from them uniformly, among everyone that I showed it to, was a certain gratitude for expressing faith in a specific sectarian manner. I think that the fact that the religion in this show is so clearly Christian, and that we are talking about the New Testament, and willing to take that somewhat sectarian stance is something that was embraced by everyone that I showed it to. I think people wanted to see some specificity in faith as they see it on television. (*New York Times,* 2005)

Seltzer claims that the series deals with a man and a woman and the struggles within their lives. He asked the press to not continue asking questions about his faith, as he saw no connection between his own religious beliefs and his fantasy creation. Matt Sullivan of *In Touch Weekly* endorses the DVD box set: "If you're a fan of *The Da Vinci Code, Left Behind* and the *X-Files,* you'll love this six-part series."

The Da Vinci Code, while centering on a biblically inspired plot, never comes across as a conversion or repentance device. *The X-Files* dealt with the fantastic, yet lacks any hint of Christotainment. Missing in both of these other contemporary examples are the normative assumptions in contemporary evangelical Christianity: moralistic platitudes, fearsome threats of the end of the world, and a savior who must be acknowledged and worshipped to achieve eternal life. Sullivan's endorsement thinly veils Seltzer's intent to keep the series as a fantasy and not as religious tool. Seltzer failed.

REVELATIONS IN BEING LEFT BEHIND

As fundamentalist Christian authors and clergy, LaHaye and Jenkins are clear in their intent in the *Left Behind* books. It is their duty to warn readers of the coming of the last days and the advent of the millennium. The *Left Behind* books clearly act as conversion tools, and their presence (in even the most unlikely places) accentuates the growing Christotained reading audience. Stores like Wal-Mart and Sam's Club create mountainous displays of new series releases and find it difficult to keep them in stock. Airport bookstores prominently display the editions, and many airports include entire "inspirational" sections featuring the *Left Behind* volumes.

Rapture politics, so adeptly laid out in the *Left Behind* series, with its end-of-times retribution scenario, is now a major dimension of the foreign policy discourse in the United States. The cultural politics of the Rapture are central to a wide array of fundamentalist lobbying groups in the nation's capital, in think tanks, and in assorted organizations throughout the country. The *Revelations* miniseries and *Left Behind* books position the Rapture and the coming of the Apocalypse as the inevitable outcome and fate for citizens of Earth. However, many pundits discount the possibility that such bizarre "literal" interpretations of the Bible could influence major social, diplomatic, or military policy decisions.

It has many times been possible for evangelical fundamentalists to slip under the radar of cosmopolitan academics and veteran career diplomats, simply because such individuals would not believe that the ideas promoted by fundamentalists could be taken seriously by large numbers of people. Obviously, eight years of George W. Bush has discounted this premise. The fundamentalist media empire, the coalition with other right-wing groups, and Christotainment have helped disseminate these ideologies by treating them as the norm. At the beginning of the second decade of the twenty-first century, political fundamentalist interpretations of biblical prophecy are molding decision making in a variety of domains. Indeed, efforts made by fundamentalist Christians to gain this level of influence and the details of their agenda are not state secrets. Leaders such as LaHaye and James Dobson have openly discussed and published their ideas about these issues for decades. For example, LaHaye has written that good Christians can no longer view secularists as benign individuals who choose not to accept Jesus or attend church. In a direct and unequivocal statement, LaHaye (1980) proposed that the fundamentalist Christian movement eliminate all secularists from political office and replace them with political operatives who are moral

Christians. It is important to note that LaHaye is not talking about replacing these leaders with anyone who falls under the wide umbrella of self-proclaimed Christianity. Much to the contrary, he was calling for these positions to be filled with a particular variety of Christian who believes, as does LaHaye, in the strict precepts of Rapturist Christianity. The black-and-white here is sobering: In LaHaye's Rapture politics, the virtuous will be taken to heaven when the time arrives; the "rest" either are tacitly in league with the Antichrist because of their belief structures or consciously support him and his work. If one believes that his or her political opponents are working for Satan and wants to bring misery to the planet, then the chance of a productive, respectful democratic dialogue is seriously undermined (LaHaye, 1980; McAlister, 2003; Frykholm, 2005; Unger 2005).

While the *Left Behind* series is decidedly religious in content and intent, *Revelations*, a self-titled secular production, is NBC's contribution to Rapture politics. The elements of Christotainment are the same in both productions; fundamentalist evangelical predictions fill the screens, without doubt, question, critique, or even the possibility that the narrative is mythical. *Revelations* follows the script laid out by John the Revelator in the Book of Revelation, and the *Left Behind* films appear as well to frighten members of the audience into belief and salvation. One can assume, many viewers of both series watch the shows without knowing that they are Christian in nature and origin. By assuming the Christonormative belief that the world is destined to end with the coming of the Antichrist and his eventual defeat by Jesus Christ, Rapture politics serves to support the continued escalation of a U.S. neocolonial military force.

A postscript to the ideological underpinnings of the two series: As a media critic, I saw both series as expensive production undertakings, resulting ironically in naïve and simplistic products, confusing scripts, over- or underacting, poor lighting and cinematography, and lacking in overall cohesiveness. Both series had elements common to undergraduate film students, both lacked sophistication, and neither could sustain any of my interest other than academic analysis in more than sixteen hours of film. These dynamics tend to play themselves out in many religious films, somehow demanding that the audience view the texts through a lens of innocence and severe ignorance. In the next section of this chapter I draw the same conclusions based on my screening of all films discussed. I propose that readers consider the notion that this naiveté is deliberate and echoes simplistic Sunday school lessons and repeated sermons that do not go beyond the literal in fundamentalist churches. When one becomes, as the

Bible recommends, "like a child" and thus, is open to the spirit, this imposed innocence prevents analysis, challenge, and doubt.

TACIT AND OVERT HOLLYWOOD CHRISTIANITY TELEVISION MORALISM

Network television has a long history of producing all-American family fare. From the saccharine days of *Father Knows Best, The Waltons, Family,* and *Eight Is Enough*, to the nonreligiously inscribed religious dramas of *Highway to Heaven, Touched by an Angel, 7th Heaven,* and *Joan of Arcadia*, tacit themes tell us what is expected of an American family. While earlier family shows did not openly articulate a specific denomination, it was apparent that every family was Christian, most probably Protestant. In *The Waltons* and *Little House on the Prairie*, the viewer is clearly aware that the family is "churchgoing." Pastors and church relationships are never qualified, but considered part of the typical layout of the town dynamics. Later shows, such as *Highway to Heaven, 7th Heaven, Touched by an Angel,* and *Joan of Arcadia*, all assist in identifying what is expected in Christian behavior. All shows normativize Christianity as the way an American family *just is*.

Highway to Heaven

The earliest distinctly Christonormative drama, *Highway to Heaven*, aired for five years (111 episodes). The late Michael Landon plays angel Jonathan Smith, sent to earth by God, "The Boss." Jonathan's duty is to team with Mark Gordon (Victor French) to assist people in helping one another and/or finding a better life for themselves and their loved ones. Human failure is the theme; people exhibit greed, anger, and ego. Some episodes deal with realistic issues, such as cancer and racism. A popular series, its cancellation is believed to have been due to the death of Victor French in 1989. The show had an overarching lesson in each episode: The "highway to heaven" is open to all who choose it.

Touched by an Angel

Touched by an Angel brings messages directly from God to its characters. Each show revolves around a person or group wrestling with a problem or undergoing a crisis. Angels appear in order to help those in need. The supervising angel, Tess, played by gospel singer Della Reese, and her apprentice Monica (Roma Downey), aid Christians who have lost their way. Each week they deliver messages of hope directly from God to those who have no hope. Two other characters that became regulars on the show were Andrew (John Dye) and Gloria (Valerie Bertinelli). Andrew is the Angel of Death; he takes those who have died to either Heaven or Hell. Gloria is a novice angel who learns about being human, sometimes adding comic relief. The show labels itself nondenominationally as "Christian," a theme that plays itself out continually. The opening theme song by Della Reese praises God for helping those in need: "When you walk down the road. Heavy burden, heavy load. I will rise, and I will walk with you. I'll walk with you, till the sun don't even shine. Walk with you, every time. I'll tell ya, I'll walk with you. Believe me, I'll walk with you."

The song offers solace and is an obvious marketing tool. The marketing is slick; the message sells well. The show enjoyed global popularity and is now syndicated worldwide. Running nine years, the series had many celebrity guest stars, including Maya Angelou, Carol Burnett, Bill Cosby, Kirsten Dunst, Faith Hill, Rosa Parks, John Ritter, and Luther Vandross; all self-identify as Christian. The show's fan base is large and includes both young and old.

Touched by an Angel's episodes vary in depth, sending a final message of hope and morality at the end. Ironically, while definitively Christian, the show does not exude a sense of perfection in the manner of other Christian TV shows. There is no sense of condemnation or guilt imposed upon the "sinner." Death is a dominant theme, and one is always aware of its inevitability. This is also the only Christian-themed program to date (whether implied or defined) that includes black actors and has any indication of cultural diversity. There is no confusion among viewers as to the Christian nature of the show; yet critics consistently ignored the religiosity, and the show was highly successful.

7th Heaven

7th Heaven is an example of a nonreligious, yet overtly Christian show. The series follows a minister, his wife, their seven children, a loveable dog, a happy home, and a wholesome community. The long-running series of eleven seasons features a Protestant cleric, Reverend Eric Camden, and his family, who deal week after week with "everyday life." Eric Camden (Stephen Collins) and his wife Annie (Catherine Hicks) initially have five children of varying ages. The oldest two, Matt and Mary (Barry Watson and Jessica Biel), are high school students. Simon and Lucy (David Gallagher and Beverly Mitchell) are in junior high, and the youngest Ruthie (Mackenzie Rosman) is just beginning school. In the third season, the show's producers add two more babies to the Camden family. The fact that the family is Protestant is rarely stated in the show, but is inscribed in every scene.

Just as most other Christian-based shows shy away from many controversial topics, so, too, does *7th Heaven*. The most heated issues are alcoholism (the preacher's sister) and premarital sex (the preacher's daughter); however, topics like homosexuality and abortion are never mentioned. Each week the Camden family endures "typical" American problems and traumas, like not having a date for the homecoming dance, knee surgery, a cruel teacher, and not getting the perfect job. Everything turns out well in the end, and family solidarity remains intact. *7th Heaven* is a wholesome television show that never fails to warm the heart. It portrays the Camdens as the *average* (white, middle-class, Christian) family as a perfect family. In fact, the show is so wholesome that even the villains are somewhat benevolent. The topics and show always relate to conservative Christian beliefs and ideologies. It comes as no surprise that producers asked Jessica Biel, who plays eldest daughter Mary, to leave the show after she posed seminude for *Gear* magazine. Biel reportedly posed for the magazine precisely to combat her wholesome image on the show, which made it more difficult to get diverse parts in Hollywood. Producers needed a wholesome feminine representation for their program, so they had to get rid of the fallen starlet.

Joan of Arcadia

God speaks to sixteen-year-old Joan Girardi (Amber Tamblyn). Joan goes to high school, has family problems like other girls, and worries about the same things as other girls, but God approaches her each week in a different person's body and tells her to what to do. God appears to Joan in the form of an elderly lady, a teenage boy, a little girl, a street vendor, the school mascot, an amateur stand-up comic, a stoner at school, and other unlikely characters, and asks her to complete a task. Joan questions, pretends not to hear, and argues with God. In one episode, as God gets on Joan's nerves, she proclaims, "So many people pray to see you; if they only knew." The audience is engaged in a more contemporary Christian discourse. With Joan's teenage persona, CBS hoped her contrarian attitude would invite a younger, hipper audience. *Joan of Arcadia* takes on a new dynamic when trying to help viewers "see the world," and simple, blind faith is not relied upon.

The show's popularity was astounding. *Joan of Arcadia* won a People's and was nominated for an Emmy. In its first season, 10.1 million viewers watched it each week. The popularity of the show was accredited to its being considered spiritual, though not judgmental or too religious. The production team and viewers were shocked when the hugely popular show was cancelled after only two seasons. Fans wrote letters, sent e-mails, and phoned CBS to have the show put back on the air, but their efforts were in vain, as CBS claimed it wanted to target a younger audience.

Joan of Arcadia did not solve all problems in every episode. Some issues spanned several episodes, and others are never resolved due to the show's abrupt cancellation. The supporting cast consists of sympathetic and diverse characters. Each episode ends with a moral, always noted by "God"; for example, "How you see the world, how you deal with it—that determines your real wealth," and "Growth is a process."

TV AS A TACIT BAPTISMAL FONT

These four television dramas all created a Christonormative discourse. While Christianity was rarely articulated, the shows were laden with assumptions that a North American audience was receptive to, and expected, Christian values and morals. Banal, ordinary, and simplistic, most shows catered to the socially and theologically uninformed and depended heavily on sentimentality. As major network programs, production quality in all shows was high, and each had a large budget. The inability to convert, or "turn," a subject was never considered, and even through death, the unseen Jesus influenced participants. The whiteness of three of the dramas also emphasized the Rockwellian context of American middle-class Christianity. The climate that allowed these shows to thrive indicates a lack of resistance and questioning regarding the issues engaged. Rather, all the programs were well received and considered wholesome and mainstream. Those involved in production would still declare that the shows were neither religious in nature nor promoted any particular agenda.

THE CRUCIFIX VANQUISHES BAD COMPANY: SHOULD I STAY OR SHOULD I GO?

Watching old movies on the black and white TV as a kid was probably my favorite pastime. I loved the creepy stuff, the Boris Karloff, Vincent Price genre. Who wouldn't like rising from the dead, flying around in the dead of night as a bat, and living in those cool castles? By the time I reached sixth grade, *Dark Shadows* was my run-home-from-school 4:00 P.M. weekday snack. Most vampire/demon films follow the apotropaism (warding off of evil) of traditional vampirism: stays awake in the dark; sun would turn him into dust; sleeps in a coffin; became a vampire through a bite on the neck; repelled by garlic; can be killed by a stake through the heart; and absolute terror at the sight of a crucifix. The "crucifixication" of bad guys has always been an enigma to my Jewish self. My early viewing saw the repellent cross as the item that frightened a vampire; traditionally, the cross was held up, the vampire raised his arm to cover his eyes, and he backed up in absolute fear...task complete.

It wasn't until I understood *what* a cross implied that I realized my ilk was unable to slay the bad guys. I'm not referring to the Catholicized plot line of *The Exorcist*; there is nothing hegemonic in the plot. It is the use of the crucifix as *the global* solution to putting a halt to a vampire's advance. In *The Exorcist*, for example, the priests clearly believe Jesus is their savior, and in their abilities to vanquish demons. No Christotainment there. Rather, the Hollywood global consent that the only symbol that works to get rid of certain death is the crucifix, is Christotainment. I have never seen a show that shows an ideological conflict by a Jew, Muslim, Hindu, atheist, etc., use one of their own symbols to slay a demon or diminish a vampire. No star of David, no crescent moon, no aum, and no Che t-shirt is ever thrust into the face of evil. The Christotained part comes in when there is no discussion about the use of the cross—only the hegemonic agreement that it is the *only* way to do the deed. So any Jew unlucky enough to run into a vampire has to grab that crucifix, or else. It is the assumption that only Christianity can save one from evil that is implicit in vampire and demon repellents.

In the past fifteen years, vampire- and demon-themed bad guys have made an impact on prime time TV. Carrying a large tween to mid-twenties fan base, shows like *Buffy the Vampire Slayer*, *Angel*, and *Charmed* have held engaged audiences and created tie-ins, films, and corporate marketing. Without religious or ideological overtones, all three shows deal with the conquest of good over evil, whether it be humans versus demons/vampires/witches or demons versus vampires versus witches, with the humans facilitating the battles for the good. Interestingly, without the religious connections, the use of the crucifix always succeeds in backing up the evildoers and rendering them powerless. In particular, *Angel* (1999–2004), a spin-off of *Buffy, The Vampire Slayer*, employs the use of the cross against demons. Angel

is a vampire with a restored human soul. His guilt from prior mur-
ders, tortures, and neck biting drives him to help those in need, weak
people who need to be shielded from demonic Earthlings, or demons.
He also is challenged to keep himself from returning to his roots as
a bloodsucker. In the five seasons of *Angel* (and countless reruns),
Angel or his comrades resort to the use of a crucifix to ward off the
demons or the possessed. While never signaling a particular religious
agenda, the underpinnings of the series deal with Angel's intent on
redemption and his messianic positioning in regard to those he saves.
There is clarity between the good (Angel) and the bad, the resur-
rection of dead good guys, and an overarching theme echoing the
Apocalypse. The incantation of the expectation of the Rapture and
the use of the cross to fight evil make the Christotained assumption
that viewers are comfortable with Angel's methods.

SILVER SCREENING CHRISTOTAINMENT AS INTENDED BAPTISM

The following discussion of theater-released films deals with repentance, conversion, and guilt, the continued simplistic themes within
Christotained Hollywood. They deal with both tacit and overt
Christonormative values and intent. None of them provides any
hint that there are alternative paths to salvation or diverse roads to
Christianity. Being a true believer is the only way to be saved. The following films are not of the blockbuster genre and are rather modest
in scope; they purvey a distinctly missionary zeal and fundamentalist
posture.

The Cross and the Switchblade

David Wilkerson (an untanned Pat Boone) is a bumbling preacher
who means well. He feels called to New York to do God's work. The
first of the Christoconversion genre, *The Cross and the Switchblade*
(1970) tells the tale of a young Latino gangbanger (Erik Estrada from
CHIPS). Reverend Wilkerson is not wanted when he invades the *bad
neighborhood*: "Don't be layin' that God stuff on me." Wilkerson
retorts. "There's somebody who cares about you people .... In fact,
he loves you just the way you are." The young pastor does not ask,
nor does God, that the gang members change, merely that they give
themselves to God and believe. "God"ll get you high, but he won't
let you down. God sent me." Wilkerson appears whenever there are
problems and conflicts, preaching the need to get to heaven. "You just

don't know what heaven's like, Preach." Wilkerson/Boone responds, "I don't have any magic cure." He tells the kids that he is just a "simple preacher" but continues to involve himself in opining about their futures.

Laced with god-awful rock music, the film takes us through a rumble, prostitution, heroin addiction, and stabbings. Renting a theater with the local church group, the reverend asks two rival gangs to take up the collection. To prove to him that they can be trusted, the kids collect the money and give every cent to the preacher. Estrada rises, cries, and receives the spirit as Wilkerson preaches: "Jesus Christ was perfect, and they crucified him. When he died on that cross, he was a man." At this point, the gang leader receives the Lord, and when told that the macho Jesus had a "spike drove into his feet," he is able to relate to this manly deity. Conversion is complete and he is invited to be saved: "It's free. All you have to do is accept it. Let Jesus Christ come in." The film ends with glory to God, converted gangbangers, a few dead bad guys, and lots of happy people of color following their newly anointed leader.

Hometown Legend

Terry O'Quinn of *Lost* (he plays the messianic John Locke) stars in this modest-budget film from 2002. Produced by Jerry Jenkins, coauthor of the *Left Behind* books, the film follows a coach who rediscovers Jesus Christ. Since the coach's kid was killed in a football game, the coach has lost his faith. In Athens, Alabama, it is said that the only two things anyone cares about are God and football. The coach returns to lead the team for one last year. Since the school is going to be closed, he wants to help the team win. The retired jerseys of the "Crusaders" are brought out for the game, and God wins the game for the team, and the coach finds his way to Jesus Christ again. His son, however, remains dead.

Flywheel

In this 2003 film, Max Kendall (Walter Burnett) is a used car salesman who attends a megachurch with his family, runs a business, and exhibits confidence to his employees. However, Max isn't an honest man. Driven by debt and greed, he insists on charging customers more than cars are worth and pockets large profits. His saved pregnant wife and son are disappointed in Max and pray for him to find Jesus. Facing financial ruin, he takes the advice of an evangelist on TV: "Your marriage is in the shape it is in today because of the choices you have made. You are in financial bondage today because of the choices you have made." He knows that he is a failure and wants to pray for himself, yet says, "I don't think God would listen to me right now, He knows I'm not an honest man." Falling on his knees (with the American flag behind him), he learns to manage money, be honest, and pay attention to his wife and son. He acknowledges: "My pride got in the way but when I let the Lord tell me how to run my life, things got better." After a long search, Max acquires a valuable flywheel for his car and is able to have his vintage MG repaired. The moral is clear: A car can be a great car, but without a flywheel, it won't go anywhere. Max's car gets the flywheel; the Lord gets Max.

Facing the Giants

Produced in 2006 by members of a local Georgia church, this film uses music reminiscent of old biblical films. The story opens on the first day of school at Shiloh Christian Academy. The football coach is grumpy, his life sucks, and his house has a bad odor. The team is on a losing streak, and he is deeply depressed. Falling on his knees, the coach prays, "You're my god. You're on the throne....Lord, give me something, show me something." During a game, team's kicker has to kick a field goal twenty yards further than he ever has before. As he gets ready to attempt the kick, his crippled father pulls himself out of his wheelchair to inspire his son. The kicker sees his father and knows that the Lord is with him. The kick is made, and the game is won. Jesus is Lord.

The coach is able to save his job, his wife finds she can get pregnant, the stink in the house was only a dead mouse, and in a coincidental plot twist, the coach is admonished, "Your attitude is like the aroma of your heart. If your attitude stinks, it means your heart's not right." Now *that* is Christotainment.

Too many films that have been made claiming conversion and change of heart, common themes wind through the reels: men losing their way, men falling on their knees, men finding God, and men winning football games or getting their cars fixed. I didn't find any films dealing with females losing faith and regaining it...each film reiterates the need for the *man*, the dad or husband, to step up and take charge by rededicating himself to Jesus and letting God take over. The man, in turn, takes over the family. White male desperation is always caused by unavoidable outside forces: losing seasons, losing jobs, losing honesty, or losing family members. By regaining God, men are able to retrieve their rightful patriarchal roles and find their places at the head of the family.

TACIT BAPTISM

World Trade Center

Other contemporary films assume Christianity and its belief system, while not centering the plot on Christ or conversion. *World Trade Center* (2006) deals with two surviving rescue workers who are caught beneath the burning rubble at Ground Zero. A man who is called by God while sitting in church saves them. Drawn to New York, he sneaks over the barricades and goes directly to rescue the two men. Never mentioning God or Christ in a direct manner, the film cuts to rays of light appearing along with cross-shaped metal at the site of the destroyed Twin Towers. An implied holiness and godly presence underlies the film, while not overtly demanding adherence to the word. The Christonormative nature of this film is subtler, but there is no doubt that it is the Christian God whose hand is made manifest (at least to two rescued workers). God doesn't rescue the other hundreds of workers from Ground Zero or the nearly 3,000 people who jumped from the Twin Towers or were incinerated in the attacks. Christonormativity was echoed throughout newscasts and discussions of 9/11, without embarrassment or acknowledgment. The metal tangled cross girders were featured on magazine covers and paintings, representative of the omnipresence of a Christian deity.

The Blind Side

Academy Award–nominated *The Blind Side* (2009) recovers earlier themes of tacit Christianization. Based on the true story of football great Michael Oher, the story is set in Memphis, Tennessee, where a wealthy white woman brings a large black young man into her home and saves him. Naturally, since the film is based on a true story, I am not disputing whether or not the film is accurate. And the messianic nature of Leigh Anne Tuohy, played by Sandra Bullock, will be saved (pun intended) for my next chapter on white liberal guilt/do-gooding. However, *The Blind Side* is significant as a Christotained version of the tried-but-true plot of poor black kid from the black side of town being redeemed and becoming part of the American Dream (in this case, a football player). Oher is admitted into Briarcrest Christian Academy (the coach fights to get him a scholarship by citing their Christian duty....his aim, to get a football recruit). Through scenes of the family in prayer, joining hands, and Bullock's character's ever-present cross pendant, viewers are aware that there is *more* than just human intervention in this story. Short of naming the life of Michael Oher a miracle, it is clear that Christianity plays a great role in the salvation and future of this football great. Reminding us of *Facing the Giants*, the familiar fusion of football and Christianity creates a formidable whole.

Whether it is explicitly noted that a film is a product of, for example, ChristianCinema.com or Epiphany Films, there is no doubt that cinematic and televised Christotainment exist in Hollywood. Not striving for Oscar- or Emmy-winning performances or productions, these shows depend on a naïve audience craving for moralistic and threatening narratives. Viewers are able to identify with the fragile nature of fallen men and find comfort in the fact that by falling on their knees and giving themselves up to God, they will be saved. The goal of Christotainment, aside from marketing, is to prepare for the end of days and eventually get to Heaven.

With the increase of Heaven-bound viewers, Neveah is one of the most popular names for baby girls. Spell it backwards.

Make no mistake, *Christotainment* works.

NOTES

This chapter is dedicated to my life viewing partner; apprenticed as a Methodist minister and never saved, Joe Kincheloe's rapture was grounded in critical theory, social consciousness....and a life of rock 'n' roll.

Parts of this research appeared in *Christotainment: Selling Jesus Through Popular Culture.* (2009). Boulder, Co: Westview Press.

REFERENCES

Frykholm, A. 2005. The gender dynamics of the *Left Behind* series. In *Religion and Popular Culture in America*, eds. B. Forbes and J. Mahan. 2nd ed. Berkeley: University of California Press.

LaHaye, T. 1980. *The battle for the mind.* Old Tappan, NJ: Fleming H. Revel.

LaHaye, T., and Jerry B. Jenkins. 1995. *Left Behind.* Carol Stream, IL: Tyndale House.

McAlister, M. 2003. An empire of their own. *The Nation.* www.thenation.com/doc/20030922/mcalister (accessed February 10, 2010).

New York Times. 2005. Gavin Palone with UPI reporter, Pat Nason. *New York Times*, March 20.

Steinberg, S. 2010. "Faith and Trust in the Lord: Christotainment and Selling Jesus through Corporate Power." Keynote speech. *Discourse, Power, and Resistance Conference.* Greenwich, UK.

Steinberg, S. and Kincheloe, J. (eds). 2009. *Christotainment: The Selling of Jesus Through Popular Culture*. Boulder, CO: Westview Press.
Unger, C. 2005. American rapture. *Vanity Fair*, December, www.vanityfair.com/politics/features/200s/ I 2/ rapture200s I 2 (accessed February 10, 2010).

Filmography

Facing the Giants. 2006. Directed by A. Kendrick. Albany, GA: Sherwood Pictures.
Flywheel. 2003. Directed by A. Kendrick. Albany, GA: Carmel Entertainment.
Hometown Legend. 2002. Directed by J. Anderson. Foley, Al: Jenkins Entertainment.
Left Behind: The Movie. 2000. Directed by V. Sarin. Columbia Tri-Star Pictures.
Left Behind: Tribulation Force. 2002. Directed by B. Corcoran. Cloud Ten Pictures and Namesake Entertainment.
Left Behind: World at War. 2005. Directed by C. Baxley. Cloud Ten Pictures.
The Cross and the Switchblade. 1970. Directed by D. Murray. New York: Gateway Productions.
The Blind Side. 2009. Directed by John Lee Hancock. USA/Canada: Alcon Entertainment.
The Exorcist. 1973. Directed by William Friedkin. CA: Warner Bros.
World Trade Center. 2006. Directed by Oliver Stone. NJ: Paramount Pictures.

4

Hollywood Incarcerated and on Death Row: Bjork, Schwarzenegger, and the Pedagogy of Retribution

Richard Van Heertum

Overview

Today, the United States accounts for less than 5 percent of the world population, but almost a quarter of the world's prisoners, a total of over 2.3 million citizens (750 per 100,000 and 1 in 100 among adults). The rise in the prison population accelerated dramatically in the 1970s with "tough on crime" laws and the inception of the drug wars (Liptak, 2008). Among the many troubling aspects of this *prison-industrial complex* is the racial composition of prisons today. Blacks are 6.4 times as likely as whites to be incarcerated and, among 25- to 29-year-olds, 12.6% are in prison, versus 3.6% of Latinos and 1.6% of whites. An estimated 32% of Black males will enter state or federal prison at some point in their lives (versus 17% of Latinos and 5.9% of white males), and over half the total prison population is in jail for drug-related crimes. Overall, an incredible 7 million people were under some form of correctional supervision in 2005, with the vast majority minorities (Justice, 2008). And the United States remains the only liberal democracy in the world that still practices capital punishment.

In this paper, I explore the relationship between the justice system, capital punishment, and Hollywood film. I argue that at the heart of the prison-industrial complex are two complementary themes that are spread and reinforced through the media: the fear of dangerous youth of color and the idea that justice is best exemplified by the death of violent, evil criminals. I start by looking at the arguments for and against capital punishment. I next turn to the Hollywood theme of violent retribution and its relationship to our notion of justice. I conclude by looking at a number of films from the past fifteen years that have directly addressed the death penalty, including *Dancer in the Dark* (2000), *Life of David Gale* (2003), *Monster's Ball* (2001), *Monster* (2003), and the archetypical film of the "subgenre" *Dead Man Walking* (1995).[1] While these films challenge hegemonic ideas, and as Kellner argues, Hollywood is a contested terrain (Kellner, 2001), the vast majority of Hollywood films either overtly or covertly tend to support capital punishment by naturalizing violent retribution, revenge, and "an eye for an eye" justice. My central thesis, then, is that capital punishment is a legitimizing force for our entire justice system and media an important vehicle for framing justice, making deconstructing film an important vehicle in altering the debate.

DEATH PENALTY: THE CONTOURS OF THE DEBATE

The United States remains the only industrialized country in the world to still practice capital punishment, placing us in ideological solidarity with Saudi Arabia, Afghanistan, China, Libya, Pakistan, Iran, Iraq, and Sierra Leone. While approximately 70 countries still permit the death penalty, very few in the "developed" world do, and of the 1,252 people that were killed in 2007, 88% were in China, the United States, Iran, Pakistan, or Saudi Arabia.[2] Even as increased evidence of racial biases and errors in the system have proliferated over the past few years (including the case in Texas of Cameron Todd Willingham, where the state may soon admit killing an innocent man) (Grann, 2009), the high-profile cases of Mumia Abu-Jamal and Stan "Tookie" Williams galvanized activists across the globe and governors in several states, including Illinois, to put a moratorium on the practice, popular support in the latest Gallup Poll (October 1–4, 2009) was 65%, with 49% arguing the death penalty "is not used enough" and another 24% "about right."[3]

The main arguments for the death penalty generally revolve around deterrence and justice. The deterrence argument is often used as the primary justification for capital punishment, based on the idea that fear of ultimately being put to death causes many criminals to rethink the choice to kill. While it is difficult to quantify the effectiveness of capital punishment on deterring crime, and some recent studies claim to substantiate this claim, a large body of evidence exists to belie their findings.[4] The justice argument regards retribution to society and retribution to the victims' families. By killing the murderer (or occasionally rapist), they pay their "debt to society" and provide relief and appeasement to the families of the victims of their crimes. A third line of reasoning sometimes invoked, although in my mind the least valid, revolves around the idea that some people are beyond redemption and thus no longer have a right to live. Finally, there is the mistaken argument that it costs less to kill someone than keep them in prison.[5] Ultimately, many ironically argue for the death penalty based on respect for human life (Stoekl, 1999).

In considering the case against capital punishment, I have located six basic arguments: (1) Moral: Is it okay to kill anyone as an individual or a state? (2) Fairness: Does the justice system discriminate along racial, gender, or class lines (Dewan, 2008; Ogletree, 2002)? (3) Justice: Are we willing to accept the possibility that someone who is innocent is put to death? (4) State power: Should the state have power over a citizen's life? (5) Cost: Is the cost of putting someone to death, which is greater than keeping them in prison for the rest of their lives, worth it? (6) Constitution: Does the death penalty as practiced in the country contravene the Sixth Amendment, prohibiting cruel and unusual punishment? I believe all of these arguments provide a strong case to end capital punishment in America. I now turn to how Hollywood has intervened in these debates.

THE PIONEER, THE COWBOY, AND THE BIRTH OF THE CONTEMPORARY AMERICAN MONOMYTH

Revenge is a favored Hollywood theme. From crime dramas and film noir, where the criminal generally has to die at the hands of the avatar of justice, to westerns where Manichean dualism established the necessity of eradicating evil, to the naturalistic violence of 1970s films like *The Godfather* and *Taxi Driver* to the present popularity of superhero, horror, and "turbo-charged" action films, Hollywood has persistently focused on the theme of justice within the frame of violence and revenge.

Yet how do we translate this addiction to revenge to popular opinions on the death penalty? George Lakoff (2002) argues that our political philosophies reside in the frames and metaphors we use to contemplate particular issues, relating experience to discursive constructs. Our political opinions thus relate to the effectiveness of the metaphors and frame used to deliver ideas and their connection to our morality, which Lakoff believes is derived from our upbringing.[6] Regarding capital punishment, he argues that conservatives see the death penalty in terms of moral accountability (pay proportional debt based on action), while liberals tend to adhere to the positive action principle, which says that a moral act adds positive value to society and an immoral act negative value. Thus, metaphors like an eye for an eye, the scales of justice, and retribution resonate with conservatives, while liberals are more moved by empathy, forgiveness, and rehabilitation.

I argue here that given our location in a media spectacle society, visual culture profoundly influences the discursive space and thus, our conceptual understanding of justice is constructed through both words and visual images of its instantiation. Thus, films, TV, video games, and popular music offer a cultural pedagogy (a la Giroux and Kellner) (Giroux, 1997, 1999, 2000; Kellner, 2001) that provides normative values and behavior and stereotypical views of class, race, gender, sexuality, and, of course, justice that might supersede more traditional institutions of civil society, like the family, church, and schools.

In looking at justice specifically, we have particular images or metaphors that offer us frames to explore our conceptualization of crime and punishment. These include the courtroom, the lawyer, the jailhouse, the gunslinger slaying the bad guy, the police officer or detective shooting the murderer, the army commando exacting revenge for our failed venture in Vietnam, or the recent spate of crime dramas where a team of experts finds the killer and metes out justice (*CSI, Criminal Minds, Cold Case, NCIS, Numb3rs, Law and Order*, etc.). In all these instances, justice is manifest in the image of good defeating evil, often in violent terms. One could go even further to argue that justice becomes the manifestation of these images. As the bullets pierce the skin of the evil killer and the red blood of their sins puddles around them, we see justice enacted. Audiences come to desire these redemptive moments, offering safety and security in the realization of justice in images. We want the restoration of order jeopardized by the presence of evil in our community.

Carol Clover, in her analysis of horror films, believes they go beyond offering audiences the sadistic (and arguably misogynist) pleasure of violence to also invoke themes of heroic victory over evil and positive feminist images (Clover, 1992). These very images are justice-oriented, with the victim-hero serving as the apotheosis of justice manifest in human activity. She claims horror films relate to the enactment of desire fulfillment within a constructed environment. I believe the aforementioned genres do the same, offering a reenactment of social anxiety about injustice and looming evil (a la Glassner's (2000) culture of fear), where the audience is the voyeuristic outsider, watching their own fears unfolded and then relieved in a controlled environment that offers them the guise of security through identification with the story and characters. Audiences arguably enter these films with expectations that are then actualized in the culminating scenes.

Films based on the struggle between good and evil have been around for most of Hollywood's history. In the 1940s and 1950s, there was the popularity of the noirish crime drama. In the 1950s through 1970s, the western reigned supreme. In the 1970s, the move toward naturalism was punctuated with a strong inclination toward violence and its role in justice. In the two *Godfather* films, for example, violence is critiqued within frames that arguably celebrate it at the same time enacting an indirect paean to capitalism, restored masculinity, and "familial" justice; a trend that continues in mafia films like *The Untouchables* (1987), *Goodfellas* (1990), *Bugsy* (1991), *Mobsters* (1991), *Casino* (1995), and *Road to Perdition* (2002); and obviously on TV with *The Sopranos*. In *Taxi Driver* (1976), an act of supreme violence by the troubled Travis Bickle (Robert De Niro) is justified given the sick acts of the pimp and his partners, who allow the twelve-year-old Iris (Jodi Foster) to pimp for them. Other examples include Charles Bronson confronting our fear of escalating urban crime with his *Death Wish* films (1974 to 1987), Dirty Harry attacking the residual evils of the cultural revolution and their manifestation in violent killers, and the working-class hero *Rocky* fighting the displacement and worsening economic situation that emerged in the 1970s and racial anxiety percolating from the vestiges of the civil rights movement.

In just the past few years, a list of revenge-inspired films includes, among others, *Inglourious Basterds*, *Live Free or Die Hard*, *V for Vendetta*, *Transformers: Revenge of the Fallen*, *Casino Royale*, *Kill Bill 1 and 2*, the *Lord of the Rings* series, *Star Wars Episode III*, *Spider-Man III*, *The Bourne Ultimatum*, *Ocean's Thirteen*, *Red Eye*, *Sin City*, *Man on Fire*, *Batman Begins*, *The Dark Knight*, *Collateral*, *The Streets of New York*, and even *My Super Ex-Girlfriend* and *Slumdog Millionaire*. The reemergence of the vigilante character in female form is particularly interesting, with Jodie Foster in *The Brave One* (2007) having her revenge codified in the end by a police officer, Detective Mercer (Terrence Howard), who had been pursuing her both sexually, and unknowingly, as a vigilante throughout the film. A subtheme involves revenge for those who abducted, hurt, or killed a child—seemingly one of the greatest social anxieties today— including *Taken* (2008), *21 Grams* (2003), *In the Bedroom* (2001),

Little Children (2006), and the older *A Time to Kill* (1996). In *Taken* (2008), the abduction of his daughter leads ex-CIA operative Bryan Mills (Liam Neeson) to leave a trail of death and destruction across Paris that includes thirty-two mostly unnamed dead bodies, all to save his daughter and "restore" a broken American family (as he is divorced from his remarried wife). In all the films, murder is justified because of the violent acts of some other.

Many of these films are built on the premise of a singular character that is the avatar of justice—or in Lawrence and Jewitt's term, the *American Monomyth* (Jewett & Lawrence, 1977, 2002). The American Monomyth often has uber-human strength, power over nature, an awe-inspiring countenance, and heroic victory over a binary evil. An exemplar from the 1980s forward is Arnold Schwarzenegger. In the films *Commando* (1985), *Raw Deal* (1986), *Red Heat* (1988), *The Terminator* (1984), *Total Recall* (1990), and even *Kindergarten Cop* (1990) he comes in to save the day and restore order to his family, the country, the universe, and then the family again by exacting violent revenge on the perpetrators of evil. Bryan Mills takes on this role in a more personalized way in *Taken*, as do Quentin Tarantino's Basterds in exacting a fictional revenge for the horrific acts of the Nazis during World War II. The graphic nature of the violence in the latter film seems to relate to this desire to see the clear visual instantiation of their suffering and death.

Even films that are sold as critiques of violence and its ineffectiveness in meting out justice often end up fitting into the metaphors and desires we are programmed over time to expect, having the effect of simply reinforcing the close relationship between violence and justice. *A History of Violence* (2005), the fascinating film from famed Canadian auteur David Cronenberg, explores the effects of violence on an American family with great nuance: from a son who violently beats up a school bully, to a wife who appears to be willingly raped, to a community unwilling to believe the truth about a man reformed from a violent past. In the end, while offering a powerful critique of violence in America, including the pornographic manner in which we often experience it, Cronenberg arguably falls prey to the very critique he offers—by using pornographically violent scenes that will probably be experienced by the audience as they often are: as the manifestation of desire and justice. And like in *Mystic River* (2003) (see Chapter 2), the final scene is an iconic image of American life, a family at the dinner table, with peace and order restored.

To return to Clover, the films establish parameters that arguably make capital punishment an anxiety-reducing source of appeasement to the constant flux of uncertainty and insecurity plaguing Americans. In a broader sense, it establishes the very justice of the larger society, through images of people held responsible for their actions and subsequently punished. And the audience expectations of particular genres (e.g., the chase and explosions in action films, the kiss in a romantic comedy, the violent death of evil in thrillers and westerns) thus almost dictates the continuation of the relationship between both director and audience and, in a larger sense, violence and justice (Altman, 1999). The structure of these films, where good defeats generally pure evil, also alleviates us of complicity in crime and justice, ignoring structural issues at the heart of both, like racism, class structure, and unequal access to quality education. These films then establish the very legitimacy of capital punishment, with the state standing in symbolically for a materially nonexistent Monomyth and the executed standing in metonymically for justice itself.

I further believe that the death penalty essentially stands in as the legitimator of the entire legal system, predicated largely on media-constructed images of justice. By destroying an absolute evil, we not only realize justice, but also see our social anxiety appeased. Without the death penalty, justice is too remote—a legal system few of us understand, prisons on the outskirts of cities and in small towns (which, since the partial privatization of the system, are sometimes based around those very prisons), and a system that seems skewed to the rich, including O.J. Simpson using his wealth to overcome, or maybe exploit, the racist nature of the system to literally get away with murder. Just like Schwarzenegger took lines from his heroic turn as a Monomyth to the governor's office of the fifth largest economy in the world, the death penalty stands in as the symbolic reenactment of justice a la Hollywood, leading us to believe it does in fact exist and good does sometimes win out over evil. The finality of execution is well suited to the visual metaphors and frames film has established for justice realized.

COUNTERHEGEMONIC FILM: OR NOT?

I will next turn to a series of films from 1995 to 2005 that dealt explicitly with the death penalty, often challenging us to reconsider it. While there are several in this "genre," I will focus my attention on the quintessential example of *Dead Man Walking* and discuss other films that fit its general thematic structure. These films generally exist within one of three frames: (1) Guilty victim that is humanized/reformed to build empathy: *Dead Man Walking, Last*

Dance (1996), *Monster* (2003), or *Redemption: The Stanley Tookie Williams Story* (2004); (2) Race to save an innocent victim: *The Green Mile* (1999) and *The Life of David Gale*; and (3) Critique of capital punishment in the subtext: *Monster's Ball, Dancer in the Dark,* or *Capote* (2005).

Moving forward, I analyze the effectiveness of these films in critiquing the death penalty, intertwining this with exploration of how they can be used by educators and cultural critics to (1) spark dialogue and debate about capital punishment and the criminal justice system, (2) get students to explore the effects of media on the development of their social and political identity, and (3) teach the rudiments of civic engagement. The films open the doorway to such an approach by addressing some of the key arguments for and against the death penalty, including challenging the morality of an eye for an eye, humanizing and building empathy for inmates on Death Row, showing the cruelty of state execution, challenging false ideas like its role as a deterrent, and in some cases offering a structural critique of the death penalty (based on race and class bias), the politics behind capital punishment, and its cynical use by politicians.

The films essentially attempt to alter our frames, asking new questions like:

> Whether death is really an image of justice?
> Whether execution is a fair punishment (and whether it is cruel and unusual)?
> Whether criminals are really monsters unworthy of our compassion?
> And whether the state has the right to kill?

Educators can then capitalize on the emotional openings these films offer with arguments and facts that can spark debate and new ways to look at the issue. Tools toward this end include critical media literacy, media production projects that can engage capital punishment from student perspectives, and information on ways to get involved in local campaigns or political action (Kellner & Share, 2007; Van Heertum & Share, 2006).

Dead Man Walking (DMW) is based on the book by famed capital punishment abolitionist Sister Helen Prejean. It follows the final days of condemned inmate Matthew Poncelet (Sean Penn) and his relationship to Prejean, played by Susan Sarandon. The plot revolves around attempting to get a stay of his execution and him taking responsibility for his actions. We are also introduced to the victim's families and a slow re-creation of the crime scene from one where Poncelet is a scared accomplice shot in black and white to the denouement when he admits to raping the girl and killing one of the victims himself before being put to death

The first technique the film uses is to humanize and build empathy for Poncelet. As Henry Giroux argues, many films in the 1980s and 1990s showed predatory, violent, and amoral youth of color that kill each other recklessly (Giroux, 1996). These films establish a culture of fear that makes it easier for audiences to ignore the injustices of the legal system and of the death penalty itself. This extends to films like *88 Minutes* (2007), *Murder by Numbers* (2002), *15 Minutes* (2001), *Silence of the Lambs* (1991), and *Manhunter* (1986) that all show sadistic killers that are dangerous and unredeemable. Scenes throughout DMW attempt to break us out of this way of thinking, humanizing Poncelet. First, he is an attractive, masculine figure that can invoke sexual desire. Second, we see scenes between he and his family, and particularly his mother, that establish his proximity to traditional American values. And most importantly, we are given inroads to his emotions and identity both inside and outside his horrible acts through his relationship to Sister Helen.

This third relationship manifests itself in two key ways. First is his admission of guilt, establishing his relationship to Judeo-Christian notions of individual responsibility and redemption, and second through the love that Prejean develops for him. This is a common approach in many of the films, with an advocate serving as the entryway or "identification vehicle" between the audiences and the pseudo-protagonist. Prejean's love and compassionate view of Poncelet offers the possibility of our building empathy ourselves and thus realizing that even these "monsters" are worthy of our mercy. She makes this very point when she tells Poncelet that people "Think of you as a monster. It's easy to kill a monster, but harder to kill a human being." This relationship, in fact, often serves as the visual frame and perspective through which the audience ultimately judges the murderer.

In *Last Dance* it is the young man of means, lawyer Rick Hayes (Rob Morrow), struggling to save Cindy Liggett (Sharon Stone), who was born on the wrong side of the track and kills a wealthy man's son and his girlfriend. In *The Green Mile* it is the sympathetic guard, Paul Edgecomb (Tom Hanks) coming to see that John Coffey (Michael Clarke Duncan) is not only innocent but has divine healing powers. In *Capote* famed writer Truman Capote (Philip Seymour Hoffman) is the vessel to build sympathy for the real-life killers Perry Smith and

Dick Hickcock, even as he is possessed by the contradictory interests of helping Smith and finishing his book (which requires an execution). In *Redemption*, it is the real-life journalist Barbara Becnel becoming the vehicle for the reformed Crips co-founder Tookie to get out his message. And in *Monster* it is naïve girlfriend Selby (Christina Ricci) humanizing the famed real-life prostitute-turned-serial killer Aileen Wuornos (the role that won beauty Charlize Theron an Oscar, partially for making herself so unattractive).

The film *Monster* seems the most powerful on this point by showing us a realistic portrayal of a Death Row inmate, which generally includes poverty, sexual abuse, and personal degradation (*Redemption* also provides a compelling case, through flashbacks, of the roots of violent behavior). Kevin Doyle, in fact, argues that DMW's "major failing" was not showing what he saw in five and a half years working on Alabama's Death Row: "Everybody there had a history of childhood or adolescent abuse or trauma, which goes a long way to explaining why they ended up where they were. That was given—to put it mildly—short shrift by Tim Robbins" (as quoted in (Shapiro, 1996, p. 1150). One could use these scenes to engage students in questions surrounding their view of these characters, whether they seem like monsters and how the media portray criminals in general.

A second major theme is to show the brutality of the process of execution. DMW attempts to do this at the end by creating parallel scenes (in alternating clips), one where Poncelet is killed by lethal injection (in real life he died in the electric chair) while the other re-creates the original crime in all its brutality (and in color, as Poncelet finally admits the truth of his participation to Prejean). It appears that Robbins's intent, based on interviews, is to juxtapose the brutality of the crime with the brutality of state killing, to ask people the real moral question surrounding the death penalty—which is that of moral equivalence.

This is also the case with *Last Dance*, with both films showing the executed dying with relative ease, though there is fear in their eyes. Never does the camera try to give us the point-of-view shot of the inmates themselves as they are strapped down, administered a shot, or first feel the shock of electricity course through their bodies. One problem thus may be representation versus identification with the person being executed. Death arguably exists beyond representation through its unknowability, but it might be possible to at least hint at the fear and pain the victim feels as they are executed.

The scene in DMW, and all the films with an execution, instead places us as the voyeuristic outsider, offering various focalizations, but tends to center on the juxtaposition between those that feel sympathy for the victim and those intent on revenge. In the end, the outstretched arms of Sarandon and the Jesus-like posture of Penn seem to orient the viewer toward recognizing this moment as wrong, though many see it differently. Wendy Lesser argues the intercutting of the execution with the crime was a "standard" convention "that is part of the language of movies" (as quoted in (Shapiro, 1996, p. 1145). There is thus an expectational issue, in so far as we see rape and murder and then the death of Poncelet, maybe undermining the message and fulfilling the general expectation of moviegoers to see revenge for brutal crimes.

In the case of *The Green Mile* it is the perspective of the guards, the community witnesses, and the man sitting behind the black curtain pulling the lever that will end three lives. Here the second execution goes wrong as the sadistic guard Percy (Doug Hutchison) purposefully neglects to wet the sponge put on the murderer's head before execution. We then witness a horrifying scene where the inmate Eduard Delacroix's (played by Michael Jeter) face is burned off, the crowd runs out screaming and throwing up, and the guards are left with no choice but to let it continue until he dies. The most effective film in this vein might be Lars Von Trier's Palm D'or winner *Dancer in the Dark* (2000), where the nearly blind, demure and poor Selma Jezkova (played brilliantly by singer Bjork) is put to death by hanging as she screams and then sings out as a largely anonymous audience watches. The protagonist dies based on a series of misunderstandings and false accusations surrounding her complicity in the killing of a neighbor, who begged her to do it after stealing the money she had saved to try and save her son from the near blindness that curses her. The scene is effective in showing the brutality and tragedy of killing, with a number of sympathetic guards and friends watching as this unjust death unfolds.

A third major theme revolves around issues of race and class. This is one of the main weaknesses of *DMW* and why there has been a lot of critique of the film. This may be largely based on Robbins's contention that he is "not a big believer in victimology. Just because someone may have had a horrible childhood or a specific psychological setup doesn't right his crimes." But some scenes at least hint at these issues. Early in the film Poncelet tells Sister Prejean "Ain't nobody with money on Death Row," and he later makes an aside to the fact that two Black men have been killed and now the politicians want to kill a white man. A third instance involves comments from the lawyer arguing for his clemency. But these factual moments are arguably less persuasive in the filmic medium, where emotional proximity to the chosen empathetic character is a key mechanism to convey information.

Millard Farmer (1996) argues that Hollywood films on the death penalty rarely engage the important question of why Blacks make up such a high proportion of those on Death Row. Here lies a wonderful opportunity for educators to offer contextual information that can bring the class and racial issues surrounding capital punishment, and crime and punishment in general, to the forefront. One way would be to read the book by Prejean, which is much stronger on this matter, or just to provide some basic facts that show the racial proportionality of conviction and of those in jail. *The Green Mile* might have been more effective on this point—offering us the view of a wrongly accused Black man—but is heavily infused with magical realism and has clear religious overtures that undermine its relationship to current class and race compositional issues. And while *Last Dance* does deals with these issues tangentially through secondary characters, it is a weak film overall and did not reach a large audience.

DMW may, in fact, undermine these issues further, though, as it appears to turn more on Poncelet taking responsibility for his actions than on a systematic or structural critique of capital punishment, leading Doyle to argue the film is about moral accountability. Sarat (2002) then argues that it exists within a conservative cultural view based on autonomous individuals who are personally responsible for actions and what proportional punishment is acceptable. Lesser agrees, arguing that DMW only works for those who already believe in Christian notions of redemption and salvation, following a moral-humanist argument structure without any nod to the structuralist arguments that many abolitionists, including Sister Helen, firmly believe are central to the larger critique. And philosopher Hugo Bedau believes the film indicates that "it's his death that gives the symmetry our aesthetic and moral sensibilities require [in light of] the terrible crime itself" (as quoted in (Shapiro, 1996, p. 1155)). The audience becomes the jury, deciding what fate Poncelet deserves.

In *Monster* and *Dancer in the Dark*, on the other hand, the question of class and poverty is clearly raised, and how money plays a huge role in justice. And *Redemption* may be the strongest film on this issue, given Williams' broader critique, including this explanation to Barbara in the film:

> I think the core of it is an embedded sense of self-hate. What I mean by
> that is that any time you spoon feed an individual derogatory images of

himself and his race...after a period of time you start to believe these images. These stereotypes depicting that the majority of Blacks are buffoons, or functional illiterates, promiscuous, violent, welfare recipients, indolent criminals. Unfortunately, too many Black people buy into these and believe that those stereotypes are true. So you lash out at those individuals that fit those stereotypes. You're basically trying to obliterate those negative images to rid yourself of that self-hating monster that subconsciously stalks you.

A fourth theme emerges to challenge the very arguments for the death penalty. DMW attempts to take on many of the assumptions of death penalty advocates. For example, Sister Helen argues over the biblical relevance of its morality with another priest, reminding viewers that a number of other crimes like adultery warrant death in the Bible and ending with the famous quote from Gandhi that an eye for an eye leaves us all blind. There are also hints of the cynical politics behind its use, with reference to the governor and the inadequate representation Poncelet received in the original trial. And the film engages the reality that families do not necessary get any relief from the death of the killer, as embodied in the father of one victim, Edward Delacroix (Raymond J. Barry), who ends up divorced, still angry after the execution, and ultimately seeks answers by praying with Prejean.

The Life of David Gale and *Last Dance* also show the cynical politics behind capital punishment and images and articulated arguments on its racist implementation. This is also the case with *The Green Mile*, where empathetic guards allow inmates to die with dignity and sympathy. Yet the central argument of *Green Mile* appears to be undermined as the protagonist John Coffey (read Jesus Christ) puts one of the two antagonists, Percy , in a trance where he kills the other antagonist Wild Bill (played by Sam Rockwell), the embodiment of pure evil. Violent redemption is thus still just—and even given a divine legitimation—and even the death penalty is an open issue, if carried out efficiently by empathetic, caring guards. This leads to the final theme of these films, the possibility of killing an innocent man or woman.

The Green Mile is one of three films discussed here that deal explicitly with an innocent victim being put to death, but Coffey ultimately accepts his fate as a gift, as he is tired of living in this evil world. The second is *The Life of David Gale*, which may be a more interesting case—even if it was a box office flop. The film follows the final four days of David Gale's (Kevin Spacey) life, as Bitsey Bloom (Kate Winslet), a famed, cynical New York reporter, unravels the crime that has led him to Death Row. As the story unfolds, we are led to believe

78   RICHARD VAN HEERTUM

the popular professor and leading abolitionist in Texas is innocent
and Bloom thus struggles, with sidekick intern Josh (Jeff Gibbs), to
save his life.

The problem with this film appears to reside mainly with identification. I'm not sure that a mainstream audience can or would
identify in a sympathetic way with either of the rabid abolitionists
Gale or Constance Jones (Laura Linney), or the obnoxious Bloom.
Gale and Jones are the embodiment of stereotypical conservative
views of liberals, willing in the end to kill themselves for their
cause. They are caustic, pedantic snobs, whose lives are outside the
American norms (Gale is shown as a good father ruined by false
rape charges; though he was cheating on his wife). And Bloom is
not much better, and it is thus hard to see where the point of entry
into her perspective emerges. Thus, its critique of the death penalty
is undermined by the form of much of the critique and the lack of
any compelling point of entry for empathy. In *Dancer in the Dark*,
the main character is also innocent and her death so tragic and sad
I remember having to go for beers with my ex-wife afterwards to
relieve the deep sense of distress the film left. But as is so often the
case, we have to look outside Hollywood for this sort of emotional
and intellectual impact.

CONCLUSION

In the end, *Dead Man Walking* and all the other Hollywood films
discussed here miss a lot of the nuance and richness of argument surrounding capital punishment. Robbins argued, in the case of *Dead
Man Walking*, that this is founded on the imperatives of filmmaking
and reception, and there is probably some truth here. Identification,
narration, and emotional connection are all key to effective filmmaking. Yet educators could build on the emotional impact of film and
provide further insights into the key issues and arguments surrounding capital punishment and how media culture influences their students' lives.

I believe this is particularly important given the proclivity of
Hollywood film to support violent retribution as the dominant image
of justice and their eliding of films specifically dealing with this issue
since 2005. In a country dominated by Christianity, it appears an
appeal to forgiveness, redemption, and rehabilitation could resonate
if properly framed. Educators may be the only ones in a position to
challenge current popular opinion and provide arguments toward a
more just and democratic criminal justice system in America.

In his concurrence in *Furman v. Georgia*, Justice Thurgood Marshall voiced the opinion that the American people were largely unaware of the information necessary to make an informed judgment on the morality of the death penalty. He felt that if the public was better informed, it would consider capital punishment to be "shocking, unjust and unacceptable." I concur.

NOTES

1. Other films in this genre include *The Green Mile* (1999), *Redemption: The Stanley Tookie Williams Story* (2004), *Capote* (2005), *Last Dance* (1996), and earlier, *The Executioner's Song* (1983, TV) and the infamous *The Thin Blue Line* (1988), where celebrated documentarian Errol Morris helps free an innocent man from Death Row.
2. From http://www.infoplease.com/ipa/A0777460.html.
3. Gallup Poll. Oct. 1–4, 2009. N = 1,013 adults nationwide. MoE ± 4. As cited from PollingReport.com: www.pollingreport.com/crime.htm. The documentary *Mumia Abu-Jamal: A Case for Reasonable Doubt* (1997) details Mumia's plight and the popular support for his release.
4. There are studies that support some deterrent effect to the death penalty. These include Yang, B. & Lester, D. (2008). The deterrent effect of executions: A meta-analysis thirty years after Ehrlich. *Journal of Criminal Justice*, 36(5), 453–460 and Cloninger, D., & Marchesini, R. (2006). Execution moratoriums, Commutations and deterrence: The case of Illinois. *Applied Economics*, 38 (9), 967–973, among many others. However, many argue the methods and assumptions of these studies often fail under closer scrutiny. For example, see Fagan, J. (2006). "Death and deterrence redux: Science, law and causal reasoning on capital punishment. *Ohio State Journal of Law*. 4, 255–320, Donohue, J. & Wolfers, J. (2006, April 2006); The death penalty: No evidence for deterrence. *Economists Voices*, Berk, R. (2005); New claims about execution and general deterrence: Deja vu all over again? *Journal of Empirical Legal Studies*, 2(2), 303–330; and Weisberg, R. (2005). The death penalty meets social science: Deterrence and jury behavior under scrutiny. *Annual Review of Law and Social Science*, 1, 151–170. One of the major problems is that many states don't actually execute anyone, most other states execute very few individuals, and the data is often biased. A good site with a long list of articles on both sides of the debate is www.cjlf.org/deathpenalty/DPDeterrence.htm.
5. A wonderful resource is the Death Penalty Information Center (www. deathpenaltyinfo.org/costs-death-penalty). According to their data, in California having someone on Death Row costs $90,000 per inmate per year, for a total of $63.3 million annually at present. In New Jersey, the New Jerseyans for Alternatives to the Death Penalty (NJADP) found that the death penalty has cost the state $253 million

since 1983. In Florida, the state spent $57 million to execute eighteen individuals between 1973 and 1988. In the most extreme case, Maryland paid $37.2 million for each of their five executions (the total cost of 162 capital cases between 1978 and 1999 was $186 million more than if there was no capital punishment).

6. Lakoff essentially argues that there are two general moral systems in the United States, one based on the strict father model (stressing individual responsibility, obedience to authority, moral strength, and nature over nurture) and the other on the nurturing parent (stressing community, moral nurturance, empathy, and nurture over nature). While this analysis is reductive, it does appear to point out the centrality of discourse and framing in politics.

REFERENCES

Altman, R. (1999). *Film/Genre*. London: British Film Institute.

Clover, C. (1992). *Men, women & chainsaws: Gender in the modern horror film*. Princeton: Princeton University Press.

Dewan, S. (May 7, 2008). As executions resume, so do questions of fairness. *The New York Times*.

Farmer, M. (January 15, 1996). Distorting 'Dead Man's' last wish. *Los Angeles Times*, p. F3.

Giroux, H. (1996). *Fugitive culture: Race, violence and youth*. New York: Routledge.

Giroux, H. (1997). *Channel surfing: Racism, the media, and the destruction of today's youth*. New York: Palgrave Macmillan.

Giroux, H. (1999). *The mouse that roared: What Disney teaches*. Lanham, MD: Rowman and Littlefield.

Giroux, H. (2000). *Stealing innocence: Corporate culture's war on children*. New York: Palgrave Macmillan.

Glassner, B. (2000). *The culture of fear: Why Americans are afraid of the wrong things*. New York: Basic Books.

Grann, D. (September 7, 2009). Trial by fire: Did Texas execute an innocent man? *The New Yorker*.

Jewett, R., & Lawrence, J. (1977). *The American monomyth*. New York: Doubleday.

Jewett, R., & Lawrence, J. (2002). *The myth of the American superhero*. Cambridge, UK: William B. Eerdmans Publishing Co.

Justice, B. O. (2008). Prison statistics update. Washington, D.C.: U.S. Department of Justice.

Kellner, D. (2001). *Media culture: Cultural studies, identity and politics between the modern and the postmodern*. New York: Routledge.

Kellner, D., & Share, J. (2007). Critical media literacy is not an option. *Learning Inquiry*, 1(1), 59–69.

Lakoff, G. (2002). *Moral politics: How liberals and conservatives think*. Chicago: The University of Chicago Press.

Liptak, A. (April 23, 2008). U.S. prison population dwarfs that of other nations. *The New York Times*.

Ogletree, C. J. (2002). Black man's burden: Race and the death penalty in America. *Oregon Law Review*, 81(1), 15–38.

Sarat, A. (2002). *When the state kills: Capital punishment and the American condition*. Princeton, NJ: Princeton University Press.

Shapiro, C. (1996). Do or die: Does *Dead Man Walking* run? *University of San Francisco Law Review*, 30(4), 1143–1166.

Stoekl, A. (1999). Execution and the human. *Intertexts*, 3(1), 3–33.

Van Heertum, R., & Share, J. (2006). Connecting power, voice and critique: A new direction for multiple literacy education. *McGill Journal of Education*, 41(3).

2

HOLLYWOOD REPRESENTS THE OTHER

From Ms. J. to Ms. G.: Analyzing Racial Microaggressions in Hollywood's Urban School Genre

Tara J. Yosso and David Gumaro García

Introduction

> Amongst other kinds of ideological labour, the media construct for us a definition of what *race* is, what meaning the imagery of race carries, and what the 'problem of race' is understood to be.
>
> Hall, 1981, p. 35, emphasis in original

Hollywood depictions of Latinas/os reflect troubling racial myths that have changed very little over the last century of filmmaking (e.g., Keller, 1985, 1994; Noriega, 1992; Pettit, 1980; Ramírez Berg, 2002; Woll, 1977, 1980). The treacherous *bandido* of old Hollywood films has evolved into a violent *cholo* in contemporary mainstream cinema, while the modernized version of the Latina spitfire and harlot remains hot tempered and sexually promiscuous. Disguised as entertainment media, this imagery projects racially charged messages about Latinas/os being biologically inferior and culturally deficient. Carlos Cortés (1995) notes that as part of the "societal curriculum," films "have a major impact in shaping beliefs, attitudes, values, perceptions, and 'knowledge' and influencing decisions and action. In short, movies teach" (p. 75). In this chapter, we examine two Hollywood films that carry this teaching potential to the realm of public education (e.g., Bender, 2003; Delgado & Stefancic, 1992; Romero, 2001). Produced over a decade apart, *Dangerous Minds* (1995) and *Freedom Writers* (2007) each claim to present a realistic depiction of a mid-1990s public high school classroom in California. As we explore these ostensibly inspirational stories about a White female teacher who challenges cynicism and bureaucracy, we find similar narratives about what is and how to fix "the problem" for urban Youth of Color in schools. We argue that instead of being uplifting or oppositional portrayals, these films echo disproven social science theories and demean Students of Color with subtle, stunning, and derogatory messages—racial microaggressions (Pierce, 1969, 1980, 1995).

Building on the foundational work of Chester Pierce (1974, 1975), Daniel Solórzano (1998) identifies racial microaggressions as stunning "acts of disregard" against Chicanas/os that include nonverbal denigrating gestures, stereotypical assumptions, lowered expectations, and assaultive verbal remarks. In their multiple forms, racial microaggressions communicate that People of Color are unintelligent, foreign, criminally prone, and deserving of socially marginal status (see Constantine, 2007; Constantine & Sue, 2007; Davis, 1989; Solórzano, Ceja, & Yosso, 2000; Yosso, 2000). These racialized assaults also carry derogatory inferences based on gender, class, sexuality, culture, language, immigration status, phenotype, accent, and surname. Indeed, scholars have identified at least three types of microaggression messages: (1) *microassaults*, or intentional and explicit derogatory verbal or nonverbal attacks, (2) *microinsults*, or rude and insensitive subtle putdowns of someone's racial heritage or identity, and (3) *microinvalidations*, or remarks that diminish, dismiss, or negate the realities and histories of People of Color (Sue, et al., 2007, p. 274).

We argue that on film, racial microaggressions carry a distinct element of intention, projected by commission and omission. The tremendous expense of creating a Hollywood film leaves very little room for accidents. To evoke specific emotions, laughter, or for dramatic effect, filmmakers often use derogatory imagery, dialogue, or other characterization techniques. Filmmakers may claim such images or dialogue are not degrading, but they cannot argue that they included those images or dialogue unintentionally. Even when telling a story about Communities of Color, filmmakers tend to completely ignore their histories and decontextualize their present realities. Again, they may be unaware of how their ahistorical narratives diminish the humanity of People of Color, but filmmakers cannot claim that they omitted these histories and contexts as a series of accidental errors. Cinematic microaggressions reinforce Hollywood's tradition of exploiting race, upholding White privilege for mass audiences and for future generations. Below, we briefly examine some of the racial microaggressions evidenced in Hollywood's urban school genre, especially in relation to Latina/o students.

THEORIZING HOLLYWOOD'S URBAN
SCHOOL GENRE

One year after the landmark *Brown v. Board of Education* case, the 1955 film *Blackboard Jungle* recounted a fictionalized story about a novice high school teacher struggling to inspire urban youth. This film inaugurated what scholars later identified as an urban school genre. Indeed, Hollywood has repeated the plotline of *Blackboard Jungle* at least nine times over the last fifty-five years (e.g., *Up the Down Staircase*, 1967; *The Principal*, 1987; *Stand and Deliver*, 1988; *Lean On Me*, 1989; *Dangerous Minds*, 1995; *The Substitute*, 1996; *High School High*, 1996; *187*, 1997; *Freedom Writers*, 2007). The now formulaic plot casts race in a central role. Establishing shots most often introduce the optimistic, naïve novice (White) teacher as he/she navigates a chaotic school hallway, only to be disrespected and overwhelmed by a classroom of predominately Black and Latina/o students shooting spit wads, dancing, and fighting with one another. A male student usually brutalizes and/or sexually threatens a female teacher in the first act. Deflated faculty work in misery to collect a paycheck, and seek refuge in the teacher's lounge, having lost their belief in the sense of service or mission. Administrators perpetuate the system with cynical, authoritative, and often hostile management. The protagonist teacher distinguishes him/herself from these pessimists, determined to make a difference. Delinquent and remedial Students of Color eventually become inspired to learn academic basics, build up self-respect, and to pursue their education (see Yosso & García, 2010).

Scholars have critiqued urban school genre films for their decontextualized portrayals of delinquent Students (of Color) who are saved from their "culture of poverty" by a heroic (White) teacher (e.g., Bulman, 2002, 2005; Chennault, 2006; Giroux, 1997, 2002; Wells & Serman, 1998). Still, very little research specifically examines Hollywood's depictions of Latinas/os within these films. For this chapter, we narrowed our focus to two films set in California, where Latinas/os comprise at least 49% of the K-12 student population. Nationally, out of every 100 Latina/o elementary school students, only 53 attain their high school diploma, the lowest achievement rate of any major racial or ethnic group (Burciaga, et al., 2010). Rather than address historically unequal schooling conditions, scholars too often blame these dismal outcomes on Latina/o students and their parents (Valencia & Solórzano, 1997).

For example, in the early 1900s, to justify segregating Mexican and Black students based on "inherent" biological deficiencies, scholars claimed, "They cannot master abstractions but they can often be made efficient workers" (Terman, 1916, pp. 91–92). Over the decades, many social scientists shifted their articulation of the problem from biological to cultural deficiency, and endorsed curricula aimed at changing inappropriate Latina/o cultural values, attitudes, and behaviors (e.g., Banfield, 1970, Bernstein, 1977; Madsen, 1964, Sowell, 1981). In this tradition, scholars also charged Latina/o parents with failing to embrace "achievement, independence, and deferred gratification" and thereby creating "stumbling blocks to future advancement" (Heller, 1966, p. 34). Schools then took on the responsibility of subtracting the knowledge systems and culture Latina/o students brought to the classroom (see Valenzuela, 1999) and depositing ostensibly superior White, middle class values (e.g., Hirsch, 1988, 1996).

Hollywood films tend to reflect these deficit arguments with portrayals of Students of Color as delinquents, sexually promiscuous, and unintelligent as a matter of biological or cultural inheritance. Filmmakers often portray Latina/o parents as uninvolved in their children's schooling and providing little useful guidance in their lives. Similar to other racialized Hollywood narratives, such ahistorical framing produces simplistic plotlines revolving around "good and evil, simple and clear-cut conflict, a them-and-us identification process where good equals us, the American (Anglo) values and social system. Them, the villains, are defined as those who reject and seek to destroy the proper set of American (Anglo) values" (Keller, 1994, p. 115). Even as they rely on this familiar plotline, filmmakers often claim to project an authentic voice of a courageous educator, based on a real-life story. Certainly, the medium of film limits the complexity of "reality-based" storytelling. Still, we find this declaration of authenticity disingenuous when filmmakers insist on repeating the same narrative, where "Conflict is typically resolved through the use of righteous force, with Anglo values winning out" (Keller, 1994, p. 115). *Dangerous Minds* and *Freedom Writers* exemplify this commercially successful, albeit unoriginal filmmaking.

A White Missionary in a Gangster's Paradise: *Dangerous Minds*

To begin our discussion of Hollywood's racially exploitative tradition of cultural deficit theorizing, we expand on previous scholars' astute analyses of *Dangerous Minds* (e.g., Chennault, 2006; Giroux, 1997, 2002), with a brief overview of the film's treatment of Latinas/os. Written by Ronald Bass and directed by John N. Smith, *Dangerous*

Minds begins in black-and-white. Rapper Coolio's ominous tune Gangster's Paradise plays over establishing shots of graffiti, street altars honoring the dead, homeless people pushing shopping carts, and drug sales in broad daylight. Then, a small group of Latina/o and Black youth with backpacks board a school bus. The film becomes colorized as the bus reaches a tree-lined street with manicured lawns, where a White man in a suit places his briefcase in a BMW. The bus arrives at the suburban school in vibrant color. This artistic technique establishes a clear, color-coded dichotomy between the dark/gray (hopeless) *barrio* and the bright/colorful (hopeful) suburban school. The unengaged, remedial students from the *barrio* embody this hopelessness. Once on campus, what the filmmakers have determined to be "the problem" is physically contained in an Academy Program class taught by Ms. LouAnne Johnson (Michelle Pfeiffer), a naïve ex-Marine who has not yet completed her teaching credential. Based on the book *My Posse Don't Do Homework*, by the real-life LouAnne Johnson, the film offers a fictionalized version of her student-teaching experiences at Parkmont High School (a pseudonym for the real Carlmont High) in Palo Alto, California.

Racial microaggressions puncture each of the classroom scenes. On her first day, Ms. Johnson excitedly enters the classroom only to be greeted by a hostile mob of dancing, rapping Black and Latina/o youth who hurl racial and sexual insults at her. Across the hall, her friend and colleague, Hal Griffith (George Dzundza) tries to teach history. When his quiet, studious White and Asian American students become distracted by the shouts from the Academy class, Griffith motions for them to stay focused, saying "Come on, come on, come on. You know what they're like!" A shaken Ms. Johnson grabs her briefcase and flees the classroom only minutes after her arrival. Humiliated and furious he did not warn her, she questions Griffith in the hall, exclaiming, "Who are these kids, rejects from hell?"

The school has "contained" these social and racial problems within the Academy Program, and Ms. Johnson becomes determined to control them. "OK, you little bastards," she says to herself. The next day, she returns to the classroom armed with a dare-to-care philosophy and a new poetry-based curriculum she apparently invented, complete with a rewards system of candy bars, a trip to the amusement park, and a restaurant dinner with the teacher. As part of her patronizing pedagogy, Ms. Johnson intervenes in her students' personal, family, and social lives. Here, the filmmakers bombard audiences with microaggressions featuring the sexually threatening Emilio Ramirez (Wade Dominguez), the remedial class clown Raul Sanchero (Renoly

Santiago), and the smart, but pregnant Black teen Callie Roberts (Bruklin Harris). Ms. Johnson exercises her role as the moral authority by teaching these youth to make "good" choices, reflective of what she considers to be "the cultural capital of white middle-class or upper-middle-class people" (Giroux, 1997, p. 49). We focus briefly on the multiple microaggressions evident in the following scenes with Raul and his family.

Raul is characterized as a remedial reader suspended for fighting with Emilio. He lives in a run-down apartment complex, with a dirt lawn and random beer drinking men standing outside. Inside the cluttered apartment, four young children gather around Ms. Johnson whispering complements such as *"que bonita"* (how beautiful). The filmmakers cast shadows across the faces of Mr. and Mrs. Sanchero, while soft light frames Ms. Johnson's face. "I warned Raul to stay out of trouble," Mr. Sanchero states. His wife nods, "He's first in our family to maybe graduate high school." Ms. Johnson tells them "What a pleasure it has been having Raul in my class this semester, you must be very proud." It is clear this thought never occurred to the Sanchero's. Shocked that Ms. Johnson has not come to complain about their son, they hesitantly follow her moral lead and say, "yes," they are proud of their son. She goes on to explain, "He's bright, funny, articulate. The truth is, he's one of my favorites." After exchanging another surprised look with his wife, Mr. Sanchero exclaims, *"¡Que milagro!"* (What a miracle). This scene contributes to the mythmaking process that alleges Latina/o parents do not value education enough to be actively involved in their children's schooling (see Valencia & Black, 2002). Indeed, it could have been written by deficit theorist Cecilia Heller (1966) who claimed that Mexican American "Parents, as a whole, neither impose standards of excellence for tasks performed by their children nor do they expect evidence of high achievement (p. 37). Such myths have been repeatedly debunked by research showing that compared to other working class families, Chicana/o parents maintain higher educational aspirations for their children than do White parents (e.g., Espinosa, Fernández, & Dornbusch, 1977; Solórzano, 1992).

In framing the story around Ms. Johnson's White, middle class, English-only experiences, the filmmakers cannot see, let alone appreciate, the funds of knowledge and indeed, the familial capital the Sanchero's may possess (e.g., Gonzalez, et al., 1995; Moll et al., 1992; Yosso, 2005). They omit Latina/o families' "pedagogies of the home" (Delgado Bernal, 2001), which foster children's aspirations with *una educación* beyond the confines of the school—an education that emphasizes integrity, communal responsibility, and respect (e.g., Burciaga, 2007). Of course, such a depiction would call into question Ms. Johnson's role as the hero-teacher who benevolently gives them the cultural capital necessary for school success. Instead of presenting a complex character who brings linguistic, familial, and social capital to school, the filmmakers depict Raul as academically deficient and dependent on Ms. Johnson. When the class reads aloud, Raul reads with hesitancy, and his peers interrupt him to correct his pronunciation. He later learns proper etiquette from Ms. Johnson after having won a fancy dinner with the teacher. Here, she takes on a parenting role in modeling table manners and demonstrating the value of investing in education. Her dinner lessons also show Raul the importance of planning for the future instead of merely surviving in the present. Ms. Johnson loans him money so he will not hustle for it on the street, and he promises to pay her back when he graduates from high school.

Even though her moral lessons and cultural knowledge positively impacted her students, Ms. Johnson resigns at the end of the school year. Her despondent students give her a candy bar as Raul exclaims, "Ah, come on Ms. J. All those poems you taught us say you can't give in, you can't give up. Well, we ain't giving you up." Callie, who has decided to continue pursuing her high school diploma even while pregnant, adds, "See, cause we see you as being our light." Upon being convinced her students need her, Ms. Johnson "chooses" to stay and in turn, they enthusiastically show her how to dance. The film functions, as "part of a larger project for rearticulating 'whiteness' as a model of authority, rationality, and civilized behavior," reinforcing "the highly racialized, though reassuring, mainstream assumption that chaos reigns in inner-city public schools and that white teachers alone are capable of bringing order, decency, and hope to those on the margins of society" (Giroux, 1997, p. 49). To neatly tell this patronizing story of a White woman bestowing her cultural and moral superiority onto supposedly culturally impoverished and amoral Latina/o and Black youth, filmmakers altered the facts from the real-life version. According to the head of the actual Academy Program, James Ryan (personal communication, March 15, 1996), and as noted by a Washington Post film reviewer, "In truth, a third of the Academy students were White" (Britt, 1995, B1). The real-life Johnson explained, the filmmakers "were in love with the idea of Michelle [Pfeiffer] being white and the kids not...They have the notion that school is only a problem for poor minority kids" (Britt, 1995, B5). In our analysis, the filmmakers also endorse the notion that "poor minority kids" are *the problem* in schools (see also Yosso & García, 2010).

NEW MOVIE, SAME FORMULA: *FREEDOM WRITERS*

Freedom Writers tells the real-life story of Erin Gruwell (Hillary Swank), who taught English for four years at Woodrow Wilson High School in Long Beach, California. Similar to *Dangerous Minds*, the idealistic and naïve Ms. Gruwell encounters a hostile class that includes Latina/o, Black, and Cambodian students. The story follows her diligent efforts to invent teaching methods that transform these antagonistic youth into self-respecting, racially tolerant, and motivated students. The film distinguishes itself from its predecessors with deliberate attempts to center students' experiences, based on 150 real-life student diaries. Still, *Freedom Writers* does not stray far from the urban school formula with its grim view of Communities of Color. Establishing shots, voiceovers, and on-screen text set the context of Gruwell's classroom experience two years after the 1992 Los Angeles uprisings, when on-screen text claims, "gang violence and racial tension reach an all time high." Writer/director Richard LaGravense admittedly narrowed the scope of the film by choosing diaries that "punched me the hardest." In fact, he comments on the DVD that he framed the film around one student's diary in particular, which "was the most dramatic for me to follow, and this was the Eva character."

Indeed, Eva Benitez's (April Lee Hernandez) individual narrative of her Chicana gang life becomes the lens through which LaGravense depicts all the students and from which he infers that violence is synonymous with Communities of Color. LaGravense introduces Eva's character in a flashback to her childhood. As her father buys her a pair of boxing gloves and teaches her to punch, she narrates, "In America, a girl can be crowned a princess for her beauty and her grace. But an Aztec princess is chosen for her blood." This line resurrects racialized myths about violence being inherent to Mexican culture and positions Eva as carrying on an ancient ruthless history. After portraying Eva's childhood exposure to violence, including a drive-by shooting of her neighbor, the wrongful imprisonment of her father, and her own gang initiation, the film jumps to the present day. Here, a group of Asian teenagers with guns disrupt Eva's leisurely walk in her neighborhood. She runs to avoid getting shot, and a block later, a group of African American teens beat her up. As these images play, Eva's matter-of-fact narration continues, "In Long Beach, it all comes down to what you look like, if you're Latino, or Asian, or Black, you could get blasted anytime you walk out your door. We fight each other for territory. We kill each other over race, pride, and respect."

The film's focus on Eva's world-view defines Long Beach as a place of random, incessant interracial conflict. While these assertions may reflect the perspective expressed in the actual diary of Ms. Gruwell's student, research with real-life gang members does not corroborate her claims. On the contrary, scholars such as Cid Martinez and Victor Rios (in press) confirm that even in neighborhoods with high incidents of violence, interracial violence rarely occurs, because rather than initiate conflict, African American and Latino gangs practice conscious avoidance of each other (see also Macallair & Males, 2000). They even engage in cooperation more often than conflict, to defend their neighborhood from being disrespected, fend off outsider threats to their economic opportunities, or to reflect on shared growing up experiences and struggles. *Freedom Writers* does not capture the complexities of this reality.

After positioning the story within Eva's conflict-driven narrative, the film introduces the bright-eyed Ms. Gruwell, meeting with a school administrator who gives her a series of class rosters and notifies her that some students are on house arrest. The camera pans down the list of "problems" brewing in Ms. Gruwell's freshman English classes, focusing on words such as, "probation officer" and "learning disability." On his DVD commentary, LaGravense suggests he emphasized these "problems" to show Ms. Gruwell's courage and to paint a sympathetic portrait of the faculty overall, noting,

> All of these teachers at this particular school had White students who were [performing] very high academically. And when the integration program was put in, 75 percent of the White kids left. And you had Latinos, African Americans, and Asian gangs coming in. And these teachers hated these kids because suddenly their jobs were a lot tougher. And the whole ranking of the school went down.

LaGravense applauds Ms. Gruwell for taking on the extra burden of educating Students of Color who seemingly destabilized an otherwise functioning school system. He justifies his racial-conflict theme based on his own perception of all Latina/o, African American, and Asian American students as gang members.

The film does provide more depth to the student characters than *Dangerous Minds*, but the breadth of their experiences remains quite limited. Indeed, every student narrative entails some sort of violence, drugs, or gang activity. When no one shows up to talk with her on parent-teacher night, Ms. Gruwell reads students' diaries and learns about their dysfunctional families and violent communities. With their voices playing over a montage of images, students "speak" to the teacher they begin to affectionately refer to as Ms. G. The Latina/o characters include, Alejandro (Sergio Montalvo), who talks about witnessing a drive-by while buying candy at the store, and beginning to carry a concealed gun to school for protection. Gloria (Kristin Herrera) writes about being beaten and having to hide her bruises. Rather than engage students in understanding and challenging gang violence or domestic abuse, Ms. Gruwell positions these social problems as a result of students' individual choices. She grabs their attention and sarcastically mocks them by calling the Nazi's the "most famous gang in history," erroneously equating students' racial prejudices with the Nazi regime's violence and White supremacist ideology. For Ms. Gruwell, racism occurs when students sit together by race/ethnic group and create their own "borders" of self-segregation in her classroom (see Tatum, 1997; Villalpando, 2003). She focuses on self-reflective class activities that enable them to recognize these personal battles occur across racial lines. Her individualistic approach parallels previous Hollywood "teacher-heroes," who encourage students to choose academics instead of the street. As Robert Bulman (2005) argues,

> Most of the urban public school films portray the individual attitude of the students as the primary obstacle to their academic achievement. These students don't have the right manners, the right behavior, or the right values to succeed in school...Their depiction as 'animals' suggests that the problems in these schools are rooted in student behavior and, furthermore, that their behavior is rooted in an inferior culture. (p. 51)

The only White student in the class, Ben (Hunter Parrish), reiterates this emphasis on the individual. His diary entry discusses a documentary film Ms. Gruwell showed about the Freedom Riders of the 1960s. As black-and-white images play of a bloodied and bruised Jim Zwerg, Ben reflects on the bravery of this White youth, who volunteered to be the first person off the Freedom Riders' bus in Alabama, knowing he would face the brunt of the anti–civil rights mob. Ben remarks, "That kind of courage is unbelievable to me. I was afraid of just being in this class. And I must have some kind of courage, because I could have lied to get out of here, but I stayed. I stayed." Taking his cues from Ms. Gruwell, Ben's monologue, though expressed in a sincere tone, absurdly equates his classmates with the violent, racist mob in Alabama and suggests he, too, is a hero in the tradition of the real-life Zwerg.

Ms. Gruwell boldly chooses to teach racial tolerance through the *Diary of Anne Frank*, but her curriculum fails to foster a deeper understanding of how students' personal crises relate to societal power structures. She misses an opportunity to transform the meaning of the individual self by, "drawing sustenance from the past experiences of the group," as Stephen Butterfield (1974) observed is a strength of Black autobiography" (p. 3). Indeed, whether through the auto-biographies of African Americans and Latinas/os or through other texts about urban youth, Ms. Gruwell provides no opportunity to historically contextualize their experiences (Moore & Vigil, 1993). She does not ask them to consider some of the socioeconomic reasons that gave rise to youth gangs (e.g., Mirandé, 1987). She does not discuss any of the history around discriminatory housing laws, which restricted access to certain neighborhoods based on skin color. Such a discussion could have also addressed the ways Whites enforced racial segregation beyond the confines of the law, with violence and threats of violence (e.g., Almaguer, 1994). This would have aided students in understanding some of the material consequences of racism's legacy in their everyday lives. The abbreviated discussion of civil rights also projects a microaggression of omission, suggesting racism no longer exists as an institutionalized societal problem and reducing the histo-ries of People of Color to particular and personal tragedies (see Yosso & García, 2008). When Eva expresses her anger at the injustice dealt to her friends and family by White police officers, Ms. Gruwell does not engage the class in a research assignment about police brutal-ity against low income Communities of Color. She focuses instead on Eva's assertion that she "hates" White people. "You hate me?" Ms. Gruwell asks. When Eva answers affirmatively, Ms. Gruwell pro-tests, "You don't know me." Eva retorts,

> I know what you can do! I saw White cops shoot my friend in the back for reaching into his pocket. His pocket! I saw White cops break into my house and take my father for no reason except because they feel like it; except because they can. And they can, because they're White.

Eva's remarks begin to unpack institutionalized racism and White privilege, but Ms. Gruwell personalizes her social critique, turning to Ben and asking, "Ben, do you have anything to say?" With this redi-rection, she callously dismisses the legitimacy of Eva's anger, avoids a discussion of racial injustice and confirms the power of her own whiteness to control the terms of the debate.

LaGravense does attempt to show some of the racial stress Students of Color may experience in predominately White, segregated settings. For example, he introduces Victoria (Giovonnie Samuels) as the only African American student in a Distinguished Scholars Honors English course. When her White male teacher Mr. Hall (Horace Hall) asks Victoria to give the class "the Black perspective," she begins an internal monologue, questioning "Do I have a stamp on my forehead that says 'the national spokesperson for the plight of Black people?" She subsequently requests a transfer to Ms. Gruwell's class. Unfortunately, LaGravense reduces the complex issue of tracking to a simple case of racial conflict. A later scene features Mr. Hall and teacher/administrator Ms. Campbell (Imelda Staunton) privately venting their concern about Victoria's "choice" to leave the honors program. Their dialogue reveals their thinly veiled racial prejudice against Ms. Gruwell's students. Still, the film falls short of naming the institutionalized racial discrimination they attempt to justify (i.e. the maintenance of a racially segregated, predominately White college preparatory track within an otherwise integrated school; see Mickelson, 2005; Oakes, 1985; Wells & Serman, 1998. This incomplete narrative also feeds deficit assumptions about Black and Latina/o parents. While Ms. Gruwell sits alone on parent-teacher night, Mr. Hall interacts with a group of parents.

Ms. Gruwell fuels the individualistic "pick yourself up by your bootstraps" theme when she asks her class to openly commit to turning over a new leaf in their personal lives with a "toast for change." She explains, "the person you were before this moment, that person's turn is over. Now it's your turn." With almost religious overtones of being "born again," she mobilizes students to change the savage inequalities they experience by changing their own self-defeating oppositional behaviors (see Solórzano & Delgado Bernal, 2001). For example, Gloria grabs a glass of sparkling apple cider for the toast and declares she will not get pregnant by age sixteen and drop out like her mom. Eva publicly commits to change in a later scene, when she defies her father and betrays her "family" by testifying against a Latino gang member instead of falsely accusing an innocent Black youth of the liquor store shooting. Other classmates also make life-changing decisions, including Alejandro, who throws away his gun. According to the film, it is not the parents, but Ms. Gruwell who provides students with the tools to develop a moral compass. This time-consuming, demanding work ostensibly contributes to Ms. Gruwell's divorce. LaGravense's portrait of the self-sacrificing Ms. G. further highlights the almost complete absence of Latina/o and Black parents throughout the film. This omission perpetuates the cultural deficit myth that Parents of Color do not value or engage in their children's education.

Though the microaggressions in *Freedom Writers* may appear less overt, and the narrative offers a more nuanced approach to portraying the experiences of urban youth in schools, the film falls back on the same cultural deficit narrative evident in *Dangerous Minds*. The filmmakers' intent to engage issues of racism resonate throughout the film, lingering in its theme song, which heavily samples Martin Luther King Jr.'s speech "I Have a Dream." Unlike Dr. King, who courageously named and challenged structures of racism crippling society, the film looks for hope in urban schools not through the collective struggle of a community against injustice, but through individuals bettering themselves. We agree that helping students gain self-confidence is a laudable goal, but we remain concerned by the messages of White superiority projected through this depiction. LaGravense cannot move away from the patronizing portrayal of *Dangerous Minds* while marketing his film as "the gripping story of inner-city kids raised on drive-by shootings and hardcore attitude." *Freedom Writers'* omission of historical context and distortion of individual cultural attitudes and behaviors recenters the teacher-hero's whiteness as the solution, and ultimately leaves the urban school formula intact 52 years after its *Blackboard Jungle* premiere.

DISCUSSION

> Once minority representations are seen and understood for what they are, the invisible architecture of the dominant-dominated 'arrangement' is exposed and there is a chance for a structural "rearrangement."
>
> Ramírez Berg, 1997, p. 116

In this chapter, we have attempted to expose "the invisible architecture" of Hollywood's urban school formula, focusing on depictions of Latina/o students in *Dangerous Minds* and *Freedom Writers*. We argue that with subtle, stunning repetition, these films position White teachers as the hope for reforming culturally wayward Latina/o and Black youth, and thereby relieve institutions (and audiences) from responsibility to change structures of inequality.

Drawing on traditions of deficit social science, the microaggressions in these films helps construct "the Latina/o problem" in California

schools as a crisis of cultural values, while ignoring the legacy of institutionalized racism shaping Latina/o educational experiences. The
filmmakers continue what Hall described at the opening epigraph
of our chapter as "ideological labour," associating Latina/o youth
and communities with moral depravity, cultural poverty, and racial
conflict. These cinematic racial microaggressions reflect the messages
sent by a multi-year conservative electoral assault against California's
working class Communities of Color, which cast English Language
Learners, and urban Youth of Color as "suspects" who burden and
menace mainstream society (Hayes-Bautista, 2004; Martin, 1996).
Indeed, the duplicitous language of California's propositions 187,
(Save our State), 227 (English for the Children), and 21 (Juvenile
Justice) only thinly disguised the cultural deficit narratives and racial
stereotypes they evoked (see Santa Ana, 2002).

George Lipsitz (1990) explains that, "commercial motion pictures invariably resonate with the value crises of the times in which
they appear...they [also] reposition us for the future by reshaping
our memories of the past" (p. 164). With their subtle and stunning
racially assaultive images, *Dangerous Minds* and *Freedom Writers*
fuel unfounded public fears about growing populations of ostensibly uneducable and uncontrollable Youth of Color (Californians for
Justice Education Fund, 2003). At a minimum, these films could
have recognized that Students of Color possess and create valuable knowledge and exhibit resilience independent of their teachers
(Delgado Bernal, 2002). Indeed, while Hollywood's urban school
genre films omit, distort, and exploit their experiences, Latina/o students resist racism well beyond the classroom (see Olmos' *Walkout*,
2006; Yosso & García, 2008, 2010).

Utilizing these films as pedagogical tools, educators can build on
a legacy of resistance to racism, and engage students in a critical race
media literacy curriculum that challenges dominant racial ideologies
projected as "inspiring" Hollywood entertainment (Yosso 2002):
Expanding on their knowledge as media consumers, students can
critique the all-too prevalent "it's just a movie" argument by con-
ducting their own research analyzing racial microaggressions and
cultural deficit theory on film. As they uncover historical patterns of
framing Latinas/os and African Americans as "the problem" in urban
schools, students can recover and document the cultural wealth of
Communities of Color, which filmmakers often omit. They can
examine the ideological links between Hollywood's racialized myths
and urban educational policies, to explore some of the real implications of this reel pedagogy.

REFERENCES

Almaguer, T. (1994). *Racial fault lines: The historical origins of White supremacy in California*. London: England. University of California Press.

Banfield, E.C. (1970). "Schooling versus education." *The unheavenly city: The nature and future of our urban crisis*, (pp. 132–157). Boston: MA: Little Brown and Company.

Bender, S.W. (2003). *Greasers and gringos: Latinos, law, and the American imagination*. New York University Press.

Bernstein, B. (1977). *Class, codes, and control: Vol. 3 towards a theory of educational transmission*. London: Routledge and Kegan Paul.

Britt, D. (1995). "In Hollywood, real life doesn't play," *The Washington Post*, August 11, 1995, B1.

Bulman, R.C. (2002). "Teachers in the 'hood: Hollywood's middle class fantasy." *The Urban Review*, *34*(3), 251–276.

——— (2005). *Hollywood goes to high school: Cinema, schools, and American culture*. New York: Worth Publishers.

Burciaga, R. (2007). Living nepantla: Chicana education doctoral students' personal and professional aspirations. Unpublished doctoral dissertation, University of California, Los Angeles.

Burciaga, R., L. Perez-Huber, D.G. Solórzano. (2010). "Going back to the headwaters: examining Latina/o educational attainment and achievement through a framework of hope." *Handbook on Latinas/os in education: Theory, research, and practice*, (pp. 422–437). New York: Routledge.

Butterfield, S. (1974). *Black autobiography in America*. Amherst: University of Massachusetts Press.

Californians for Justice Education Fund. (2003, May 17). "First things first: Why we must stop punishing students and fix California's schools: A report on school inequality and the impact of the California High School Exit Exam." Oakland: Author.

Chennault, R.E. (2006). *Hollywood films about schools: Where race, politics, and education intersect*. New York: Palgrave Macmillan.

Constantine, M. G. (2007). "Racial microaggressions against African American clients in cross-racial counseling relationships." *Journal of Counseling Psychology*, *54*(1), 1–16.

Constantine, M. G., & Sue, D. W. (2007). "Perceptions of racial microaggressions among Black supervisees in cross-racial dyads." *Journal of Counseling Psychology*, *54*(2), 142–153.

Cortés, C.E. (1995). "Knowledge construction and popular culture: The media as multicultural educator." In, J.A. Banks & C.A. Banks (eds.), *Handbook of research on multicultural education*, (pp. 169–183). New York: Macmillan.

Davis, P. (1989). "Law as microaggression". *The Yale Law Journal*, *98*(8), 1559–1577.

Delgado, R. & Stefancic, J. (1992). "Images of the outsider in American law and culture: Can free expression remedy systemic social ills?" *Cornell Law Review*, *77*, 1258–1297.

Delgado Bernal, D. (2001). "Living and learning pedagogies of the home: The *mestiza* consciousness of Chicana students." *International Journal of Qualitative Studies in Education, 14*(5), 623–639.

——— (2002). "Critical race theory, LatCrit theory, and critical raced-gendered epistemologies: Recognizing students of color as holders and creators of knowledge." *Qualitative Inquiry, 8*(1), 105–126.

Espinosa, R.W., Fernández, C., Dornbusch, S.M. (1977). "Chicano perceptions of high school and Chicano performance." *Aztlan: A Journal of Chicano Studies, 8,* 133–155.

Freire, P. (1973). *Pedagogy of the oppressed.* New York: The Seabury Press.

Giroux, H. (1997). "Race, pedagogy, and whiteness in Dangerous Minds." *Cineaste, 22*(4), 46–49.

——— (2002). *Breaking in to the movies: Film and the culture of politics.* Malden, MA: Blackwell Publishers.

Gonzalez, N., Moll, L. C., Tenery, M. F., Rivera, A., Rendon, P. Gonzales, R. & Amanti, C. (1995) "Funds of knowledge for teaching in Latino households." *Urban Education, 29*(4), 443–470.

Hall, S. (1981). "The whites of their eyes: Racist ideologies in media." In, G. Bridges & R. Brunt (eds.). *Silver linings: Some strategies for the eighties,* (pp. 28–52). London: Lawrence & Wishart.

Hayes-Bautista, D.E. (2004). *La nueva California: Latinos in the golden state.* Berkeley: University of California Press.

Heller, C. (1966). *Mexican American youth: Forgotten youth at the crossroads.* New York: Random House.

Hirsch, E. D., Jr. (1988). *Cultural literacy: What every American needs to know.* New York: Vintage Books.

——— (1996). *The schools we need and why we don't have them.* New York: Doubleday.

Keller, G. D. (Ed.). (1985). *Chicano cinema: Research, reviews, and resources.* Binghamton, NY: Bilingual Press/Editorial Bilingüe.

——— (1994). *Hispanics and United States film: An overview and handbook.* Tempe, AZ: Bilingual Press/Editorial Bilingüe.

LaGravenese, R. (Director). (2007) *Freedom Writers.* [DVD] Hollywood, CA: Paramount Pictures.

Lipsitz, G. (1990). *Time passages: Collective memory and American popular culture.* Minneapolis: Minnesota University Press.

Macallair, D. & Males, M. (2000) "Dispelling the myth: An analysis of youth and adult crime patterns in California over the past 20 years." San Francisco, CA: Center on Juvenile and Criminal Justice.

Madsen, W. (1964). *Mexican-Americans of South Texas.* New York: Holt, Rinehart and Winston.

Martin, P. (1996). "Proposition 187 in California." In, D. Hamamoto & R. Torres (eds.). *New American destinies: A reader in contemporary Asian and Latino immigration,* (pp. 325–332). New York: Routledge.

Martinez, C. & V. Rios (in press). "Examining the relationship between African American and Latino street gangs: Conflict, cooperation and avoidance in two multi-racial urban neighborhoods." In E. Telles, G. Rivera Salgado, & M. Sawyer (eds.). *Black-Latino relations in the United States*. Russell Sage.

Mirandé, A. (1987). *Gringo justice*. University of Notre Dame Press.

Moll, L. C., Amanti, C., Neff, D. & Gonzalez, N. (1992) "Funds of knowledge for teaching: Using a qualitative approach to connect homes and classrooms." *Theory into Practice, 31*(2), 132–141.

Moore, J. & Vigil, J.D. (1993). "Barrios in transition." In, J. Moore & R. Pinderhughes (eds.). *In the barrios: Latinos and the underclass debate*, (pp. 27–49). New York: Russell Sage.

Oakes, J. (1985). *Keeping track: How schools structure inequality*. New Haven, CT: Yale University Press.

Olmos, E.J. (Director). (2006). *Walkout*. [DVD] Los Angeles, CA: HBO Video.

Pettit, A. G. (1980). *Images of the Mexican American in fiction and film*. College Station, TX: Texas A&M University Press.

Pierce, C. M. (1969). "Is bigotry the basis of the medical problems of the ghetto?" In J.C. Norman, (ed.), *Medicine in the ghetto*, (pp. 301–314). New York: Meredith Corporation.

——— (1974). "Psychiatric problems of the black minority." In S. Arieti, (ed.), *American handbook of psychiatry*, (pp. 512–523). New York: Basic Books.

——— (1975). "Poverty and racism as they affect children." In I.N. Berlin. (ed.), *Advocacy for child mental health*, (pp. 92–109). New York: Brunner/ Mazel Publishers.

——— (1980). "Social trace contaminants: Subtle indicator of racism in TV." In S. B. Withey & R. P. Abeles (eds.), *Television and social behavior: Beyond violence and children. A report of the committee on television and social behavior social science research council*, (pp. 249–257). Hillsdale, NJ: Lawrence Erlbaum Associates.

——— (1995). "Stress analogs of racism and sexism: Terrorism, torture, and disaster". In C. V. Willie, P. P. Rieker, B. M. Kramer, & B. S. Brown, (eds.), *Mental health, racism, and sexism*, (pp. 277–293). Pittsburgh, PA: University of Pittsburgh Press.

Ramírez Berg, C. (1997). "Stereotyping in films in general and of the Hispanic in particular." In, C. Rodríguez (Ed.), *Latin looks: Images of Latinas and Latinos in the U.S. media*, (pp. 104–120). Boulder, CO: Westview Press.

——— (2002). *Latino images in film: Stereotypes, subversion, and resistance*. Austin: University of Texas Press.

Romero, M. (2001). "State violence and the social and legal construction of Latino criminality: From *el bandido* to gang member." *Denver University Law Review, 78*(4), 1081–1118.

Santa Ana, O. (2002). *Brown tide rising: Metaphors of Latinos in the contemporary American public discourse*. Austin: University of Texas Press.

Smith, J.N. (Director) (1995). *Dangerous Minds*. [DVD] Burbank, CA: Hollywood Pictures.

Solórzano, D.G. (1992). "Chicano mobility aspirations: A theoretical and empirical note." *Latino Studies Journal, 3,* 48–66.

——— (1997). "Images and words that wound: Critical race theory, racial stereotyping, and teacher education." *Teacher Education Quarterly, 24*(3), 5–19.

——— (1998). "Critical race theory, racial and gender microaggressions, and the experiences of Chicana and Chicano scholars." *International Journal of Qualitative Studies in Education, 11,* 121–136.

Solórzano, D. G., & Delgado Bernal, D. (2001). "Examining transformational resistance through a critical race and LatCrit theory framework: Chicana and Chicano students in an urban context." *Urban Education, 36*(3), 308–342.

Solórzano, D.G., M. Ceja, & T.J. Yosso. (2000, Winter/Spring). "Critical race theory, racial microaggressions, and campus racial climate: The experiences of African American college students." *Journal of Negro Education, 69*(1/2), 60–73.

Sowell, T. (1981). *Ethnic America: A history.* New York: Basic Books.

Sue, D. W., Capodilupo, C. M., Torino, G. C., Bucceri, J. M., Holder, A. M. B., Nadal, K. L., & Esquilin, M. (2007). "Racial microaggressions in everyday life: Implications for clinical practice." *American Psychologist, 62*(4), 271–286.

Tatum, B. D. (1997). *Why are all the Black kids sitting together in the cafeteria?: And other conversations about race.* New York: Basic Books.

Terman, L. M. (1916). *The measurement of intelligence: An explanation of and a complete guide for the use of the standard revision and extension of the Binet-Simon intelligence scale.* Boston: Houghton Mifflin Company.

Valencia, R.R. & Black, M.S. (2002). "'Mexicans don't value education!': On the basis of the myth, mythmaking, and debunking." *Journal of Latinos and Education, 2*(2), 81–103.

Valencia, R.R. & Solórzano, D.G. (1997). "Contemporary deficit thinking." In R.R. Valencia (Ed.), *The evolution of deficit thinking in educational thought and practice* (pp. 160– 210). Washington, DC: Falmer Press.

Valenzuela, A. (1999). *Subtractive schooling: U.S.-Mexican youth and the politics of caring.* State University of New York Press.

Villalpando, O. (2003). "Self-segregation or self-preservation? A critical race theory and Latina/o critical theory analysis of findings from a longitudinal study of Chicana/o college students." *International Journal of Qualitative Studies in Education, 16*(5), 619–646.

Wells, A.S. & T.W. Serman. (1998). "Education against all odds: What films teach us about schools." In, G. Maeroff. (Ed.), *Imaging education: The media and schools in America* (pp. 181-194). New York: Teachers College Press.

Woll, A.L. (1977). *The Latin image in American film.* Los Angeles, CA: UCLA Latin American Center Publications.

——— (1980). "Bandits and lovers: Hispanic images in American film." In, R.M. Miller (Ed.), *The kaleidoscopic lens: How Hollywood views ethnic groups* (pp. 54–72). New York: Jerome S. Ozer.

Yosso, T.J. (2000). A critical race and LatCrit approach to media literacy: Chicana/o resistance to visual microaggressions. Unpublished doctoral dissertation, University of California, Los Angeles.

———— (2002). "Critical race media literacy: Challenging deficit discourse about Chicanas/os." *Journal of Popular Film and Television, 30*(1), 52–62.

———— (2005). "Whose culture has capital? A critical race theory discussion of community cultural wealth." *Race, Ethnicity, and Education, 8*(1), 71–93.

Yosso, T.J. & D.G. García. (2008). " 'Cause it's not just me': *Walkout's* history lessons challenge Hollywood's urban high school formula." *Radical History Review, 102,* 171–184.

———— (2010). " 'Who are these kids, rejects from hell?' Analyzing Hollywood distortions of Latina/o high school students." *Handbook on Latinas/os in education: Theory, research, and practice,* (pp. 450–473). New York: Routledge.

HOLLYWOOD'S CINEMA OF ABLEISM: A DISABILITY STUDIES PERSPECTIVE ON THE HOLLYWOOD INDUSTRIAL COMPLEX

Tony Kashani and Anthony J. Nocella II

> Check it out. Dustin Hoffman, "Rain Man," look retarded, act retarded, not retarded. Counted toothpicks, cheated cards. Autistic, sho'. Not retarded. You know Tom Hanks, "Forrest Gump." Slow, yes. Retarded, maybe. Braces on his legs. But he charmed the pants off Nixon and won a ping-pong competition. That ain't retarded. Peter Sellers, "Being There." Infantile, yes. Retarded, no. You went full retard, man. Never go full retard. You don't buy that? Ask Sean Penn, 2001, "I Am Sam." Remember? Went full retard, went home empty handed.
>
> Kirk Lazarus (played by Robert Downey Jr.) in
> the film *Tropic Thunder* (2008)

Does Hollywood exploit people with disabilities? This is a loaded question, pregnant with polyvalent responses. On the one hand, it is safe to assume the employers within the corporate cinema globally known as Hollywood adhere to all the liberal laws that are put in place to protect people with mental and physical disabilities. On the other hand, representation of people with mental and physical disabilities seems to be highly problematic, given the number of films that are produced, which either get entertainment value out of dramatizing the disability of the characters and/or exoticizing them to get an emotional rise out of the audiences. In short, what unites most Hollywood narratives that have the disabled either as central characters or minor players is its exploitation of people with disabilities, using them as a means to move the plot.

In this chapter we argue that no matter how one looks at it, Hollywood does too much of exploitation and not enough of advocacy for people with disabilities via its representations within its narratives. Moreover, we put Hollywood cinema under the critical examination lens, and in thinking through its modes of representation, maintain that its cultural machinery generates story after story filled with ableist themes. It follows that these narratives implicitly teach their audiences that social Darwinism is the norm in society. It is important to note that our argument is not about a few films released by the system; our argument is institutional, as we intend to take the entire system to task. If Hollywood is a purveyor of social attitudes, then it must be held accountable for its ethics (Kashani, 2007).

Given our stance in positing Hollywood as an ableist institution, we ought to qualify this by explaining how we define ableism. Although this term can be construed in different ways depending on the context in which it is used, we address abelism in its categorical sense. In many ways, disability used to generate shame and marginalization in society, both for people with disabilities as well as their families. However, history has shown us that as a society we have made strides in correcting this moral mistake, predicated on many years of struggles, which went into high gear in the 1960s and continues to this day. Thus far, the most important piece of legislation in the societal fight against ableism seems to be the Americans with Disabilities Act of 1990 (Greenberg and Page, 2003). Not unlike racism and sexism, ableism is also embedded in society in such a way that the so-called "normal people," which is to say those folks without visible physical or mental disabilities, are often not even aware of their ableist attitudes and tendencies (Foucault, 1980).

To be sure, "disability" is a contested terrain (Davis, 1997), given the fact that all members of the human species have limitations; abilities in some areas and disabilities in other areas. Nonetheless, there are those of us who struggle and are oppressed more than others. What is disability and why does it have a negative connotation? Disability can be construed as a pejorative term because of the implications of being broken and not working properly. The politically correct term, "people with disabilities," is a replacement for words like crippled, lame, freak, crazy, and retarded, all of which mean similar things and are used commonly in U.S. society (Taylor 1996) and beyond. It is important to note that many people may use the PC version, but still have the discriminatory feeling about it. These terms often conjure up negative images that are most commonly used to insult and label someone. "You are being lame," "Stop freaking out,"

"You are so retarded," "That dude is crazy," "What, are you mad?" "Don't be insane?" and "What are you, crippled or something?" Thus, for example "feebleminded," "retarded," "special educational needs," "special needs," and "learning difficulties" are all examples of negative implications about the disabled (Armstrong, Armstrong, & Barton, 2000: p. 3).

As you are reading this chapter, some Hollywood executives—knowing full well that cinematic representation is perhaps the most powerful means of communication (Denzin, 1991; Giroux, 2002; Kashani, 2009)—are having private conversations about the ways in which they can get a story about a "retarded" person or a "paraplegic," or a "freak," and so on, into a successful blockbuster for a great profit. They might be pointing to the success of films like *Avatar* (2009) and the *X-Men* series (2000, 2003, 2006, 2009). They may or may not be aware of their ableist attitudes; nonetheless they practice it. They may even be referring to each other and their own ideas by using words like lame, freak, crippled, weak, psycho, and retarded. How often do you hear a response from someone when they (usually a man) rejecting an idea, calling it "retarded?" This is similar to the notion of that person (usually a man) rejecting an idea or action and calling it "gay."

THE BENEFICIARIES OF ABLEIST CINEMA

Ableism is a form of discrimination and can make it hard for people with visible and invisible disabilities to find employment, attend college, and have families of their own. On the other hand, many Hollywood stars without visible disabilities have had tremendous success playing characters that had distorted images of disabilities. Tom Cruise in *Born on the 4th of July* (1989), Dustin Hoffman in *Rain Man* (1988), Russell Crowe in *A Beautiful Mind* (2001), Will Smith in *I, Robot* (2004), Brad Pitt in *Twelve Monkeys* (1995), Julia Roberts in *Steel Magnolias* (1989), Denzel Washington in *The Bone Collector* (1999), Cuba Gooding Jr. in *Radio* (2003), and of course Tom Hanks in *Forrest Gump* (1994). All of these bona fide stars benefited greatly from acting disabled. Although some of these films have raised awareness about certain disabilities (e.g., *Rain Man* (1988) with autism) and offered negotiated readings for media-literate audiences, for the most part, we argue, they have exploited people with disabilities to make money and perpetuate ableism.

How does it work? Cinema operates on the principle of projection and identification (Allen & Gomery, 1985, Kashani, 2009) and given the star power of Hollywood and the ways in which its consumers identify with the stars, the central message communicated with these films is that it is desirable to portray a person with disabilities, but it is not okay to be one. The case of *Rain Man* (1988), winner of four Academy Awards, including best actor for Dustin Hoffman, best writing for Barry Levinson, best writing (original screenplay) for Ronald Bass (screenplay) and Barry Morrow (screenplay/story), and best picture for Mark Johnson is indeed an empirical example of our thesis.

Everyone who has viewed *Rain Man* (1988) knows that Dustin Hoffman is not autistic, and yet he receives the industry's highest award for constructing an image of a person with autism. Although the film generated a general awareness regarding autism, raising the collective consciousness of American society, it capitalized on the cliché concept of "idiot- savant" to sell a formulaic character-centered, coming-of-age road movie about brotherly love. *Rain Man* (1988) creates an exotic character out of Raymond, an autistic savant who has the uncanny ability to read cards at a Las Vegas casino, but is unable to function in society at large, and therefore has to be confined to a residence for people with mental disabilities. It is important to note that *Rain Man* (1988) does not have a single character of any significance who is actually a person with real mental disabilities—that person is a caricatured image of one with autism.

Does the story ever delve into the societal problems of people with mental disabilities? Aside from some superficial and very brief scenes between Raymond, his doctor, and Charlie (the self-centered, neoliberal brother played to near perfection by Tom Cruise) discussing the social stigmas and difficulties of independent living for Raymond, the film is a melodrama about sentimental love and the inevitability of humanity's shortcomings, therefore reinforcing the notion that independence (rather than interdependence, which is promoted by disability studies) is what is valued in society. Dustin Hoffman, a method actor par excellence, depicts a composite character brilliantly, but had he more meaningful material in the writing and direction where sensitivity toward people with mental disabilities would take center stage and societal problems were pronounced in more profound manner, we contend the film would be rich and educational for its audiences. Cursory glances at institutional abelism are not enough, given the pedagogical power of the rest of this professional melodrama.

In the twenty-first century, Hollywood seems to have turned the clock back a bit. In *Tropic Thunder* (2008), which we have noted earlier, one of the protagonists, Kirk Lazarus, played by Robert Downey Jr. is not only ableist with his language, but made up in blackface (the appalling racist practice of white actors putting on black wax on their faces and depicting African Americans in often demeaning and humiliating fashion). Although the ways in which *Tropic Thunder* (2008) attempts to generate humor are explicitly racist, sexist, and ableist, the makers of the narrative seem to be indifferent to the film's oppressive pedagogy. The film, written, directed, and acted by Ben Stiller—who is no stranger to disability exploitation— had gross revenue of $188,072,649 at a budget of $100 million. It is hardly debatable that a profit of $88 million is a healthy sum for neoliberal executives of Hollywood. Given the logic of neoliberalism, where ethics do not matter and the marketplace is an ethics in itself, is it any wonder that in Hollywood anything goes in the name of profit? This also begs the question: What does this say about our society and our value system as a people?

ETHICS OF HOLLYWOOD'S ABLEISM

From an ethical standpoint, all domination, no matter the form (e.g., racism, sexism, homophobia, ableism, and ageism), is wrong. Take a deeper look and you will notice that exploitation is modus operandi for all ruling systems in our society. We are, of course, pointing to economic, political, and cultural institutions that, in a cartel-like fashion, support each other for control, domination, and authoritarianism. This was the way of colonialism, and it is the way of the Hollywood industrial complex. Paradoxically, there are Hollywood films that intend to do justice for people with disabilities. For example *Tiptoes* (2003), which does a fair representation at times of expressing the culture of little people, identified by many in society and in the film as "dwarfs," while keeping those that are little people actors in the film on the margins and off the cover of the DVD. Dwarfs, midgets, half-people, freaks are labels to marginalize and reinforce abnormally a group of people, in this case, little people. The film centers on a couple, Carol, played by Kate Beckinsale, and Steven, played by Matthew McConaughey. Steven comes from a family that has had dwarfism. In fact, his twin brother, played by 5'-10" Gary Oldman, is a little person. Not surprisingly Steven and Carol get married and have a dwarf child. The plot ostensibly revolves around the difficulties of dwarfism. To ensure the marketability of the film, a story that on the surface intends to do justice for the dwarf community instead reinforces the marginalization and oppression of little people. In an insightful analysis of the film, Kay Olson, an activist blogging against ableism, writes

> ...a movie about dwarfism with all average-size actors playing any character with billing. The secondary characters and extras include dozens of little folks, so it was a very conscious casting choice to not let dwarfs represent themselves in any major substantive character-developed way. And while it's good to see a film about dwarfism, exploring the unique difficulties and cultural events that bring little people together, they remain—if you'll forgive me—the sideshow to the average-sized people who spend the film talking about them or, in Oldman's case, acting as one of them. False representation, however earnest or talented the actor, is still a form of silencing and control (Olson 2007).

Olson's blog points to egoism of Hollywood and in turn holds a mirror in front of all of us. In our inquiry, one ethical question kept coming back to the surface. Why do the public endorse these films by buying tickets and/or renting them at their local video store? Is it because Hollywood has cultivated a consumer attitude toward cinema that renders the cinematic experience into a culinary experience? Is it because neoliberal practices generate apathy amongst people who ought to know better? Does a neoliberal society reach a state of meaninglessness that oppression becomes just another word?

Following the logic of neoliberalism, in a deregulated media paradigm, a widespread depoliticization of disability has taken place, giving Hollywood license to practice what we call cinema of freakism. Films such as the *X-Men* series (2000, 2003, 2006, 2009) with their freakish superheroes (male and female) and villains who are led by a man in a wheelchair, grossing revenue of $1.565 billion, are emblematic of the cinema of freakism. The *X-Men* series apply freak philosophy to their narratives whereby the "mutants" have super-human powers. But the *X-Men* mutants are also subject to Hollywood's Manichean treatment. The good guy mutant/bad guy mutant nexus carries the bulk of the narratives, especially in *X-Men 3: The Last Stand* (2006).

The *X-Men* films are based on the popular comics of the same name. The comic book as a medium of communication has questionable ethics, to be sure. The comic world is grounded and built on the logic of the "freak" saving the world or destroying it, but no matter the action, we should always be fearful and keep "them" at a distance, prepared to imprison and kill them if possible. Generally speaking, the pedagogy of popular comics is potent, given its successful history in selling serial stories to kids and juvenile adults. The central lesson to youth is, and always has been, to fear and never trust the one who is different from the majority (i.e., those with visible disabilities); therefore, only trust those that are similar, equal, the same, and thus normal.

The 2007 film *300* (another comic book adaptation, in which a solider is denied admittance to the great 300 Spartans due to his being seen as disabled) is yet another unethical but highly successful example of ableist cinema. In the narrative, the "great fighting 300 Spartans" battle the Persians, who are depicted as "uncivilized." In the movie the Spartan king, Leonidas, is approached by a Greek, who is strong and loyal but a person with physical disabilities, to join the Spartans to fight. However, King Leonidas judges this man as a weak liability, rather than a powerful and strong soldier with wit. The solider with disabilities pleads his case to be part of the Spartans, but the king, after observing the soldier perform a few defensive and offensive moves, decides he is not suitable to join the Spartans. This devastates the solider so much that he becomes a traitor for what the movie portrays as the uncivilized, wild, freakish, darkskinned, and therefore inferior Persians. The meaning of the story is that the Spartans, as a perfect society constructing the notion of normal, could never have a person with disabilities among them, but for the uncivilized and evil Persians, he is the perfect match. This theme pedagogically suggests that all marginalized groups are the same—non-Spartan is equitable to nonperfect, and, of course, not normal.

The ableist cinema seems to have received a serious boost by the success of its most recent superhyped James Cameron (yet another mythologized privileged white director as lone genius) vehicle, *Avatar* (2009). This is a Pocahontas story about genetically engineered humans and person who is a paraplegic, sure to be followed by many sub-par copycats at a theater near you.

CONCLUSION

We should like to stress the fact that the concept of disability is a social construct. This is not dissimilar to concepts of race, gender, and nature, all developed through a binary logic that here takes the form of normal ability versus abnormal disability. What we argue is that normal does not exist; thus, there exists no such thing as a purely normal person in actuality, hence this is an ideological construction (Gramsci, 1989). Therefore, the normal and abnormal are false and when established and reinforced in cinema, yield a form of exploitation of the one who is portrayed as abnormal and not the one who is not. It is society that makes people disabled and not the person's innate qualities. Moreover, as our society is intensely capitalistic, we maintain that representations of normalcy and ability aim to gird status quo economic ideals. We suggest a reading of cinema that interprets disability and/or freakishness in cinema as signifiers of anticapitalist potentials. For example, the mutants of *X-Men* can be read this way, provided the audience is media literate. If we wish to have a society working toward social justice, then as its engaged citizens we must aim to transgress normalcy and ableism, respecting difference, and in turn, supporting total inclusion of all.

History has shown that terminology is a tricky game to play: one that always has the potential to foster a negative side to it. "Disability" and "disabled people" are the most endorsed and used terms by disability rights activists, theorists, advocates, and allies. As discussed earlier, there are negative images of the term "disability," but the disability rights movement has reclaimed the term, more out of a universal global understanding of what the definition of disability means and who it is referring to. It is also the only term used to hold significant legal and medical value. "The term disability, as it has been used in general parlance, appears to signify something material and concrete, a physical or psychological condition considered to have predominantly medical significance" (Linton, 1998: p. 10). This does not suggest that the term should and must be resisted. Most disability activists would not argue for resisting the term, but instead reframing the term. The classic predicament in all names for particular identities is that not everyone will understand the term or not even be aware that it exists.

Authenticity is something that democratic media must stay true to (Marcuse, 1969). Indeed, there are many fictions, as well as documentary films, that promote and support disability rights and values behind disability studies *The Cost of Living* (2006) about the valuing of ourselves in relation to others; *How's Your News?* (2006) a transformative film about a group of people with disabilities interviewing everyone and anyone, both famous and not, from coast to coast; *Aaltra* (2005), a comedy that makes one think about the false constructed notions in society around us; and the winner of two Primetime Emmys *Autism: The Musical* (2007) a powerful film that brings to the public's attention a major "epidemic." These films are not obscure or hard to find. The disability community is indeed growing and developing films series on college campuses, such as the well-known Beyond Compliance Coordinating Committee (BCCC)

Film Series at Syracuse University. In the margins with Cinema Touching Disability in Austin, Texas; DisABILITIES Film Festival hosted by DisABILITY History and People, Inc., in Buffalo, New York; and DisTHIS! Film Series in New York City, along with many more around the world, a cinema of advocacy for the disabled is thriving and becoming more powerful. Will Hollywood learn some lessons here?

The twenty-first-century youth consume information at an alarming rate, faster than they can critically examine. They are sponges soaking information through downloaded (Hollywood) films, cable television, Wi-Fi Internet, interactive Wii video games, and music on their iPod, which shape their opinions and constructed reality. It is this fact that educators need to recognize and be prepared to critically engage with in order to reach youth—our future. Hollywood is an important site of pedagogy (Giroux, 2002). If teachers do not adapt to the growing forms of new media to teach, study, and conduct research, there will develop a massive gap between educators and students, which will soon tear down education, and soon to follow democracy. Hollywood is too eager to fill that gap. The twenty-first-century teachers and professors must be public educators who are also public intellectuals (Giroux 1988, Giroux & Giroux, 2006), engaging with all venues of multimedia—Facebook, online journals, MySpace, Twitter, podcasts, blogs, websites, Flicker, YouTube, Skype, instant messenger, and even texting. Public pedagogues (i.e., the twenty-first-century teacher) have an ethical responsibility to engage with the community by utilizing all forms of multimedia inside and outside the classroom in a nonjargon-based, noncorporate-endorsed manner. To be sure, this ought to include disability advocates and pedagogues, who are also anticapitalists and against all forms of domination. This form of pedagogy values technology that is inclusionary based, against authoritarian and oppressive forms of detached teaching, and for emancipatory learning (Giroux & Giroux, 2006; Nocella, 2008, 2010).

The Hollywood industrial complex shapes and aids in the social production of the dominant paradigm (i.e., neoliberalism), fostered by the hegemonic power promoting normalcy, ableism, sameness, and conformity. These "values" are reinforced by social control, political power, and economic investment. As more and more industrial complexes emerge, freedom, creativity, and diversity declines. Industries, institutions, and systems of domination do not yield freedom and democracy, but rather, order, conformity, consumerism, and normalcy.

References

Allen, R. C. & Gomery, D. (1985). *Film history: Theory and practice.* New York, NY: Knopf.

Armstrong, F., Armstrong, D., & Barton, L. (2000). *Inclusive education: Policy, contexts and comparative perspectives.* London, UK: David Fulton Publishers.

Davis, L. (1997). *The disability studies reader.* New York, NY: Routledge Press.

Denzin, N. K. (1991). *Images of postmodern society: social theory and contemporary cinema.* Thousand Oaks, CA: Sage.

Foucault, M. (1980). *Power/knowledge* (C. Gordon, Trans.). New York: Pantheon.

Giroux, H. A. (1988). *Teachers as intellectuals: Toward a critical pedagogy of learning.* New York, NY: Bergin & Garvey.

Giroux, H. A. (2002). *Breaking in to the movies: Film and the culture of politics.* New York: Blackwell.

Giroux, H. A., & Giroux, S. S. (2006). *Take back higher education: Race, youth, and the crisis of democracy in the post-civil rights era.* New York: Palgrave MacMillan.

Gramsci, A. (1989). *Selections from the prison notebooks* (10th ed.). New York, NY: International Publishers.

Greenberg, E. S. & Page, B. I. (2003). *The struggle for democracy.* New York, NY: Longman.

Kashani, T. (2007). Dissident cinema: Defying the logic of globalization. In J. Harris & V. Seizys (eds.), *Contested terrains of globalization* (pp. 241–254). Chicago, IL: Changemaker Press.

Kashani, T. (2009). *Deconstructing the mystique: An introduction to cinema.* Dubuque, IA: Kendall/Hunt.

Linton, S. (1998). *Claiming disability. Knowledge and identity.* New York: New York University Press.

Marcuse, H. (1969). *An essay on liberation.* Boston, MA: Beacon Press.

Nocella, II, A. J. (2008). Emergence of disability pedagogy. *Journal for Critical Education Policy Studies.* Volume 6, Number 2.

Nocella, II, A. J, Best, S., and McLaren, P. (2010). *Academic repression: Reflections from the Academic Industrial Complex.* Oakland, CA: AK Press.

Olson, K. (Thursday, May 31, 2007). "Movie review: Tiptoes." The gimp parade. http://thegimpparade.blogspot.com/2007/05/movie-review-tiptoes.html.

Taylor, S. (1996). Disability studies and mental retardation. *Disability Studies Quarterly.* Vol. 16, No. 3.

7

INTERNATIONAL CITIZENRY IN THE AGE OF THE SPECTACLE

Shoba Sharad Rajgopal

> Whether we like it or not, cinema assumes a pedagogical role in the lives of many people. It may not be the intent of a filmmaker to teach audiences anything, but that does not mean that lessons are not learned
>
> bell hooks, 1996: p. 2

INTRODUCTION

Hollywood cinema is an instrument of ideology par excellence, where nonwhites, both from within the nation and without, occupy a subordinate role, from D. W. Griffith's bizarre representation of the supposed heroism of the Ku Klux Klan in *Birth of a Nation* (1915) to the more recent brazen exercises in Eurocentrism such as Gary Synder's *300* (2007). This is a mindset that envisions the world from a single, privileged point, which has been naturalized as "common sense" to such an extent that most people from the West are not even aware that it exists as the dominant paradigm, so much so that postcolonial film theorist Ella Shohat terms it "unthinking Eurocentrism" (Shohat and Stam, 1994). Shohat and Stam describe it as an implicit positioning rather than a political stance (Shohat and Stam, 1994: p. 4), and it is a mindset that causes the West to perceive the world only as its reflection, with everything that is different as being against the norm. Indeed, the overt propaganda of master Third Reich propagandist Leni Riefenstahl is not as dangerous as the covert propaganda of Hollywood cinema today, masked as it is in the feel-good "winning hearts and minds" model. In today's world where the mass media have immense reach and power, they play a crucial role in developing and disseminating stereotypes that eventually take over the mindset of entire countries, with disastrous ramifications. This chapter deconstructs much of the representation of the non-American citizen in Hollywood cinema, through a non-Eurocentric international lens, utilizing the lens of cultural studies and transnational feminist theory. Richard Dyer's powerful analysis of whiteness in the cinema argues that the equation of being white with being human secures a position of power (Dyer, 1997). Thus, the nonwhite person is placed in a position of powerlessness and even a certain lack, which can only be transformed by accepting the hegemony of the white, and in Hollywood cinema, this representation is even more specific.

Ethnic studies theorist Arturo Aldama categorizes the representation of the person of color in Hollywood cinema as the "colonial gaze" (Aldama, 2001), where Hollywood's worldwide hegemony results in the popularity of macho characters like Rambo even in Southeast Asia, despite the fact that this is the ideology of Western imperialism. This is the case with a plethora of Hollywood films that cast the Chicana/o/ the Asian/ the Muslim/ the Hindu/ the Native American as the West's Unspeakable Other. We may no longer have blatant racism as evinced in the early Fu Manchu films where sinister Orientals spy on enemies through panels in the wall and gongs are struck at key moments as Dr. Fu Manchu intones ludicrous lines such as "My flower daughter, the knife would wither your petal fingers" (1931). But the subtle racism of Hollywood's more recent productions is far more insidious in that they are much more difficult to decipher for the average filmgoer. They are unlikely to connect the icy Asian vixen of *The Year of the Dragon* (1985) and *Kill Bill Volume 1* (2003) to the old openly racist representations of the Asian woman in Hollywood films of the 1940s and 1950s. It is left to Asian American theorists and activists to critique the representation of Asian women in today's films as either sexy villains, as in *Kill Bill Volume 2*'s O-Ren Ishii, or as disempowered victims of their culture, such as Sayuri in *Memoirs of a Geisha* (2005), who need to be rescued by the benevolent hand of the West (Spivak, 1988; Mohanty, 1991; Alquizola, 2003). Not surprisingly, these representations of Asian women are all by non-Asian men from the West, from the author James Golden (author of *Memoirs of a Geisha*) to the directors Rob Marshall and Quentin Tarantino, respectively. As for the Asian men of Hollywood cinema, they are either emasculated nerds or brainwashed terrorists out to destroy the West.

Transnational feminist theorist Zillah Eisenstein hones in on a crucial point that has been suppressed by the U.S. media, namely the fact that Eric Harris, one of the two key participants in the Columbine massacre, had described in his diary his plan if he did not die in the school attack: to get on a plane and ram it into a building in New York City. But it is the Arab men who rammed their planes into the Twin Towers who have become the universalized symbol of Islamic extremism, despite the fact that it is white men like Harris and Timothy McVeigh of the Oklahoma City bombings, who have committed great acts of violence against the United States. Violence by white men does not transfer to whites in general because whiteness is not racialized by whites (Eisenstein, 2004: p. 61). As such, these representations of immigrants and internationals mask a far more sinister agenda of justifying neocolonial policies in non-Western nations, whose leaders are reduced to stereotypes, much as with the Empress Tzu Hsi of ancient China.

In today's world, even more than the print media, it is the visual media of film and television that play a very important role as "a teaching machine," to use the phrase of Henry Giroux (Giroux, 2006), in the construction of collective memories and identities. The cinema has in fact been described by Ella Shohat as the world's storyteller par excellence (Shohat and Stam, 1994), and is as such ideally suited to relay the projected narratives of nations and empires. It is not coincidental that this important arm of mass media was born at a moment when a poem such as Rudyard Kipling's "White Man's Burden" could be published, as it was in 1899 to celebrate the U.S. acquisition of Cuba and the Philippines. In fact, the first Lumiere and Edison screenings in the 1890s closely followed the "scramble for Africa" that erupted in the 1870s (Shohat and Stam, 1994).

Under the circumstances, it is hardly surprising that cinema came to play a major role in creating and disseminating a hegemonic colonial discourse wherein films were churned out on a regular basis to demonstrate the role of Empire as "mission civilisatrice," based on the imperialistic novels of writers like Edgar Wallace and Rider Haggard. The colonizer's perspective was seen as the norm, be it in the Tarzan films based on the books of Edgar Rice Burroughs or the historical films set in the far-flung recesses of the British colonies, such as *Gunga Din* (1939) and *Lives of a Bengal Lancer* (1934). The importance of this overt propaganda cannot be missed, as in the earlier British version of the film *Around the World in 80 Days* (1956), where Phineas Fogg strides onto the screen with the strains of "Rule Britannia" in the background.

These are dangerous times when being an "international" and especially an international person of color in the West is akin to being in the crosshairs. It is a time when, as Henry Giroux describes in a recent article, the growing dominance of a right-wing media "forged in a pedagogy of hate" spews forth "a toxic rhetoric" in which the public sphere is largely for white people, which is under constant threat of annihilation by immigrants and people of color (Giroux 2009). In such a worldview, all internationals of color are suspect, potential terrorists to be constantly surveyed. Some might argue that this toxic worldview is that only of talk radio, which is the purview of extremists, and that Hollywood remains the bastion of liberalism that it always was. But to comprehend the nexus between Hollywood and politics, one needs only to examine the timing of the opening of specific films. *300* for instance, the Hollywood film based on a graphic novel that depicts the confrontation of Sparta and Persia at the Battle of Thermopylae, opened on the eve of *Norooz*, the Persian new year. It is a time when Iranians celebrate the arrival of spring, and not a particularly opportune season to be represented as barbaric, demented savages baying for the blood of Western nations. The timing could not have been more appropriate to ramp up war hysteria at a moment when Iran-U.S. relations had been at their lowest. In many ways it is similar to the timing of the immensely popular film of the 1990s, *Not Without My Daughter* (1991), which opened just before the first Gulf War, and arguably helped fuel the lurking anti- Arab sentiment in the United States even though the film was ostensibly set in Iran, not Iraq.

The Indiana Jones films had been playing havoc with South Asian sensibilities for years, seen in the bizarre representation of East Indians in the film *Indiana Jones and the Temple of Doom* (1984), where Hindus are represented as a cult of crazed savages, devouring monkey brains and performing ritual murder. The critical fact that most traditional Hindus are vegetarian and that Hindus worship the "monkey god" Hanuman, and therefore it is taboo for them to consume simian flesh, seems to have escaped the director. Indeed, in the world of Hollywood cinema, Eastern religions are commonly perceived as "fraudulent, cultish, and fanatical," rarely as equally legitimate as the spiritual doctrines of the monotheistic Judeo-Christian tradition (Sethi, 1994: p. 241). Some would argue that things have changed for the better with characters like Apu and Taj becoming popular Asian figures of U.S. pop culture. On its own, they would not be problematic, but when we take into consideration the fact that the only well-known South Asian representations in the U.S.

mainstream media today are of bumbling cartoon figures is disturbing. As the country careened towards the end of the century, the situation only deteriorated further, with Asians, particularly those from South and Southwest Asia, being perceived anew in a very negative light (Eisenstein, 2004). It is in such a racialized world that the events of September 11, 2001, took place.

South Asians awoke to a world in which they went from being the face of the model minority to suddenly the face of Osama bin Laden. After this watershed date, the primary target of hate crime incidents reported to the FBI changed from blacks to Asians/Arab immigrants or those who were perceived as belonging to these groups (Nguyen, 2005: p. xii; Fernandes, 2007; Alden, 2008). Deepa Fernandes terms the U.S. "the immigration-industrial complex," which criminalizes immigrants of color, deploying the extensive government apparatus to incarcerate and deport them with hardly any process of law (Fernandes, 2007). This is truly ironic, as this is a country made up primarily of immigrants, where *mestizaje*, to coin a term developed originally from Anzaldua's categorization of "the new *mestiza*" (Anzaldua, 1987), is a new state of being beyond binary oppositions, and unlike the simplistic black and white world defined by Samuel Huntington's "Clash of Civilizations" (Huntington, 1996). Edward Said's description in his last radio interview of our world today as one of "unresolved geographies, embattled landscapes" (Said, 1993) holds the key to the major conflicts between and within nation states, wherein it is through projecting the very alienness of the immigrant of color that one can define one's own right to citizenship.

Anne McClintock defines it eloquently in her important study of Victorian racism. "Imperialism is not something that happened elsewhere—a disagreeable fact of history external to Western identity." Rather, imperialism and the invention of race were "fundamental aspects of Western, industrial modernity." The invention of race in urban areas became central not only to the self-definition of the middle class, but also to the policing of the "dangerous classes": the working class, the Irish, Jews, prostitutes, feminists, gays and lesbians, criminals, the militant crowd, and so on (McClintock, 1995: p. 5). This is as true of the United States today as it was of Britain in the Victorian era that McClintock describes. The utilization of the word *"firengi"* in the Star Trek chronicles to designate a race of vile and aberrant beings illustrates this point, for the original term in Hindi stood merely for "foreigner" without any value judgments therein.

Indeed, cultural theorist Sunaina Maira's suggestion that in the post-9/11 world, Asian American studies could benefit from reexamining the representations of Asian popular culture holds good, for it is apparent that the Orientalization of Arabs and South Asians remains a powerful rhetorical tool, even a "moral imperative," for justifying U.S. foreign policy, as images of "backward" women and "fanatical" men suggest the need for the benevolent hand of Empire to rescue the brown woman from the brown man (Maira, 2005; Spivak, 1988). Asian activists have linked this xenophobic representation to "racial demonization," giving the example of the New York *Post*, which had carried a headline entitled "The Face of Hate," with the face of a swarthy, bearded man of South Asian or Middle Eastern descent (Sethi, 1994: p. 242).

Moreover, this new picture of the Asian as a menace coincides with a strange intersection of the old paradigm of the Asian as terrorist with the new paradigm of certain Asian economies as emerging world powers, benefiting from the collapse of the American economy through the policies of economic outsourcing. Interestingly, the rise of China and India as potential world economic powers is seen as a new threat, while the rise of the European Union had not aroused as much resentment. The fear of the outsider is compounded by resentment that this Other with the face of the alien is responsible for the gradual erosion of the American Dream. Lisa Lowe has described this return of the Yellow Peril paradigm as predominant at a time of domestic crisis coupled with anti-Asian nativist backlash through an exclusionist rhetoric in which Asian labor undercut white labor, with Asia emerging as "a double front of threat and encroachment" (Lowe, 1996: p. 5). These are the sentiments exploited by governments to maintain the status quo through its ideological instruments, defined by the Frankfurt School as "the culture industry" (Horkheimer, 1972). Proponents of this school hold that the culture industries churn out mass-produced products that generate a highly commercial system of culture, which in turn sells what Noam Chomsky describes as "necessary illusions" (Chomsky 1999), which help us justify the values and lifestyles of the American way of life. Indeed, Robert McChesney's contention that our news media have internalized the notion that corporate power is largely benevolent, capitalism is synonymous with democracy, and the United States is a force for good in the world (McChesney, 2005) is symptomatic as much of the entertainment industry as it is of the news media. Media theorists Carl Boggs and Tom Pollard term it "the Hollywood war machine," which works as "a crucial instrument for the legitimation of empire" (Boggs & Pollard, 2007: p. 11).

Even if this vision of the public as appearing too much like "tabula rasa" fails to hold ground, can it not be possible that the media present beliefs and attitudes to a mass audience that largely supports and believes in that system and now feels free to openly display those same attitudes? If that was the case with D. W. Griffith's magnum opus *The Birth of the Nation* (1915) in the early years of the last century, perhaps it is no less so with *Borat: Cultural Learnings of America for Make Benefit Glorious Nation of Kazakhstan* (2006) a century later, or *300* (2007), two of the three Hollywood films I shall examine here. *Borat* is the brainchild of British comedian Sacha Baron Cohen, ostensibly the saga of a journalist from the central Asian republic of Kazakhstan who finds himself in a modern, civilized United States, and is a critique of both American and Kazakh culture. But what is disturbing in this film is that the bulk of the satire is directed at the outlandish Other, portrayed as an ignorant racist lout who is openly anti-Semitic and sexist. This goes back to the Foucauldean concept of "discourse," further elaborated by Edward Said (Said, 1978), which recognizes that knowledge and power are always constructed within and are indelibly marked by power relations. He elaborates further in a much later book *Covering Islam* (Said, 1993) on this discourse affecting media coverage in the West through news practices such as the selection of specific sources and story-telling techniques, and even the cultural assumptions of journalists who represent people from "the Muslim world" in Orientalist frames (Said, 1993: p. 48–49). If this is commonplace in the news media, it is no less so in the entertainment industry.

Indeed, culture today has become the battleground for different ideologies, and has become associated with ideas of the nation, as a measuring ground for an "us" against "them" mentality. Cinematic representations of different groups and ethnicities thus tend to reflect a multitude of perspectives and ideologies, depending on who stands behind the camera, for the cinema is a key carrier of contemporary cultural myths through which our reality is lived. Hollywood films must therefore be comprehended as part and parcel of an ideological system that disempowers minority groups through what Jimmy Reeves and Richard Campbell term "a discourse of discrimination" within which they are portrayed as "the pathological Other"(Reeves & Campbell, 1994). Sacha Cohen's earlier avatar as Ali G in the British television series *Da Ali G Show* is a different picture, for that is openly a comedy show. But *Borat* reaches out to wider audiences, some of which may not recognize even the most blatant satire for what it is. The feeble remonstrance of the Kazakh government notwithstanding, many in the United States who view the film have never seen any other representation of Kazakhs to lend the portrait balance. The film suggests Kazakhs drink horse urine; consider prostitution, rape, and incest respectable; and are openly anti-Semitic.

The question we must ponder is: Why could Hollywood not have picked a fictitious country rather than a real country and that too in Central Asia, a much misunderstood and misrepresented part of the world, especially considering the ongoing war against Islamic peoples worldwide? In fact, what it does is reify a certain Orientalized perception of inhabitants of Central Asia as uncivilized barbarians. This representation of Asians/Arabs in Hollywood today may be compared to that of American Indians in Westerns as "The Unspeakable Other" whose vanquishing was necessary for the reign of peace and order. Under these circumstances, it is right and proper for South and Central Asia and the entire Middle East to be portrayed as open for the "mission civilisatrice" of Empire, or its new avatar of necolonialism or globalization, accompanied by its handmaiden, the popular cinema. The cataclysmic 9/11 attack resulted in an ideological discourse founded on a "duty to intervene" that is supposedly justified by the defense of "democracy," the "rights of peoples," and "humanitarianism" (Prashad, 2002; Eisenstein, 2004; Chomsky, 1999). As such, cinematic representations of those who remain on the fence are often as severe as that of the actual "enemy," with cultural nationalism at its core. The central message of such discourse is that, unless proven to be "good," every Muslim was proven to be "bad." All Muslims were now under obligation to prove their credentials by joining a war against "bad Muslims" (Mamdani, 2004: p. 15). Literature and cinema often become insidious political forces of mass deception whereby the public are robbed of their ability to see the substance for the shadow and comprehend the reality behind the stereotype.

There have been more than a few recent international films that portray a sympathetic representation of people of color in the West, such as *Monsieur Ibrahim et les fleurs du Coran* (2004), by François Dupeyron, which follows the universally appealing story of a young boy's coming of age in 1920s France. Through its sensitive portrayal of the friendship between a lonely white boy and an elderly Turkish immigrant, the film reflects French attitudes toward immigrants in the early years of the twentieth century. But there have been very few sensitive portraits of immigrants or internationals in the stables of Hollywood. Instead, the picture of the Asian or Arab Other as unidimensional caricatures constantly appears and reappears in film after film, from those of the 1990s to those of today: *Not Without*

My Daughter (1991), *True Lies* (1994), *The Siege* (1998), *The Mummy Returns* (2001), *The Kingdom* (2007), and so on, *ad infinitum*. These characters are, without exception, shown as subhuman agents of destruction lacking any motive or purpose apart from a blind hatred of the West and all that it stands for, namely democracy, freedom, and so on. One of the few exceptions to this rule can be the characters of the critically acclaimed *Crash* (2004), the directorial debut of Canadian Paul Haggis. The film is about the collision of races, cultures, and classes in Los Angeles, and depicts the inability of people to look beyond surface impressions based on race and class. But even such a rare Hollywood film that deals with the complexities of living in a multicultural society arrives at a tepid and feel-good conclusion, that the racist white cop is in reality a heroic figure, who tenderly cares for his aged father and ultimately rescues women, regardless of their race. This takes away much of the sting of the earlier portrait of a racist and sexist cop out to humiliate nonwhite people for the sheer hell of it. *The Visitor* (2008), Tom McCarthy's sensitive portrayal of the unlikely friendship between a university professor and a Syrian illegal immigrant, is even more remarkable in its nuanced representation of an illegal Arab immigrant and his mother. Initially, and accentuated by the strange circumstances of their first encounter, the quiet Caucasian professor and his unusual houseguests, the illegal immigrants from Syria and Senegal respectively, are apprehensive of each other, but gradually they learn to understand and empathize with each other. The internationalism of the theme is underscored both by the international cast and by the fact that the soundtrack was written and performed by revolutionary Nigerian musician Fela Kuti, who created his own unique style of Afrobeat by fusing elements from different genres of world music, and set against the backdrop of the New York City skyline. The symbolism of the musical instruments utilized in the film cannot be missed either: the piano as symbolic of Western music with its rationality and intellectualism, which is unable to reach the soul of the lonely Walter, versus the *djembe*, the African drum, an instrument that Tareq describes as one that needs feeling rather than thinking. Indeed, this is an unusual instrument for the dour and diffident Caucasian professor, but as he learns it from his young Arab friend, the lonely widower opens up and begins to live for the first time in many years.

One of the most significant scenes in the film occurs in the detention center, where Walter and Tareq are seated facing each other with the glass wall between them, and Tareq asks Walter to show him what he has been practicing. The two men from different parts of the world whose lives are connected by music, then begin to play together like brothers in the cold and impersonal atmosphere of the detention center, using the table between them as a drum. Walter's exposure to the *djembe* heals him and appears to symbolize the film's message that our lives are enriched by other lives and cultures. It is a powerful argument for multiculturalism as the glue that holds American society together, and the film is the only one of its kind that discusses the very real problems faced by individuals labeled illegal immigrants and treats them like real human beings. Yet the fact remains that this was an independent film and not a Hollywood production. This is the case, too, with two other powerful films of the decade, *America So Beautiful* (2001) and *House of Sand and Fog* (2003), both of which depict the lives of Iranian immigrants in the United States and the tragic nobility of the expatriates, but neither of these films are Hollywood productions, and therein lies the rub. No doubt, given the explosive political climate in the Middle East, humanizing suspected potential terrorists in a film is an experiment that few mainstream filmmakers would dare to take. And can we blame them considering the fact that the group of filmmakers who worked on *9/11*, a group of short films depicting the impact of the attack on innocent Arab and Muslim lives, was vilified by some as a support of terrorism?

Indeed, the only Hollywood film of recent times to depict South Asian Muslims in a more nuanced light is Stephen Gaghan's *Syriana* (2005). The two major Asian characters represented in the film are a young Pakistani man, Wasim, who is a temporary worker in Saudi Arabia, and Prince Nasir, the Saudi aristocrat whose idealism and hopes for the betterment of his country are thwarted by the diabolic plot of the CIA. Both Wasim and Prince Nasir are portrayed in a sympathetic light, despite the fact that Wasim eventually becomes a suicide bomber and launches an attack on an American tanker. Wasim's plight is symptomatic of much of the economic underclass of the Third World, which has fallen prey to the ravages of global-ization and forced them to leave their countries in search of better opportunities. The conditions of these temporary workers and the total lack of protection under which they make their daily lives, while simultaneously the oil corporations make huge profits on the backs of the workers who are treated as if they are subhuman, is tantamount to the "coolie" labor of old, with the workers ground underfoot by global multinational corporations. Indeed, what the film suggests is that it could be these dreadful conditions that make men like Wasim fall prey to the fundamentalism of the *madrasa*. Yet Wasim remains a sympathetic figure, a sensitive young man whose other side we get to see, playing soccer with his friends and sharing jokes with them, and who shares with his father the dream of one day being able to bring the mother there, too, and build a home where they could live in peace. It is a poignant moment in the film, for both the son and the father are conscious of how unlikely this is, and their awareness of being mere pawns in the maw of big oil corporations controlled by the West only adds fuel to the fire that rages within the breast of the idealistic young man.

Yet, such films are rare in Hollywood where stereotypes of international citizens still rein supreme. The year 2007 witnessed the historically inaccurate representation of the battle of Thermopylae with Zack Snyder's *300*. The film takes place during the Persian Wars in Greece and has been the subject of considerable controversy with the circulation of an Internet petition signed by some 10,000 Iranians, distressed that their Persian identity could be savaged by Hollywood cinema. It represents Spartans as tall, handsome white men with rippling muscles, while the Persians are represented as black masked demonic hordes, the monstrous Orcs of their decadent monarch. The scene that pits them against each other presents this blatant racism and homophobia in its essence. In a key scene, the Spartans are dragged by the Persians to face the Persian monarch, Xerxes. Let us take a close look at how these two races are represented. Whereas the Spartans, symbolized by their King Leonidas, are represented as handsome, powerfully built, white heterosexual men in their prime, the Persians are portrayed as effeminate, evil, debauched creatures, symbolized by their monarch Xerxes who appears as a bizarre, pierced, bejeweled, and androgynous giant of dubious sexuality. Horrified by this spectacle of ultimate evil, the righteous Leonidas recoils and is ordered to kneel in submission before the decadent Xerxes, which of course is the moment when he rebels and calls for his men to attack. It recalls Said's theorization of Orientalism, which suggests not that Arab/Asian men are effeminate, but that the West constructs them as such.

The racism of this representation is equaled only by its overt homophobia, with the Spartans symbolizing the hetero-patriarchal righteousness of Europe against the barbarism and sexual deviance of the Oriental Other. Just as was the case with *Not Without My Daughter* close to two decades ago, here, too, there is no attempt whatsoever to depict the other perspective, making it all the more easy to perceive them as vermin who should be destroyed to save the world. No Persian character is painted in a favorable light; and where in the earlier film the local people who help the heroine are dissidents or outlaws, in this, there are no helpful or humane Persians at all, they are all monsters, slaves to their despotic ruler. In both films, screened as they were at a time when anti-Iranian/Asian hatred is at its most virulent, there is no nuanced portrayal of "the enemy." Indeed, the Asian/Muslim/Arab/Persian cultures are perceived as totally alien and incomprehensible, the inscrutable Other to the Occidental/ Christian norm. Indeed, *300* claims that the heroism of the 300 white men saved the entire Western civilization from imminent destruction by the barbaric hordes from the decadent East. Film theorist Tony Kashani points out how through this film, Hollywood has tapped into contemporary political discourse, as we are told once more, "to beware of the Persians (the Iranians)" (Kashani, 2009: p. 142). It is all too apparent that at the dawn of the twenty-first century, the lines between East and West are as starkly drawn as they had ever been, with race once again becoming a polarizing force.

The exceptions to this paradigm are a handful of films. Both *Buffalo Soldiers* (2001) and *Jarhead* (2006) depict the military from the perspective of the ordinary soldiers, much as was the case with *Full Metal Jacket* (1987) a decade earlier. They present Marines as perplexed, afraid, and conflicted young men, rather than as the doggedly determined military machines of mainstream representation. Both *Syriana* (2005) and *Babel* (2006) depict the strange interconnectedness of the world, where events in one part of the world are changed completely by actions in another, and both have a strongly implied critique of the politics of Empire. Even more clearly, *Lions for Lambs* (2007) and *In the Valley of Elah* (2007) question the U.S. invasion of Afghanistan and Iraq, respectively, but the indifferent box office response to these films suggests that the public is reluctant to face a strong critique of U.S. foreign policy on screen. Paul Haggis's film suggests, as do Redford's and Gaghan's, that today's military sacrifices are being made on false premises. The last war film of the year 2009, released the same week that the country heard of the additional troop deployment to Afghanistan, was Jim Sheridan's *Brothers* (2009), which examines the devastating impact of the war in Afghanistan on ordinary American families. Interestingly, it is far from being a regular Hollywood film, as it is by an Irish director, based on the remake of a Danish film and with the screenplay by David Benioff, whose previous film was also set in Afghanistan, namely *The Kite Runner* (2007). Interestingly, the latter was made by a German filmmaker based on the best-selling novel of 2003 by an Afghani American writer, Khalid Hussein. But films like these are rare in the corporate world of Hollywood, which does not dare to suggest that racism, sexism, homophobia, xenophobia, and now increasingly Islamophobia are prevalent in American society and affect our perception of how we view the world.

Mainstream cinema serves a specific purpose, that of masking the machinations of empire by legitimating war and its horrific casualties, by creating dangerous enemies that have to be destroyed in order to maintain the status quo. As Carl Boggs and Tom Pollard point out, for Hollywood cinematic narratives to function effectively, "a Manichaeistic framework is required, pitting good against evil, light against dark, order against chaos, democracy against tyranny" (Boggs & Pollard, 2007: p. 54). In such a scenario today, internationals and especially Arabs/Asian Muslims play a crucial role, that of reflecting the "Other", either to be despised as our "Public Enemy #1," with whom you would not wish to share your country, let alone your streets, as seen in numerous anti-Arab films, as pointed out by media theorist, Jack Shaheen (Shaheen, 2009: p. 2), or to be pitied as the helpless victim, usually a woman, badly in need of rescue, of course by a Caucasian hero. The message sent through these films is that the world needs to be saved from the ravages of the barbarians from out "there," through the courage and determination of the chosen few (male, of course) heroes from "our" part of the world. Leonidas arises once again from the ashes of Thermopylae, but in Snyder's saga he is more of a symbol of white supremacist ideology than of freedom for all. Indeed, the myths induced by Hollywood images serve a purpose, that of constructing the world as badly in need of Manifest Destiny, as defined by the U.S. juggernaut. Constant exposure to these myths lead to a stronger readiness to support U.S. military operations, with international citizenry serving as the fall guys, utilized by the myth machines to create a skewed picture of the world, where they are either the "good guys" or "the bad guys," depending on whose interests they serve.

REFERENCES

Aldama, A. J. 2001. *Disrupting savagism: Intersecting Chicana/o, Mexican Immigrant, and Native American struggles for self-representation.* Durham: Duke University Press.

Alden, E. 2008. *The closing of the American border: Terrorism, immigration, and security since 9/11,* New York: Harper Collins.

Alquizola, M. & Hirabayashi, L. 2003. Confronting gender stereotypes of Asian American women: Slaying the dragon. In J. Xing and L. Hirabayashi (eds). *Reversing the lens: Looking at race, class, gender and sexuality.* Niwot: University of Colorado Press.

Anzaldua, G. 1987. *Borderlands/La frontera, the new mestiza*. San Francisco: Aunt Lute Books.

Boggs, C. & Pollard, T. 2007. *The Hollywood war machine: U.S. militarism and popular culture*, Boulder: Paradigm Publishers.

Chomsky, N. 1999. *Necessary illusions: Thought control in democratic societies*. Cambridge: South End Press.

Dyer, R. 1997. *White*. New York: Routledge.

Eisenstein, Z. 2004. *Against empire: Feminisms, racism, and the West*. New Delhi: Women Unlimited.

Fernandes, D. 2007. *Targeted: Homeland security and the business of immigration*. Haymarket Books.

Giroux, H. 2006. *The Giroux reader*. Boulder: Paradigm Publishers.

——— 2009. "Living in a culture of cruelty: Democracy as spectacle." http://www.truthout.org/090209R

hooks, b. 1996. *Reel to real: Race, sex and class at the movies*. Routledge: New York.

Horkheimer, M. & Adorno, T. W. 1972. *Dialectic of enlightenment*. New York: Herder and Herder.

Huntington, S. 1996. *The clash of civilizations? The debate*. New York: Council on Foreign Relations.

Kashani, T. 2009. *Deconstructing the mystique: An interdisciplinary introduction to cinema*. Iowa: Kendall Hunt Publishing Company.

Lowe, L. 1996. *Immigrant acts*. Durham: Duke University Press.

Maira, S. 2005. Trance-formations: Orientalism and cosmopolitanism in youth culture. *East Main Street: Asian American popular culture*. New York: New York University Press.

Mamdani, M. 2004. *Good Muslim, bad Muslim: America, the cold war and the roots of terror*. New York: Pantheon Books.

McChesney, R. 2005. *Tragedy & farce: How the American media sell wars, spin elections, and destroy democracy*. New York: New Press.

McClintock, A. 1995. *Imperial leather: Race, gender and sexuality in the colonial context*. New York: Routledge.

Mohanty, C. T. 1991. Under Western eyes. In C. T. Mohanty, A. Russo, Lourdes Torres (eds.), *Third World women and the politics of feminism*. Indiana University Press, Bloomington.

Nguyen, T. 2005. *We are all suspects now: Untold stories from immigrant communities after 9/11*. Boston: Beacon Press.

Prashad, V. 2002. *War against the planet: The fifth Afghan war, imperialism and other assorted fundamentalisms*. Left Word Books.

Reeves, J. L., and Campbell, R. 1994. *Cracked coverage: Television news, the anti-cocaine crusade, and the Reagan legacy*. North Carolina: Duke University Press.

Sadris, A. 2007. Greeks and Persians in Snyder's *300*.

Said, E. 1978. *Orientalism*. New York: Pantheon Books.

——— 1993. *Culture and imperialism*. New York: Alfred A. Knopf.

Shaheen, J. 2009. *Reel bad Arabs: How Hollywood vilifies a people.* Brooklyn, New York: Interlink Publishing Group.

Sethi, R. C. 1994. "Smells like racism: A plan for mobilizing against anti-Asian bias." In Aguilar-San Juan, K. (ed.), *The state of Asian America: Activism and resistance in the 1990s.* Boston: South End Press.

Shohat, E. & Stam, R. 1994. *Unthinking eurocentrism: Multiculturalism and the media.* London: Routledge.

Spivak, G. C. 1988. Can the subaltern speak? In C. Nelson & L. Grossberg (eds.) *Marxism and the interpretation of culture.* Basingstoke: Macmillan Education. pp. 271–313.

8

LGBT-Themed Hollywood Cinema after *Brokeback Mountain*: Renegotiating Hegemonic Representations of Gay Men

Michael A. Raffanti

Introduction

Transcending its status as a financially and critically successful Hollywood film, Ang Lee's *Brokeback Mountain* (2005) became a major cultural phenomenon. In the six months between its premiere at the Venice Film Festival and its defeat as Best Picture at the 2006 Academy Awards, *Brokeback* unleashed a torrent of media frenzy about the sociocultural and economic significance of the lesbian/gay/bisexual/transgender (LGBT)-themed (so-called "gay cowboy") film.

Although widespread media attention to *Brokeback* dissipated quickly after the Academy Awards, for some the film represented a breakthrough that would give rise to an economically viable gay cinema in mainstream Hollywood. Sadly for those who have suffered Hollywood's marginalizing silence and stereotypes, post-*Brokeback* mainstream gay cinema has not developed momentum toward authenticity and social relevance. Instead, the systemic process of "cultural hegemony" (Gramsci, 1971; Artz & Murphy, 2000) which mediates relations between power and culture under capitalism, is actively renegotiating the status of gay cinema in Hollywood. Such a renegotiation, I argue, was instigated by *Brokeback*'s perceived threat to dominant social constructions of masculinity as well as the film's status as a serious, profitable, and stereotype-defying production that might alter entrenched notions of gayness that have become a Hollywood commodity.

This chapter examines the dynamics of Hollywood as a system that continually seeks to assert its cultural hegemony. This is illustrated through an analysis of the hegemonic negotiations made necessary by *Brokeback*'s arguably counterhegemonic status. The process of negotiation and systemic correction regaining is exemplified by *Brokeback*'s Academy Awards journey and the subsequent release of three films: *I Now Pronounce You Chuck and Larry* (2007), *Milk* (2008), and *Brüno* (2009). While the dearth of gay-themed mainstream films is one piece of evidence, this trio of films sends mixed messages that demonstrate an uncertainty in the system that has yet to be resolved. Hollywood's hegemonic forces seem to be negotiating a cinema of tolerance that nonetheless maintains Hollywood's control and exploitation of gay visibility and images.

HEGEMONY OF THE HOLLYWOOD SYSTEM

Mainstream U.S. cinema is a system that is embedded in wider sociocultural and economic systems, or a "web of systems" (Kashani, 2009: p. 106). As an institution owned by a small number of corporations controlled overwhelmingly by an elite group of white businessmen, the goal of the Hollywood system is to increase profit and expand its power globally. Through dominating all aspects of film production and distribution, Hollywood asserts control over cinematic content. Such control is essential to maintaining the ideology of the pro-corporate patriarchy that sustains it.

This is a system with a voracious appetite that will devour parallel systems that show any viability of taking away profit. Ever vigilant and insatiable, Hollywood's dominant faction co-opted the success of independent cinema after *sex, lies and videotape* (1989) became a hit and cultural phenomenon. The independent film companies became subsidiaries of the major studios, thus forming "Indiewood" (Biskind, 2004). The control by conglomerates reduces the diversity of cinema and marginalizes films of substance and controversy, instead opting for homogeneity. Understanding the profitability of aiming for the lowest common denominator, Hollywood continuously relies on the same formulas and stereotypes. By foreclosing the possibility that films can have a mass audience without Hollywood's imprimatur, stereotypical images of LGBT and other marginalized groups will be perpetuated on film and therefore in the public consciousness. Such dynamics reflect Herbert Marcuse's (1964)

"One-Dimensional Man" theory in which market forces offer the false notion of freedom. That is, Hollywood's utter dominance of U.S. cinema offers limited options; all the "choices" reinforce the social norms so that there is no real choice. This one-dimensionality restricts the public's opportunity for an authentic understanding of LGBT experiences.

The dynamics of Hollywood's worldwide film domination can be understood through Marxist philosopher Antonio Gramsci's notion of cultural hegemony, which he describes as "the 'spontaneous' consent given by the great masses...to the general direction imposed on social life. This consent is 'historically' caused by the prestige (and consequent confidence) which the dominant group enjoys because of its position and function in the world of production" (1971, p. 12). According to Gramsci, the social role of intellectuals in a capitalist society is to organize public consent to power the elite's social domination. Filmmakers, both as artists and entrepreneurs, are intellectuals who (sometimes unwittingly) mediate consent to "the values, norms, perceptions, beliefs, sentiments, and prejudices that support and define the existing distribution of goods..." (Jackson Lears, 1985: p. 569) For example, public consent to negative LGBT representations in the media need not take the form of conscious commitment. Rather, so long as dominant images are "uncritically absorbed" into public consciousness, the dynamics of cultural hegemony have been successful.

Hegemony is not a closed system of domination; counterhegemonies are always an option. Gitlin (1994) argues that there is flexibility and collaboration in Hollywood's hegemonic processes; the film industry must take into account public tastes and tolerances. Cultural hegemony "is not a closed system. It leaks. Its very structure leaks, at the least because it remains to some extent competitive" (Gitlin, 1994: p. 531).

Independent filmmaking has indeed offered authentic LGBT images that compete with the stock and trade "sissy and dyke" stereotypes. But LGBT power to purvey its own images is limited by strong social forces. Heterosexual culture is so privileged that "heteronormativity" is the measuring stick for all social relationships and ways of being. As Warner (1993) explains, "Het culture thinks of itself as the elemental form of human association, as the very model of inter-gender relations, as the indivisible basis of all community, and as the means of reproduction without which society wouldn't exist" (p. xxi).

Hegemony "has continually to be renewed, recreated, defended, and modified. It is also continually resisted, limited, altered, challenged by pressures not at all its own" (Williams, 1977: p. 112). Truly independent films exert counterhegemonic pressures by appealing to the higher levels of what Pierre Bourdieu (1984) has labeled as "taste culture." Independent film offers thought-provoking and stereotype-disrupting stories and images of the "other America" (Levy, 1999: p. 52). As other, LGBT lives have been targets of cultural devaluation, distortion, derision, and condescension at the hands of Hollywood studios, independent cinema, including the revolutionary "New Queer Cinema," generated an authentic cinema that challenged stereotypes through films such as *Paris Is Burning* (1991), *Poison* (1991), *My Own Private Idaho* (1991), *The Living End* (1992), and *Go Fish* (1994). After Hollywood assimilated independent cinema within its grasp, films portraying LGBT lives remained in production because they had shown some promise of turning a profit so long as costs were kept low. Knegt's (2008) *Forging a Mainstream Gay Cinema* analyzes what he calls "Gay Indiewood": the subsystem of specialty division filmmaking that has produced a number of LGBT-themed films. Gay Indiewood represents the renegotiated relationship in which such films continue to be produced, but within parameters controlled by mainstream Hollywood. Knegt identifies the following Gay Indiewood films: *Kissing Jessica Stein* (2001), *The Deep End* (2001), *The Hours* (2002), *Monster* (2003), *Home at the End of the World* (2004), *Kinsey* (2004), *Capote* (2005), *Transamerica* (2005), and finally, *Brokeback Mountain* (2005) as falling within this canon. As I argue next, *Brokeback*'s popularity and challenges to essential stereotypes created a new round of hegemonic negotiation and systemic readjustment that is not yet resolved.

BROKEBACK MOUNTAIN AND HEGEMONIC NOTIONS OF MASCULINITY

Independent film prior to the advent of Indiewood and Gay Indiewood certainly represented a counterhegemonic force to the Hollywood system. To be sure, independent film did not pose a threat to Hollywood's economic domination; it did, however, show potential to snare the taste culture market, which is both a profitable and influential segment. With appropriation of indie filmmaking into the major studios, that threat was averted and Gay Indiewood produced relatively authentic cinema telling stories of LGBT people. In some ways, *Brokeback Mountain* was a culmination of this project owing to its financial success and cultural capital.

Yet, because it was so groundbreaking, perhaps counterhegemonic, the film set in motion a new round of hegemonic negotiations—greatly characterized by homophobic backlash—that remains underway.

What made *Brokeback* stand out as a threat to the established order? Barounis (2009) suggests what I believe to be the crux of the danger: "It would be difficult to dispute the fact that Jack and Ennis [the romantic lead characters in the film] emblematize a particular brand of frontier masculinity, one that until now has been historically off-limits in mainstream cinematic representations of homosexuality" (p. 64). Hollywood's reaction stems from its need to sustain the patriarchal ideology that privileges and perpetuates a particular notion of masculinity that is in opposition to both gayness and femininity (which dominant society conflates). By encroaching on the Western genre (Spohrer, 2009) situating the story in the conservative, rural Mountain West, and doing so with rugged, good-looking, masculine characters who engage in anal intercourse, *Brokeback* disrupted the status quo and therefore unleashed systemic forces to keep Gay Indiewood in check. To understand this dynamic, one must consider the role of masculinity in the Hollywood ideology juxtaposed with stereotypes of gay men.

Two overriding cultural stereotypes of gay men emerged over a century ago. First, medical literature, in defining homosexuality, initiated the notion of gender inversion—gay men are women trapped in men's bodies. Second, the highly publicized Oscar Wilde trials engrained the notion of all gay men as effete, delicate, and effeminate. Rooted in these stereotypes, the history of cinema has presented gay men as "pansies" and "sissies" (Barrios, 2003: p. 9); and, as is all too clear, "nobody likes a sissy" (Russo, 1986: p. 4). Why? As Russo and others argue, for a man to be perceived as being like a woman is the ultimate form of humiliation and disempowerment.

Hollywood masculinity is a stereotyped notion in its own right. According to Kimmel (2005), the hegemonic concept of masculinity is "a man *in* power, a man *with* power, and a man *of* power. We equate manhood with being strong, successful, capable, reliable, in control" (p. 30). Despite the prevalence of action heroes and other hypermasculine types, there is no monolithic concept of masculinity in Hollywood cinema; it is a social construction that Hollywood has mythologized as being essential. Cohan and Hark (1993) maintain that masculinity has always been contested by alternative constructions such as James Cagney's hysterical mama's boy in *White Heat* (1949), Fred Astaire's song and dance spectacles, or Clint Eastwood's victimization by a female stalker in *Play Misty for Me* (1971). Because masculinity is "a construction, a performance, a masquerade" (Jeffords, 1993: p. 7), the concept is susceptible to counterhegemonic pressures such as those presented by *Brokeback*'s rugged gay male characters.

Although masculinity evolves, there are firm boundaries to the concept. Indeed, it remains taboo in our culture and in film to represent or talk about certain aspects of masculinity, sexuality, and the male body (Lehman, 2001). Anal sex is at the top of that list. As Lehman (2001) notes, "Serious homophobia...is particularly related to anal sex between men. Recent Hollywood films including *Sleepers* represent such sex as rape, dangerously collapsing the meanings of homosexual sex with rape" (p. 4). Further, Wlodarz (2001) argues that although Hollywood has assimilated some "harmless" gay male images into the mainstream in romantic comedies such as *My Best Friend's Wedding* (1997) and *The Object of My Affection* (1998), gay sexuality remains taboo. According to Bersani (1988) in "Is the rectum a grave?" homophobia of gay men is rooted in anxieties around anal sex in particular because it is tied to the "the suicidal ecstasy of being a woman" (p. 212).

Although images of anal sex appear in U.S. multiplexes, Wlodarz explains that Hollywood will only allow such acts to be presented as rape (e.g., *The Prince of Tides* (1991), *Pulp Fiction* (1994), *The Shawshank Redemption* (1994), *Sleepers* (1996), and *American History X* (1998)). These rape scenes are exploited as a dramatic device that everyone in the audience understands as the most disgusting act that can be perpetrated on a straight male. In patriarchy, the "penetration of a man is generally considered to be a fate worse than (or equal to) death (Wlodarz, 2001: p. 72). This is so because it represents an abdication of power and control, running contrary to hegemonic notions of masculinity. As Wlodarz (2001) observes, "One reason that anal sex between men *must* be represented as rape is that the absence of a form of consent not only opens the door for the narrative presentation of the recuperation of straight male subjectivity (they didn't *want* to be fucked, and thus they can be 'cured') but it also encourages the expression of violent homophobia which is conveniently transformed into a classic revenge narrative that slyly masks its inherent prejudices" (p. 73).

Similarly, Kimmel (2005) argues that the construction of manhood is rooted in a fear of being seen as having feminine characteristics. Men are defined by not being like a woman; thus, straight men are apprehensive of having any traditionally feminine qualities unmasked. Kimmel posits, "Women and homosexual men become the 'other' against which heterosexual men project their identities... gay men have historically played the role of the consummate sissy in the American popular mind because homosexuality is seen as an inversion of normal gender development" (pp. 37–38).

Given the problematics of masculinity, it is no wonder that *Brokeback Mountain* caused cultural anxiety and Hollywood backlash. The film was provocative in part because the sexuality between Jack and Ennis evolves naturally. As Barounis (2009) observes, "Gay male sexuality in the film seems to spring directly from an inborn aggression and competitive instinct. It is figured as a natural corollary to male horseplay—the violent, almost primitive, crashing together of two male bodies. And, above all else, it is organic" (p. 64). *Brokeback* represents this natural sexuality through attractive, accessible, and masculine actors (Heath Ledger and Jake Gyllenhall) whose portrayal includes not only kissing (still somewhat taboo), but also a scene of anal sex (absolutely taboo). This brand of gay male sexuality gave rise to an intense homophobia. Gay Indiewood had pushed the envelope in an unprecedented manner, threatening to take away gay stereotypes as a commodity and to create a cognitive dissonance among audiences about notions of masculinity, one that takes away the notion of gay as "Other."

Gayle Rubin's (2007) theory of the "charmed circle" of respectable sexualities notes that media and other discourses help to distinguish "abject desires from normative sexuality" (p. 159). The charmed circle includes "monogamous, private, vanilla, procreative, same-generation, and heterosexual sex" (p. 159). Some gay sex is gaining ground, such as monogamous, vanilla, coupled, but most is still "on the bad side of the line" (p. 160). Anal sex between men has much to overcome to enter this charmed circle, and Hollywood will not be complicit in this happening. The backlash described in the coming pages is a result of *Brokeback*'s "gay cowboys" pushing the boundaries of masculinity too far.

Oscar Backlash

The Academy Awards are an annual spectacle of tremendous importance in the film industry and beyond. Becoming an Oscar-winning film bestows cultural cache and often increases a film's economic success. With the stakes so high, it is no surprise that *Brokeback Mountain*, as a boundary-pushing film, created a media firestorm with its multiple nominations and status as favorite for Best Picture. In fact, the

2006 Academy Awards process became a crucible in which the aspirations of LGBT (particularly gay men) for mainstream media acceptance would be negotiated through the process of hegemony. With high-profile nominations not only for *Brokeback*, but also for the Gay Indiewood films *Capote* and *Transamerica*, the media hyped the awards as the "Gay Oscars." As progressive and conservative elements weighed in on the *Brokeback* phenomenon, the unprecedented media coverage "masked hysteria and homophobia" (Rich, 2007: p. 45). The threat to dominant conceptions of masculinity was reflected in the language of commentators such as Fox News' Bill O'Reilly, who surmised that if the cowboys from the Western film *The Good, The Bad, and The Ugly* happened upon Jack and Ennis, "Gunfire would be involved I imagine" (Rich, 2007: p. 45). Highlighting hegemonic masculinity's aversion to anal sex between men, a couple of radio and televisions commentators referred to the film as "Fudgepack Mountain." Relentless satires, parodies, and jokes in the media exemplified the use of humor to relieve collective anxiety. Rich points out that the most common jokes about "catching gayness" by seeing the film illustrates a new-fangled version of the old-fashioned contagion theory (p. 46).

Universal (parent of Focus Features, which produced the film) was clearly nervous about the ramifications of the film. Rather than develop a promotional campaign for the Oscars that highlighted the relationship between Jack and Ennis, the posters depicted Jack and Ennis separately—Jack with his wife and child and Ennis with his wife. There was also a poster picturing Ennis at a Fourth of July fireworks celebration with his wife and children that evoked a commitment to family and country (and perhaps heterosexuality). As Knegt (2008) concludes, "The ads are undeniably homophobic in their silence...[the film's] content was compromised for financial gain" (p. 99). The studio chose to pander to conservative Academy voters to win Best Picture and generate more box office receipts—the way to do this was not through emphasizing the gay content. The film was sold as a universal "love is a force of nature" campaign rather than as a gay love story.

The nomination of *Brokeback Mountain* and the other LGBT-themed films permitted Hollywood to pat itself on the back for its tolerance and generosity toward sexual minorities. The dominant culture creates a myth of its own tolerance by occasionally allowing marginalized people some measure of mainstream success. But Hollywood as a hegemonic force, will only go so far in its generosity and openness to alternate ideologies and ways of being. Thus, despite having swept the pre-Oscar awards season, Hollywood voters did not bestow the top honor to *Brokeback*, instead selecting a surprise winner, *Crash*. Even this choice indicated Hollywood's celebration of itself as a progressive system, as the film portrayed issues of racism and White privilege. It was too much to ask that a film as radically stereotype-altering as *Brokeback Mountain* and as threatening to myths of masculinity could receive Hollywood's most prestigious prize. But the hegemonic nego-tiation commenced during *Brokeback*'s Oscar journey continues and can be analyzed through three subsequent films—*I Now Pronounce You Chuck and Larry*, *Milk*, and *Brüno*.

I Now Pronounce You Chuck and Larry:
Reaffirming Stereotypes

Universal's 2007 Adam Sandler-Kevin James comedy *I Now Pronounce You Chuck and Larry* tells the story of two straight firefighters who pose as gay domestic partners in order to obtain financial benefits. The film was panned by critics, but did well at the box office, gross-ing over $110 million. As a "message film," *Chuck and Larry* set out to show how two stereotypically heterosexual men (firefighters) could overcome their homophobia by being perceived as a gay couple.

According to Duralde (2007), "If there's anything that *I Now Pronounce You Chuck and Larry* can't be faulted on, it's good inten-tions." The producers sought and received a pre-release seal of approval from the Gay and Lesbian Alliance Against Defamation (GLAAD). It was believed the overall arch of the film would over-come the (many) homophobic jokes and stereotypes that appear in the film. For example, when discussing the idea to enter into the fake partnership, Sandler and James engage in the following homopho-bic banter: Sandler: Domestic partnership? You mean like faggots? James: No, I mean yea but, no, not us. Obviously. Just on paper. Sandler: Paper faggots? James: Well, the accepted vernacular is gay . . . but yes.

In another example, which appeared in the film's trailer, Sandler seeks laughs by punching James in the face rather than kiss him at their ceremony, telling the minister, "That's how we roll in our house, baby."

Gay stereotypes are played for laughs throughout the film, despite its claims to evoke tolerance. There are the usual homophobic refer-ences to gay male sex. Fire chief Dan Aykroyd tells the leads, "What you shove up your ass is your own business." Later, having learned the "message" of their union, he reflects, "And most importantly, they showed us that no matter whom we choose to love, be they heterosexual, homosexual, asexual, bisexual, trisexual, quadrisexual, pansexual, transsexual, omnisexual or that thing where the chick ties the belt around your neck and tinkles on a balloon, it has absolutely nothing to do with who we are as people." Gayness is equated, as usual, with kinky sex acts rather than genuine emotion.

Playing on stereotypical notions of gender inversion and the privilege of homonormative arrangements, the film employs a running gag where everyone assumes that Chuck is "the woman" in the relationship. Another stereotype involves a supporting character played by Ving Rhames who is initially a scary, tough guy. Chuck and Larry's feigned relationship inspires Rhames to come out and drop the masculine image for his true effeminate self by doing a naked version of "I'm Every Woman" in the fire station shower room. This transition from tough to sissy enhances the myth of masculinity by making him "other," no longer one of the guys.

What are we to make of *Chuck and Larry* in the context of cultural hegemony and LGBT-themed cinema? The film seems to pick up where the Oscars left off in terms of holding itself out as tolerant on the one hand and reasserting the use of homophobic stereotypes on the other. Otherness must be preserved to maintain traditional control over images of marginalized people. Perhaps well intentioned, the *Chuck and Larry* script and casting were destined to reinforce rather than weaken hegemonic conceptions of gayness and masculinity. Duralde (2007) captures the essence of this failure at engendering tolerance: "I'm sure [Sandler] thinks that audiences will follow Chuck's arc from homophobe to Friend of Gays Everywhere... It's nice to think that once the convulsive laughter has died down, audiences will instantly start to question just what it was they found so hilarious about seeing their hero punch [James] in the face at the altar—inspiring, ultimately, a whole generation of impressionable, *Little Nicky*-quoting Sandler fanatics to be far more tolerant of straights who pretend to be gay in order to cash in on the attractive array of domestic partnership benefits not yet available to the heterosexual community." By using such stock and trade Hollywood images, the filmmaker reestablishes consent to a social order that marginalizes the LGBT other as fodder for laughter and an object of fear.

MILK: DOWNPLAYING SEXUALITY

Focus Features, the same Universal subsidiary that produced *Brokeback Mountain*, released *Milk* in 2008. It is a biopic that narrates openly

gay San Francisco Supervisor Harvey Milk's rise in politics and ultimate assassination. This was a high-profile film that earned several
Oscar nominations, with Sean Penn taking home the Best Actor
prize. Thus, unlike *Chuck and Larry*'s fodder for mainstream laughs,
this was a serious film directed by openly gay Gus Van Sant who had
directed the New Queer Cinema film *My Own Private Idaho.*

Milk portrays its protagonist in heroic terms, a "great man" in
the tradition of other powerful figures who will themselves to political success. Penn plays the role with passion and intensity, and the
stock stereotypes give way to authentic characterizations. In short,
Milk continues, to a great extent, the authentic and heteronormative-
disrupting LGBT images evoked in *Brokeback Mountain.* The protagonist is openly gay, intelligent, an astute politician, and a tireless
advocate.

San Francisco's 1970s Castro district was a sexually charged community within a sexually charged city, regardless of sexual orientation.
Thus, one would expect in an authentic Gay Indiewood film to see
this environment depicted more fully. But as one commentator points
out, there is a "near-absence of a vibrant social and sexual community in the Castro...sexual energy is curiously absent from the film.
This would seem to be a careful strategy since Black's screenplay is
not unmindful of the power of sex. Indeed, the early flashback of
Harvey Milk meeting Scott Smith implies that the implicit freedom
and social transgression of gay male sexuality is a motivating force for
Milk's transformation from a quiet Babbitt to a queer power broker"
(Bronski, 2009: p. 72).

Depicting such dynamics of LGBT sexuality in a mainstream film
would have been radical; instead, this dynamic is downplayed. One
commentator asks, "Did Black and Van Sant sidestep this sexual
culture because they wanted to desexualize Harvey Milk's world?"
(Bronski, 2009: p.73). This is part of the hegemonic negotiation process; the up-front, raw sexuality of *Brokeback* created so much stir
and backlash, that aspect of film perhaps needs to be toned down
for mainstream palatability. The filmmakers also had to consider the
looming AIDS crisis; depicting the promiscuous culture that helped
to fuel the crisis could have detracted from the film's message or permit the discourse to be hijacked by conservative commentators.

As another sign of trepidation, the release date of the film was
in question. It could have been released earlier in 2008 and perhaps
have played a political role in California's Proposition 8 anti–same-sex
marriage campaign. The film's parallel narrative of Milk's campaign
against a 1970s anti-LGBT ballot measure could have been a timely

and powerful vehicle supporting the LGBT community and raising consciousness among undecided voters. Instead, the compromise was that the film was released in San Francisco two weeks before the election but did not go into wide release until after same-sex marriage rights suffered defeat. Why the move to distance itself from that debate? As an open system, political issues certainly affect decision making around film—the profit-motive is central, as well as a consideration of avoiding controversy. It was deemed better to approach homosexuality as an educational endeavor through highlighting the biographical aspects of the film and making sexuality a "secondary consideration" (Knegt, 2008: p. 77).

BRÜNO: CLARIFYING GAY OTHERNESS

The most recent LGBT-themed mainstream film is the most controversial of the three discussed here. Like *Chuck and Larry*, *Brüno* is ostensibly meant to increase tolerance, in this case, by satirizing homophobia. Assuming such admirable intentions, the film represents Hollywood's cultural hegemony vis-à-vis LGBT images, reasserting itself by staking out the boundaries of masculinity. In contrast to the complex and ambiguous characterizations of Jack and Ennis in *Brokeback*, Sacha Baron Cohen's Brüno is an extreme stereotype, a complete "Other." As Barnes (2009) reports, "There is no ambiguity about Brüno: he is a limp-wristed, sex-crazed queen. Universal's promotional materials show him dressed in hot pants, leopard bikini underwear and riding nude on a unicorn."

The film's premise is that after losing his job as the host of a trendy Austrian television program, Brüno embarks on an international journey in search of fame. This framework, replicating the successful formula in the "mockumentary" *Borat: Cultural Learnings of America for Make Benefit Glorious Nation of Kazakhstan* (2006), provides Cohen with the opportunity to ambush unsuspecting community members. In theory and perhaps in practice this technique compels them and the film audience to challenge their own stereotypical notions, fears, and prejudices.

Cohen introduced the character of Brüno on a television show, and the studio hoped the personage would profitably translate onto the big screens. Apparently, they believed some changes were on order to more vividly portray Brüno as gay other. Thus, the Brüno that appears in the film version has undergone a feminizing process: "This Brüno has plucked eyebrows and longish hair with blonde highlights. He wears mauve lipstick. Mr. Baron Cohen also appears to have shed several pounds of arm, leg and torso hair through waxing or elec-trolysis" (Barnes, 2009).

In anticipation of LGBT complaints about Brüno's characteriza-tion and experiences (unlike *Chuck and Larry*, this film did not seek or receive GLAAD approval during production), a Universal Pictures spokesperson stated, "While any work that dares to address relevant cultural sensitivities might be misinterpreted by some or offend others, we believe the overwhelming majority of the audience will understand and appreciate the film's inarguably positive intentions, which we've seen demonstrated whenever we have shown it" (Patten, 2009).

Lane (2009) states that despite intentions of exposing homophobia, "Brüno feels hopelessly complicit in the prejudices that it presumes to deride. You can't honestly defend your principled lampooning of homophobia when nine out of every ten images that you project onscreen comply with the most threadbare cartoons of gay behav-ior." If teaching tolerance is one of *Brüno's* goals, *Brüno*, like *I Now Pronounce You Chuck and Larry*, is not designed to deliver such a mes-sage. That is, "a schoolboy who watches a pirated DVD of this film will look at the prancing Austrian and find more, not fewer, reasons to beat up the kid on the playground who doesn't like girls. There is, on the evidence of this movie, no such thing as gay love; there is only gay sex, a superheated substitute for love" (Lane, 2009).

As an attempt at progressive pedagogy, the satire is questionable, given the target audience. One gay actor noted, "When you see a Brüno clip in a room full of gay men, everyone laughs and it's fine. When you see a Brüno clip in a room full of straight men, they're all laughing, and it's a different thing. You start to go, 'Hmmm, I don't know how I feel about this'" (Patten, 2009). Brüno's humor is decid-edly low-brow; however, for the satire to work, the highbrow audience is expected to understand that *homophobia* rather than *homosexual*ity is the true target of the humor. But will the homophobic viewers of the film grasp that they are the butt of the joke?

The film plays into the hands of homophobes by rehashing the ste-reotypical gay male as effeminate and sex-obsessed. Among the images portraying gayness, Brüno appears on a talk show with his adopted African baby, a "man magnet" wearing a T-shirt that says "Gayby." Later, the same child is shown in the background of photographs in which Brüno and another man seem to be having sex in a hot tub. In another scene, hotel workers enter a room to find Brüno and a sexual partner chained up, wearing G-strings, a plunger protruding from one of their mouths. The workers discovered a tarp on the wall with fecal stains and gerbils in a drawer. As one gay member of Hollywood notes, "It makes you sickened by gay sex, even if you are someone who participates in it" (Patten, 2009). Other scenes seek laughter by playing on the masculine aversion to anal sex. For example, Brüno approaches the hotel front desk with a remote control stuck in his rectum. As one man explained his Christian beliefs, Brüno asks the non sequitur question meant to evoke a homophobic response, "You didn't put any voodvind instruments up your Auschwitz?"

Savvy filmgoers, it is supposed, will see that these extreme, raunchy images are meant to satirize what many straight Americans are willing to believe about the practices and mores of gay men. Thus, Hollywood again can view itself as tolerant and progressive toward LGBT issues by calling out homophobes. But as a mainstream film produced with a profit motive, the stereotypes and fears are a commodity to be recycled and exploited again and again, as they have been throughout the history of Hollywood film. *Brüno* exemplifies the continual flux of hegemonic relations—Brüno is a post-*Brokeback* reassertion of old values of Hollywood—gay men as immoral sissies—but at the same time there is an awkward attempt at provoking reflection and achieving tolerance.

CONCLUSION: THE FUTURE?

This chapter has examined post-*Brokeback Mountain* gay cinema in the Hollywood mainstream. I have argued that the film's stereotype-challenging material, financial success, and cultural capital created a stir in Hollywood's patriarchal system, setting in motion a renegotiation of cultural hegemony. The circumstances surrounding *Brokeback*'s misleading Oscar campaign and eventual upset defeat for Best Picture were the first indication of a backlash. In the three films examined here, *I Now Pronounce You Chuck and Larry*, *Milk*, and *Brüno*, Hollywood's hegemonic forces appear to be negotiating a cinema of tolerance that nonetheless maintains Hollywood's control and exploitation of gay visibility and images, exploiting them on an as-needed basis.

What are the chances of mainstream cinema embracing serious, nonexploitative filmmaking around LGBT themes, continuing and expanding upon the authentic images portrayed in *Brokeback Mountain* and *Milk*? As noted earlier, the theory of cultural hegemony leaves "some room for antagonistic cultural expressions to develop (Adamson, 1980: p. 174). Of course, the dominant players in Hollywood have tremendous control over which films will achieve wide distribution. Economic forces are not in favor of an expanded, authentic LGBT cinema at the moment. The advent of specialty studios as subsidiaries of major studios has rendered all such filmmaking prohibitively expensive. If the perception remains that straight audiences will not embrace LGBT cinema, mainstream films will not be made. The result is that images appearing on multiplex screens will continue to be stereotypes rather than the diverse LGBT reality that includes all ranges of masculinity and femininity, economic status, racial and ethnic background, and familial arrangements.

The United States' neoliberal (pro-corporate, free market, privatizing) political-economic system also influences the prospects of LGBT cinema (Knegt, 2008). In matters of sexuality, neoliberal hegemony, aligning with neoconservative and religious fundamentalist elements, has embraced so-called "family values" as the cultural norm, shunting "alternative lifestyles" to the social margins. Significantly, a growing segment of the LGBT population (mostly affluent White males) has rejected progressive queer politics and adopted neoliberal stances toward inclusion in the dominant sector of society. Duggan (2002) argues that this "new homonormativity" is "a politics that does not contest dominant heteronormative assumptions and institutions" but rather incorporates them, seeking a "demobilized gay constituency and a privatized, depoliticized gay culture anchored in domesticity and consumption" (p. 177).

The new homonormativity moves toward the center-right, abandoning LGBT rights activism and neglecting alliances with race and gender rights activists. Gay neoliberals adopt a "model of narrowly constrained public life cordoned off from the 'private' control and vast inequalities of economic life" (p. 177). Knegt (2008) convincingly argues that the dynamics of Gay Indiewood parallel the new homonormativity's transition from progressive activism to mainstream identity/equality political processes. That is, Gay Indiewood served to suppress the radically counterhegemonic New Queer Cinema by forging a mainstream LGBT cinema that is controlled by Hollywood's system of independent film. Knegt explains, "'Indiewood' (and thus 'Gay Indiewood'), economically counters the 'leftist' strategy of the 'new independent cinema'... by aligning itself with the very institution that independent film defines itself *against*: Hollywood [emphasis in original]" (p. 67). Neoliberal interests, in effect, reduce the ability of truly independent filmmakers to present LGBT images that counter Hollywood's commoditized representations. Giroux (2005) recognizes this dangerous monopoly over public pedagogy as it relates to nondominant social groups:

Within the discourse of neoliberalism that has taken hold of the public imagination, there is no way of talking about what is fundamental to civic life, critical citizenship, and a substantive democracy. Neoliberalism offers no critical vocabulary for speaking about political or social transformation as a democratic project (p. 10). Thus, transforming entrenched and profitable images of masculinity and gayness is an overwhelming task, one made more difficult when neoliberalism co-opts a powerful segment of the nondominant group.

As Artz and Murphy (2000) assert regarding hegemony, "Power is best secured if subordinates buy into the arrangement, agree to the terms, and make the relationship theirs" (p. 2). This economically powerful gay constituency, with an emphasis on tolerance of the LGBT private sphere that is modeled on heteronormativity, is unlikely to push for an authentic mainstream cinema that offers complex, realistic images of LGBT life. If authentic media representations are to become part of the public consciousness and vie for control over the images of sexual minorities, it may very well be in a parallel system such as the new media, so long as net neutrality remains in effect.

REFERENCES

Adamson, W. (1980). *Hegemony and revolution: Antonio Gramsci's political and cultural theory*. Berkeley, CA: University of California Press.

Artz, L., & Murphy, B. (2000). *Cultural hegemony in the United States*. London: Sage.

Barnes, B. (2009, June). From Sacha Baron Cohen, a plea for tolerance in tight shorts, or not. [Review of the film *Brüno*]. *New York Times*. Retrieved September 22, 2009 from http://www.nytimes.com/.

Baron, C., Vince, W. & Ohoven, M. (Producer), & Miller, B. (Director). (2005). *Capote* [Motion picture]. United States: United Artists & Sony Pictures Classics.

Barounis, C. (2009). Cripping heterosexuality, queering able-bodiness: *Murderball, Brokeback Mountain* and the contested masculine body. *Journal of Visual Culture* 8(1), 54–75.

Barrios, R. (2003). *Screened out: Playing gay in Hollywood from Edison to Stonewall*. New York: Routledge.

Bersani, L. (1988). Is the rectum a grave? *In AIDS: Cultural analysis, cultural activism* (ed.) D. Crimp, pp. 197–222. Cambridge: MIT Press.

Biskind, P. (2004). *Down and dirty: Miramax, Sundance, and the rise of the independent film*. New York: Simon & Schuster.

Bourdieu, P. (1984). *Distinction: A social critique of the judgment of taste*. Trans. R. Nice. Cambridge: Harvard University Press.

Bronski, M. (Spring 2009). *Milk*. Cineaste, 71–73.

Cohan, S., & Hark. I. (eds.) (1993). *Screening the male: Exploring masculinities in Hollywood cinema*. London: Routledge.

Cohen, S. B. & Roach, J. (Producer), & Charles, L. (Director). (2006). *Borat: Cultural Learnings of America for Make Benefit Glorious Nation of Kazakhstan* [Motion picture]. United States: 20th Century Fox.

Cohen, S. B., Roach, J., Mazer, D. & Hill, J. (Producer), & Charles, L. (Director). (2009). *Brüno* [Motion picture]. United States: Universal Pictures.

Daley, R. (Producer), & Eastwood, C. (Director). (1971). *Play Misty for Me* [Motion picture]. United States: Universal Pictures.

Duggan, L. (2002). The new homonormativity: The sexual politics of neoliberalism. In R. Castronovo & D. Nelson (eds.) *Materializing democracy: Toward a revitalized cultural politics*, pp. 175–194. Durham, NC: Duke University Press.

Duralde, A. (2007, July 18). [Review of the film *I Now Pronounce You Chuck and Larry*.] Retrieved October 1, 2009 from http://www.afterelton.com/movies/2007/7/chuckandlarryreview?page=0%2C1

Edelman, L. F. (Producer), & Walsh, R. (Director). (1949). *White Heat* [Motion picture]. United States: Warner Bros.

Fox, R. & Rudin, S. (Producer), & Daldry, S. (Director). (2002). *The Hours* [Motion picture]. United States: Paramount Pictures & Miramax Films.

Gerrans, J., Hu, M. & Stark, J. (Producer), & Araki, G. (Director). (1992). *The Living End* [Motion picture]. United States: Desperate Pictures & October Films.

Giroux, H. (2005). The terror of neoliberalism: Rethinking the significance of cultural politics. *College Literature* 32(1), 1–19.

Gitlin, T. (1994), Prime time ideology: The hegemonic process in television entertainment. In H. Newcomb, Horace, ed. *Television: The critical view (5th ed.)*. New York: Oxford University Press.

Gramsci, A. (1971). *Selections from the Prison Notebooks*. Q. Hoare & G. N. Smith (Trans. & eds). New York: International Publishers,

Haggis, P., Cheadle, D., Yari, B. & Schulman, C. (Producer), & Haggis, P. (Director). (2005). *Crash* [Motion picture]. United States: Lion's Gate Entertainment.

Hardy, J. & Newmyer, R. (Producer), & Soderbergh, S. (Director). (1989). *sex, lies, and videotape* [Motion picture]. United States: Paramount Pictures.

Hogan, P. J. (Director). (1997). *My Best Friend's Wedding* [Motion picture]. United States: Tri-Star Pictures.

Hulce, T., Hart J., Koffler, P., Roumel, K., Sharp, J., Vachon, C. & Wells, J. (Producer). Mayer, M. (Director). (2004). *A Home at the End of the World* [Motion picture]. United States: Warner Independent Pictures.

Hytner, N. (Director). (1998). *The Object of My Affection* [Motion picture]. United States: 20th Century Fox.

Jackson Lears, T. J. (1985). The concept of cultural hegemony: Problems and possibilities. *American Historical Review* 90 (3), 567–593.

Jinks, D. & Cohen, B. (Producer), & Van Sant, G. (Director). (2008). *Milk* [Motion picture]. United States: Focus Features & Universal Pictures.

Jeffords, S. (1993). Can masculinity be terminated? In S. Cohan, & I. Hark (eds.) *Screening the male: Exploring masculinities in Hollywood cinema*, pp. 245–262. London: Routledge.

Kashani, T. (2009). *Deconstructing the mystique: An interdisciplinary introduction to cinema.* (2nd ed.) Dubuque, IA: Kendall-Hunt.

Kimmel, M. (2005). *The gender of desire: Chapters on male sexuality.* Albany: SUNY Press.

Knegt, P. (2008). Forging a mainstream gay cinema: Negotiating gay cinema in the American hegemony. MA Thesis, Quebec: Concordia University.

Lane, A. (2009, July) Mein Camp: "Brüno." [Review of the film *Brüno*] *New Yorker.* Retrieved September 20, 2009 from http://www.newyorker.com/arts/critics/cinema/2009/07/20/090720crci_cinema_lane?currentPage=1

Lehman, P. (ed.) (2001). *Masculinity: Bodies, movies, culture.* New York: Routledge.

Levy, E. (1999). *Cinema of outsiders: The rise of American independent film.* New York: New York University Press.

Livingston, J. (Producer & Director). (1991). *Paris Is Burning* [Motion picture]. United States: Miramax Films.

Macy, W. H. (Producer), & Tucker, D. (Director). (2005). *Transamerica* [Motion picture]. United States: The Weinstein Company & IFC Films.

Marcuse, H. (1964). *One-dimensional man.* Boston: Beacon Press.

McGehee, S. & Siegel D. (Producer & Director). (2001). *The Deep End* [Motion picture]. United States: Fox Searchlight Pictures.

Mutrux, G. (Producer), & Condon, B. (Director). (2004). *Kinsey* [Motion picture]. United States: Fox Searchlight Pictures.

Parker, L. (Producer), & Van Sant, G. (Director). (1991). *My Own Private Idaho* [Motion picture]. United States: Fine Line Features.

Patten, D. (2009). Gay Hollywood Comes Out … Against "Brüno.'" *The Wrap.* Retrieved September 22, 2009 fromhttp://www.thewrap.com/chapter/exclusive-criticism-gay-insiders-led-Brüno-reshoots_3721.

Rich, B. R. (2007). Brokering *Brokeback*: Jokes, backlashes, and other anxieties. *Film Quarterly* 60(3), 44–48.

Rubin, G. (2007). "Thinking sex: Notes for a radical theory of the politics of sexuality." In R. Parker and P. Aggleston (eds.), *Culture, society and sexuality: A reader*, New York: Routledge, pp. 150–187.

Russo, V. (1986). *The celluloid closet: Homosexuality in the movies* (rev. ed). New York: Harper & Row.

Sandler, A. & Shadyac T. (Producer), & Dugan, D. (Director). (2007). *I Now Pronounce You Chuck & Larry* [Motion picture]. United States: Universal Studios.

Schamus, J., Ossana, D. & McMurtry, L. (Producer), & Lee, A. (Director). (2005). *Brokeback Mountain* [Motion picture]. United States: Focus Features & Paramount Pictures.

Spohrer, E. (2009) Not a gay cowboy movie? *Brokeback Mountain* and the importance of genre. *Journal of Popular Film and Television* 37(1), 26–33.

Theron, C., Damon, M., Peterson, C., Kushner, D. & Wyman, J. (Producer), & Jenkins, P. (Director). (2003). *Monster* [Motion picture]. United States: Newmarket Films.

Troche, R. & Turner, G. (Producer), & Troche, R. (Director). (1994). *Go Fish* [Motion picture]. United States: Samuel Goldwyn Company.

Vachon, C. (Producer), & Haynes, T. (Director). (1991). *Poison* [Motion picture]. United States: Zeitgeist Films.

Warner, M. (ed.) (1993). *Fear of a queer planet: Queer politics and social theory*. Minneapolis: University of Minnesota Press.

Williams, R. (1977). *Marxism and literature*. Oxford: Oxford University Press.

Wlodarz, J. (2001). Rape fantasies: Hollywood and homophobia. In P. Lehman (ed.) *Masculinity: Bodies, movies, culture*, pp. 67–80. New York: Routledge.

Wurmfeld, E. & Zions, B. (Producer), & Herman-Wurmfeld, C. (Director). (2001). *Kissing Jessica Stein* [Motion picture]. United States: Fox Searchlight Pictures.

3

HOLLYWOOD AGES

9

MODES OF YOUTH EXPLOITATION IN THE CINEMA OF LARRY CLARK

Douglas Kellner

OVERVIEW

Since at least the 1950s, Hollywood cinema has been exploiting youth as a consumer society developed during the postwar epoch first in the United States and then globally, with youth positioned and constructed as key forces of consumption. Using youth culture and the resources of youthful bodies to produce popular films for young audiences, Hollywood naturally exploited youth, its bodies, lifestyles, culture, and personalities, as well as its hopes and dreams and fantasies and fears. Further, many postwar Hollywood films have presented very negative representations and pointed to youth as a social problem, associated with promiscuity, crime, violence, and destructive tendencies. The Hollywood juvenile delinquency films in the postwar period began this trend, and youth of color, and working-class youth in particular, have been increasingly stigmatized in the past decades.[1]

To be sure, there are tensions and contradictions in representations of youth in Hollywood films. On one hand, Hollywood presents beautiful youth and high-maintenance consumption as a societal ideal, and on the other, youth is frequently represented as a force of disruption and danger. Frequently, youth receive negative representations as objects of sexual degradation, drug addiction, and senseless violence, whereas other films have more positive representations of youth, in some cases, because youth are involved in their production and can partially give voice to their own perceptions, hopes and fears, and views of the world.

In fact, media culture and Hollywood film are contested terrains in which the social constructions of youth that have occurred throughout the past decades replicate social struggle and discourses where youth are vilified or marginalized, or given voice through their own cultural forms such as popular music, some youth films, subcultural styles, and now the Internet and social networking sites. Thus, while the vilification of youth continues in Hollywood films, during the past decades positive representations and narratives concerning youth have also appeared, mostly in the work of young directors and crews who are part of their communities.[2]

To talk of the exploitation of youth in Hollywood film requires a provisional definition of exploitation and recognition of different modes and levels of exploitation. Indeed, exploitation is itself a complex concept: To exploit something is simply to use it in ordinary language, while in the Marxian category, exploitation involves extraction of unpaid labor from human labor power and creative activity through which an oppressive and exploitative social system produces and reproduces itself and capital.[3] Hence, I would contrast youth films that exploit youth for commercial and ideological purposes with films that attempt to empower youth and to articulate their problems and aspirations in a society that pays lip service to youth while abusing it in multiple ways.

In this paper, I first discuss the genre of youth film and the social construction of youth through film and media culture. Then I look at a paradigm case of the exploitation of youth in a negative sense through detailed analysis of the cinematic work of Larry Clark, which consistently exploits teen bodies as objects of voyeurism and sexual fetishism, providing a panorama of highly prejudicial images of youth as consisting of highly sexualized bodies, often drugged out or passive victims of circumstances.

During the 1960s, the genre of "exploitation" film described tawdry, low-budget films that exploited sex and violence in popular genres like the crime film or horror film.[4] In this study, I argue that Larry Clark is an exploitation director in this sense and he will emerge as a test case for the extreme exploitation of youth in contemporary American cinema.

YOUTH FILMS AND THE SOCIAL CONSTRUCTION OF YOUTH

"Youth" is socially constructed in the discourses, representations, and social practices that are dominant in specific historical eras and societies.[5] In U.S. society, media culture and film have been traditionally an important site for the social construction of youth (as well as of gender, race, class, and other elements of social identities). In assessing how youth culture films construct contemporary youth, a distinction must be made between the self-representations of youth and the representations of youth by adults in the media industries, ones that are often hostile or exploitative. Traditionally, representations of youth have been subject to distortion and even demonization. In the 1950s, while American television produced idealized visions of the middle-class family and youth, Hollywood produced a wave of anti-youth films targeting violent youth as asocial rebels, as juvenile delinquents, as threats to existing society in genres like the motorcycle films, gang films, and social-problem films like *Blackboard Jungle* (1955).

Things changed somewhat, however, when, during the 1960s, Hollywood production moguls discerned that it was youth who were the largest audience for films, that young people embraced cinema that represented them in a positive, or what they considered to be a realistic, light, and that youth affirmed films that celebrated the counterculture of the period and youth rebellion. Hence, there were waves of films presenting youth sympathetically, like *The Graduate* (1967), *Bonnie and Clyde* (1967), and *Easy Rider* (1969), that affirmed values of youth subcultures and that positively portrayed the 1960s counterculture and youth revolution, such as *Monterey Pop* (1968), *Woodstock* (1970), *Zabriskie Point* (1970), and so on.[6]

It should also be noted that Hollywood itself was deeply affected by the 1960s counterculture, that its sex, drugs, and rock and roll became a major part of the Hollywood film subculture itself, particularly with its younger members. Many of these individuals, such as Peter Fonda, Dennis Hopper, Jack Nicholson, and those involved with BBS Productions, made films themselves; thus, in a sense, the youth culture was representing itself without the constraints of corporate control and censorship.[7] Of course, most of the youth movies of the post-1960s wave were controlled by production studios, subject to corporate control and censorship, and did not represent youth culture adequately or positively. Moreover, youth continued to be villainized in conservative films and TV cop shows of the 1960s like *Dragnet*, *The Mod Squad*, and the like, which sensationalized youthful criminals.

Youth films themselves, moreover, suffered a decline in the early 1970s as their audiences fell off, signaled by the decline and eventual demise of BBS by the mid-1970s. This period was also marked by the rise of the Hollywood blockbuster and spectacle with films like *The Godfather* (1972), *The Exorcist* (1973), and *Jaws* (1975) encouraging studios to produce films that would appeal to a large mass audience,[8] thus decentering the concerns of youth. Consequently, for some years it was once again adults who were representing youth and presenting adult visions of youth, often negatively, as in *Animal House* (1978), *Porky's* (1982), *American Pie* (1999), and other mindless youth films, or the cycle of stalk and slash films that portrayed the torture, mutilation, and murder of young teenagers who engaged in promiscuous sex. There were, to be sure, some exceptions, such as the John Hughes's films presenting sensitive portrayals of youth; Jonathan Kaplan's *Over the Edge* (1979), about teen revolt in a Southern California suburb; Amy Heckerling's *Fast Times at Ridgemont High* (1982), which sympathetically portrayed the problems of middle-class youth; or *River's Edge* (1986), which provided a sympathetic look at the difficulties and complexities of the lives of working-class youth.

Thus, from the 1960s to the present, youth films have both exploited and vilified youth *and* documented the situation and problems of youth, representing youth in a variety of classes, subcultures, and ethnicities in a variety of fashions. Media culture is a contested terrain and conflicting constructions of youth battle for the attention of old and young alike. Cycles of films show contemporary youth from the inner-city ghettos and barrios to the affluent suburbs and once-peaceful small towns as suffering a wide range of problems with no easy solutions. Moreover, many of these films were made by younger filmmakers, as independents have once again—as in the late 1960s and 1970s—achieved a favorable position within the film industry. Independent films dealing with youth were made on low budgets and turned over high profits, including Richard Linklater's *Slacker* (1991) and *Dazed and Confused* (1993), Spike Lee's films dealing with African American youth like *Do the Right Thing* (1994), Allison Ander's Latino youth in *Mi Vida Loca* (1993), and Kevin Smith's lower-middle-class dudes in *Clerks* (1994).[9] Hence, a wave of youth films by younger writers and directors provided self-presentations of youth by themselves, often outside of the control of the Hollywood commercial system.

Indeed, there have been cycles of youth films produced by young blacks, Chicanos, Asian Americans, women, gays and lesbians, and others previously excluded from the Hollywood production system. Hollywood cinema exhibits a more pluralized culture, with individuals and groups producing cultural expressions of their experiences that had been previously excluded from mainstream culture—or at least finding their subcultures represented in the mainstream. Although youth films often are structured by adults' representations of youth, with all the obvious exclusions and biases, a surprising number of young filmmakers have made films in recent years, accessible in video, DVD, or digitization, if not general release, that articulate the experiences of subcultures previously invisible in Hollywood. Some of these are problematic first-time efforts, but provide self-presentations of a diversity of groups and thus contribute to development of a more multicultural society and culture.

In particular, young black filmmakers have made a cycle of 'hood films about the violence and social decay facing black youth in urban ghettoes. The films of Spike Lee, Matty Rich's *Straight Out of Brooklyn* (1991), Mario van Peebles' *New Jack City* (1991) and *Panther* (1995), made with his father Melvin, John Singleton's *Boyz N' the Hood* (1991) and *Poetic Justice* (1993), the Hughes brothers' *MenaceIISociety* (1993), as well as *Fresh, Juice* (1994), *Jason's Lyric* (1994), *Clockers* (1995), and other films featuring young blacks vividly show that black communities are in grave jeopardy, that they have been abandoned by the government and leaders of the investment world, and that kids become criminals not because they are born evil ("natural born killers"), but in response to appalling life conditions (although, as Henry Giroux has argued, they also reproduce negative stereotypes of youth of color).[10] Latinos, too, suffer oppression as an urban underclass and media and political focus on illegal immigration has brought their plight to general attention. The growing influence of Hispanic culture is reflected not only in the superstardom of the late crossover artist Selena, but in a growing number of films by directors such as Robert Rodriguez and Gregory Nava. A cycle of films show Latino youth negotiating the cultural differences between Hispanic and Anglo America. Gregory Nava and Anna Thomas's *El Norte* (1983) portrays a brother and sister from Guatemala attempting to deal with the problems of adjusting to a complex American society. The independent film *Pain Flower* (1996) insightfully portrays the lives of young Chicanos in a Tex-Mex border town and the tensions between assimilating to mainstream culture and keeping their cultural identities—a theme also present in John Sayles's 1996 film *Lone Star*. In films of the 2000s, growing up Latino has been explored in films like *Raising Victor Vargas* (2006) and *Quinceañera* (2006), while *Sangre de mi Sangre* (2007) and *Sin Nombre* (2009) have dealt with challenges of immigration.

Young Asian Americans and other ethnic youth had, however, taken to video and documentary and fictional shorts to try to tell their stories in the 1990s, although in the 2000s cheaper digital cameras and computerized editing have made it possible for a renaissance of independent film, including films by youth of different social groups and ethnicities. The result is an extremely rich emerging cinematic and video culture consisting of a vibrant tapestry of young and independent voices. One has to encounter the independent film and video movement to find these new products, but it is to be hoped that new technologies and modes of distribution like the Internet, Netflix, Amazon, and Roku will make readily available a wide range of new media that will articulate the experiences and visions of individuals and groups long excluded from media culture.[11] Such media production by the young is very encouraging because precisely through learning how to produce media one also becomes a more savvy critic and user of the media.

There is still a large number of Hollywood comedies and dramas, however, that arguably involve the exploitation of youth and youth culture, presenting youth as objects of laughter and derision, embodying out-of-control libido, destructive tendencies, and mindless pranks. But there are no negative representations of youth in the history of Hollywood and perhaps world cinema that can compete with those of Larry Clark.

THE VOYEURISTIC AND FETISHISTIC CINEMA OF LARRY CLARK

Photographer Larry Clark became famous for his book collections *Tulsa* (1971) and *Teenage Lust* (1983), which featured photographs of the barely clad bodies of young drug addicts, often in a stoned haze, or engaging in graphic sexual activity. Clark puts this iconography to use in his first film *Kids* (1995), written by an eighteen-year-old New York teenager Harmony Korine and directed by Clark. The harrowing film portrays the trials and tribulations of urban youth, most of whom were unprofessional actors and Korine's friends, deploying a quasi-documentary style to capture the texture of the everyday life of inner-city youth and their dead-end lives.

Chronicling a day in the life of a group of multiracial New York City kids, the film takes its audience into a frightening world of drugs, dangerous sex, AIDS and sexually transmitted disease, and violence. The film opens with Telly (played by seventeen-year-old actor Leo Fitzpatrick), a teenage Casanova, French-kissing a young girl with whom he wants to have sex and who is his preferred mode of virgin. The opening images hone in on the open mouths and barely clothed bodies of the teenagers, fetishizing their body parts and voyeuristically documenting their sexual interaction and the young girl's sexual initiation. After Telly begins to achieve his goal, the girl repeatedly complains that the penetration is hurting, but he continues ever rougher in his plummeting of her passive body.

Telly splits and brags about deflowering the girl to his buddy Casper (Justin Pierce), another completely amoral and nihilistic young teen who spends his whole time trying to get high and eventually, a la Telly, to get laid. The two wander aimlessly through New York City streets, robbing a Korean grocer, urinating in public, and jumping over a subway turnstile. Visiting a crash house for teens, they take more drugs in group activities that include very young African American boys smoking "chronic." Telly confesses his obsession with deflowering virgins and his desire to take another one that very day whom he plans to meet later. The scene is intensely voyeuristic as the camera slowly pans young multiracial bodies, lightly clothed and spread out on a couch or on the floor, ingesting drugs, laughing, and mostly talking of drugs and sex. Another scene hones in on a group of young women also talking unabashedly about sex, and the voyeuristic Clark once again provides close-ups and tight shots of the teenage girls' bodies and highlights their sexual experience as they recount intimate details of their erotic activities. Again the camera pans slowly over the girls, focusing on their faces, breasts, legs, and other body parts, a blatant fetishizing of teen bodies.

In Washington Square Park, Telly and Casper gratuitously insult a couple of gay guys walking by, and in an altercation with a black guy, the young thugs gang up on him and violently beat and perhaps kill him, as they bash him with their skateboards. Visiting Telly's breast-feeding mom, they steal money from her purse and then go out for a night of partying.

The plot is then set in motion when Jennie (Chloe Sevigny), accompanies her friend Ruby (Rosario Dawson) to take an AIDS test. While Ruby has had multiple sex partners, many with unprotected sex, Jennie has had sex only with Telly, who the audience knows goes for virgins and eschews condoms. Ironically, it is Jennie's HIV test that turns out to be positive, and the rest of the film shows her listlessly wandering through Manhattan searching for Telly. At a club where vacuous youth listen to throbbing techno music, she learns that Telly is at a friend's house whose parents have gone out of town. Just as the film earlier portrayed in detail the multicultural youth consuming vast numbers of mind-obliterating drugs in a crash pad, at the party scene, we see scores of teenagers taking drugs and engaging in sex, including Telly, who has taken a young virgin into the bedroom of the absent parents' house to deflower her.

Jennie arrives at the party, finds Telly in bed with a young girl, then passes out from her own overload of drugs. While unconscious, she is sexually assaulted by Casper, presumably circulating the deadly virus further. It is as if contemporary youth are robbed of agency and can only passively submit to their fate and the next mind-numbing round of drugs and temporary opiate of sex.

Kids can be read as an extremely grim morality tale of a world without morals, which warns about the dangers of AIDS and sexually transmitted diseases. The profanity, casual sex, continuous drug and cigarette use, petty crime, and violence in the urban youth culture portrayed is extremely disturbing—prompting harsh critical attacks on the film when it came out. Young subteen black boys are shown smoking strong weed and passing out in a stupor—a preview of a life to come. The teenage girls and boys casually have sex with each other and face the risk of deadly disease.

The film features a world of kids without families. Obviously, many of the urban youth portrayed come from broken homes with single mothers and no fathers present. Parents are rarely seen in the film, and they are portrayed as ineffectual and unable to provide support and guidance for their kids, a theme that constitutes a standard genre of the 1990s TV talk shows. Yet the kids themselves form a tight community of multiracial closeness and solidarity. They live in a world of their own, share each other's bodies, pleasures, and fears, closely bonding together against the outside world. Their youth community thus seems to be the only haven in the heartless world. Yet it is clear that this "haven" is not enough to save them from despair and a failed life. In the last line in the film, one of the teens coming to from an all-night party looks into the camera and asks: "Jesus Christ! What happened?," a question the audience might be asking itself on their way out of the theater as they contemplate the plight of today's youth and the continuing erosion of moral norms.

Far from being a genuine moralist, Clark arguably exploits the anti-AIDS cautionary morality tale to provide exploration of teen bodies, sexuality, and drug use that is attractively and powerfully portrayed in his still-disturbing and engaging film. Like his collection of photographs of youthful bodies with blank expressions, *Kids* is highly voyeuristic and almost pornographic in its fetishizing of young bodies and depiction of explicit sexual and drug-imbibing behavior. The movie can also be seen as a horror film with Telly as a vampire sucking the lives out of young girls, but the real horror is the youth subculture as a whole, defined by meaningless sex, drugs, and violence, wasting lives with no direction or alternatives, no values and nothing but the sensations of the moment, providing a tragedy of today's youth without education, culture, or future.

Most of the rest of Clark's succeeding films take place in this world and continue to exploit youth in a voyeuristic and fetishized fashion. His characters rarely have an intelligent thought, anything interesting to say, or any values and viable goals for life. Clark chooses the most pitiful, broken, and empty youth for his films, and while he revels in exploration and unveiling of their young bodies and sexual activities, he never explores their pasts, aspirations, fears, or hopes.

Clark's follow-up film, *Another Day in Paradise* (1998), enters the world of the drug-addicted losers of his photography collection *Tulsa*, focusing on the lives of a pair of teen junkies and their surrogate parents who take them to a more advanced world of drug usage and crime. The film opens with a teen couple in bed, as Clark's camera establishes their look through focus on their body parts. The young boy Bobbie (Vincent Kartheiser) gets up to go out, while the girl Rose (Natasha Gregson Wagner) stays asleep in the bed, a defining passivity that will characterize her throughout the film.

Bobbie breaks into a community college and begins to rob a vending machine of small change when he is accosted by a black security guard, who mercilessly beats him, positioning Bobbie as a petty criminal and loser. The scene cuts to a badly bloodied-up Bobbie being tended to by an older dude Mel (James Woods) and his partner Sid (Melanie Griffith), who are priming the younger couple to join them in a life of crime. In a scene that will set up the subsequent mis-en-scene, Mel shoots up Bobbie with heroin, the painkiller that will hook him up with Mel's subsequent plots as he and Rose become increasingly addicted.

At first, Bobbie and Rose are treated to a shopping spree where they are outfitted with cool new duds and initiated into the joys of conspicuous consumption. Mel and Sid draw the two into a close family situation bonded by drugs as they set off on a new life of crime, evoking the exuberance of a road movie. A night at a honky tonk where they get loaded immerses them in the joys of the night life, although the teens must be carried home and are seriously hung over the next day. Mel and Sid treat the pair, however, with what appears to be genuine affection as a surrogate family seems to be developing.

Based on a novel by ex-con Eddie Little, the subsequent sequences of *Another Day in Paradise* portray the road trip leading to an inevitably botched crime. Interestingly, Gus Van Sant admitted that he was influenced by Larry Clark's photographic iconography in shooting his tale of young addicts on a crime spree to feed their habit in *Drugstore*

Cowboy (1989). The plotline of *Another Day in Paradise* closely follows *Drugstore Cowboy*'s story of an older addict couple joining with younger addicts who are taught how to steal and maintain their habit, and in both stories the younger woman addict dies of an overdose. However, while Van Sant provides a sympathetic look at the lives, joys, and compulsions of addiction, Clark provides a comic book caricature of hyped-up junkies on a wild crime spree while highlighting fetishistic images of the teen junkies. Moreover, the Matt Dillon character in *Drugstore Cowboy* comes to see that the junkie life is a path toward destruction and death, and chooses another way of life, while Clark puts his doomed junkies on a fast path to destruction (with a slight exception, as we will see next which is also an "appropriation" of Van Sant's story).

Clark's hyped-up junkies in *Another Day in Paradise* encounter a collection of American Gothic types along the way, giving Clark a chance to produce American freak show iconography. A hypocritical "reverend" (James Otis) who sells the crews guns and who later serves as medic after their robbery job goes sour, provides an occasion for Clark to revel in the stereotype of the crazy reverend, while an over-the-top gay dude (Lou Diamond Phillips) leads the would-be junkie criminals to the robbery that goes awry, providing another character in Clark's American freak show pantheon.

While the film shows how the family can be exploitative, as well as a haven from a heartless world, and the hypocrisy of religion, the tawdry story ends with Bobbie escaping from the clutches of his criminal surrogate family after they discover that Rose has overdosed and died, and are forced to go on the run after a botched robbery. In the concluding segment, Sid encourages Bobbie to run away in a cornfield as they stop for gas, providing the hope that perhaps he may escape the life of crimes, addiction, and destruction that awaits him.

According to the Internet Movie Database, Clark shot *Bully* (2001), *Teenage Caveman* (2002), and *Ken Park* (2002) in nine months,[12] which perhaps marks the most appalling period of the exploitation of teen bodies in the history of world cinema. *Bully* (2002) goes further than Clark's previous films into pornographic depiction of the bodies and sexual activities of a group of utterly nihilistic youth in South Florida. The film takes the form of a true story of a murder based on Jim Schutze's novelistic version of the crime, in which a group of young people kill a teen acquaintance who is bullying the main character and who has also raped one of the girls.

Bully introduces Bobby Kent (Nick Stahl), who repeatedly and mercilessly bullies and beats up Marty (Brad Renfro), a high school drop-out surfer dude who has no future and no ability to resist Bobby's bullying. In an opening sequence, the two guys pick up some highly sexualized girls in the sandwich shop where they work and within moments they are having sex. If this wasn't enough, another early scene shows Bobby and Marty going to a male strip club and Bobby ordering Marty to get on stage and strip and then be pleasured by a leering older male. In another early scene, Bobby rapes Ally (Bijou Phillips), one of the girls picked up in the opening scene, whose best friend, Lisa (Rachel Miner), has fallen in love with Marty.

While parents are not completely absent in *Bully*, as in Clark's previous films, they are totally ineffectual and have no restraining or moral influence on their out-of-control kids. Marty begs his parents to move away from the neighborhood in which he is bullied and has no future prospects, but the parents turn a deaf ear. Bobby's straight-arrow father tells him to stay away from Marty, who is a loser, and tries to get him to go into business with him, but the father is largely ignored by his wayward and conniving son.

After Bobby repeatedly humiliates Marty and rapes Ally, Lisa decides that they must kill Bobby, and both Ally and Marty agree, assembling a motley crew of losers, stoners, and a would-be gangster to plot Bobby's death. While the teens' erotic and aggressive instincts created the chaotic behavior of the first sections of the film, the concluding sections show the group ineptly plotting Bobby's murder and then savagely attacking him in a deserted stretch of wetlands, before throwing his body into a canal where sand crabs devour it. Members of the group are quickly overcome with guilt, go back to the scene of the crime, confess the murder to sundry friends and family members, and then are rounded up by the law and swiftly brought to justice.

Clark's next exploration/exploitation of youth, *Teenage Caveman* (2002), combines camp and teen'ploitation in a futuristic fantasy of a group of teens rediscovering modern civilization after an apocalypse drove them to live in caves. Part of Lou Arkoff's Creature Feature films, which presented monsters made by Stan Winston and remakes of 1950s and 1960s shlockploitation films released by his father's Samuel Z. Arkoff AIP studio, Clark's pastiche of a 1950s Roger Corman film inserts his standard themes in the schlocky B-ploitation genre material.

Out on a hunt, a teen cavedude David (Andrew Keegan) is bullied by an elder, who he stabs in the head with a spear. He then hides the body. Returning to the cave, the boy's father, a Manson-like leader, blows off his son's transgression and instead is eager to get a cute blonde, Sarah (Tara Subkoff), to whom his son is sweet on, to blow him. After a hypocritical antisex speech by the father, who claims to speak for God, the son confronts him trying to rape the blonde Sarah and kills him by hitting him in the head with a metal religious crucifix. Andrew is hung out on a cross to provide food for animals and rock-throwing fun for feral children. A gang of teens, whom Andrew has taught to read with *Penthouse* magazines, free him, and they escape from the cave, an obvious allegory of kids splitting a repressive and hypocritical communal scene, like an uptight religious community.

On their own in violent postholocaust weather, a storm hits and the teenage cavemen and young women wake up in a modern penthouse apparently owned by a charismatic and sexually voracious couple, Neil (Richard Hillman) and Judith (Tiffany Limos). The couple invites the teens to take a bath and lures them into a Jacuzzi, giving Clark an opportunity to explore their naked flesh (although Sarah puts her arms across her breasts to signify that she is shy). The couple next insists on initiating the innocent caveteens into sex, providing some soft porn moments. Playing with horror iconography, the first enthusiastic virgin to be deflowered soon literally explodes with her guts and organs flying in all directions, as Judith fiercely masturbates.

It emerges, from what serves as a narrative for the sex and violence scenes, that the couple has been injected with a genetic virus that allows them to live forever as super-humans, instantly curing all wounds, although obviously not everyone can survive the virus, making its transmission a dangerous game (AIDS anyone?). In true Larry Clark fashion, the cavekids are also initiated into drugs and alcohol, allowing long scenes of drinking, drugging, and sex, which inevitably spreads the virus and eventually takes most of the teens' lives (although Neil cuts off the head of a libidinous dude who is bragging how hard he fucked Neil's girl Judith, and the head is bounced around like a toy for the rest of the film). Equally twisted, Neil jams his arm in anger into Judith's body and accidentally yanks out her internal organs, leaving her smiling face, breasts, and legs to provide a weird sculpture of a partial body without essential organs.

To bring the entertainment to a close, David and Neil transform into monsters as they fight over deflowering, or in David's case, perhaps protecting, the virgin Sarah. Together, David and Sarah violently murder Neil, and anticipating *Twilight* (2008), David tells Sarah she must return to the cave because living with him is too dangerous, though seconds later they are having sex. The final scene shows David returning to the cave people as a charismatic leader and then leading the children away from the cave for sexual initiation rites and perhaps future pedophilic Larry Clark films.

Teenage Caveman is something of a curiosity in Clark's oeuvre, showing that there is no form of exploitation film too schlocky or sleazy for him to exploit. By contrast, Clark's relatively unseen chef d'oeuvre *Ken Park* (2002) summarizes his cinematic style, vision, iconography, and concerns. Refused release in many countries where the film was banned, *Ken Park* has become difficult to see. In Australia, where it was banned, "On 3rd July, 2003 a public screening from an imported DVD was shown at the Balmain Town Hall (New South Wales, Australia) but shut down after a raid by the Police. No arrests were made." Further, "UK distributor Hamish McAlpine dropped the film after Larry Clark punched him in the face at a celebratory dinner,"[13] and on the DVD commentary to *Bully*, Clark curses his producer and claims that he has refused to distribute the film in either the UK or the United States (I got hold of a Russian-distributed DVD through Amazon).

The screenplay, written by Clark protégé Harmony Korine, is based on newspaper clippings, tabloid television, and "stories by Larry Clark," according to the titles on the film. Conceived and written before *Kids, Ken Park* is perhaps Clark's quintessential teen-ploitation flick. Set in a California suburb, the film opens with skateboarders and zooms in on title character Ken Parks, who, after impressive skating exploits, pulls out a gun and shoots himself, presumably, we eventually learn, because his girlfriend refuses to have an abortion. The scene then cuts to a series of episodic vignettes of Ken's skateboarding friends, starting with Shawn who bullies his brother and then goes next door and asks his girlfriend's mother if she would like him "to eat her out," to which she responds deadpanned, "I'm folding." After helping her fold the wash, Shawn gets down to business and voraciously licks her vagina in meticulous close-ups with the mother giving him directions in a scene that produces an indeterminate amount of orgasms (when asked by Shawn how many times she'd come, the mother says she doesn't know and we believe her).

Next, we are introduced to Claude, a skinny skater whose pregnant mother (Amanda Plummer) is sweet to him, but whose bully father is nasty, exploding in rage when the son refuses to lift weights with him, bad-mouthing his skateboarding style and activity as he crushes his son's skateboard. Later in the film, after a night of drinking with an equally loutish and bloated buddy, the father drunkenly stumbles into his house, enters his half-clothed sleeping son's bedroom, lays down to sleep beside him with his arm around him, and then goes down under the covers to suck his son's cock, who awakes in horror and kicks his father in the head a couple of times, and then plots to leave the dysfunctional family.

While Clark's previous films showed empty and vacuous teens engaging in meaningless sex and drugs, *Ken Park* gives equal time to the parents, who are an even more perverted and loathsome lot than the appalling kids. Peaches, played by Clark regular Tiffany Limos, who allegedly conceived the story but didn't collaborate on the screenplay, is introduced with her father studying what appears to be a Hebraic religious text. We learn that the religious fanatic father has lost his wife, who looks just like his beautiful young daughter, while he tearfully tells his story to a nice guy who comes over to visit Peaches. While Curtis is introduced as a student from Bible study class, as soon as the father goes to his daily visit to his dead wife's grave, the couple gets into a dry-humping bondage ritual, tying Peaches to the top of her bed. The increasingly explicit sexual games are interrupted by an early return by the father who brutally beats the guy. After a scene in which the father reads biblical scripture to condemn his bawling daughter to damnation as the whore of Babylon, we see them in later scenes with the girl dressed in her mother's bridal attire as the demented father marries his daughter (we are spared ultra-pornographic incest this time).

And then there is charming young Tate (James Ransone) who viciously verbally assaults his grandmother when she enters his room with a fruit plate and nastily abuses his grandfather who he continuously accuses of cheating during a Scrabble game. A long masturbatory sequence depicts Tate asphyxiating himself with a scarf on his door and coming in his hand, as Clark's cinematographer focuses in on the dripping wads of cum dribbling down his hand. Soon after, we see Tate brutally murdering his grandparents and then getting arrested.

Hence, while Clark's previous films immersed themselves in youth sex and drug culture, Clark exploits extreme violence as well in *Ken Park*, and in each scene there is dramatic tension as viewers wait for the inevitable violence to explode. The film concludes, however, with Claude, Peaches, and her boyfriend Curtis in a long and explicit ménage à trois. In the film's only articulated idea, Claude speaks of reading a book that claimed that sexual gratification was the only thing worth living for, and he affirms that sex is the only thing that matters to him, a sentiment expressed by the predatory HIV distributor Telly in *Kids*, an idée de clef that emerges as the One Idea to hold together Clark's tawdry oeuvre.

Interestingly, in interviews Clark constantly denies that his films are pornographic,[14] and it is true that genuinely pornographic films aim at titillating and exciting viewers, while Clark's panoramas of teen sexuality tend to disgust and shock. His displays of sexual activity are unusually clinical and usually without passion or love.

The final film I will discuss is Clark's 2006 *Wassup Rockers*, which explores the world of young Latino skateboarders deeply immersed in punk rock culture. Using first-time actors who he discovered while they were skateboarding in Venice Beach, California, the film opens with a split-screen fetish of the film's central character, fourteen-year-old Jonathan (Jonathan Velasquez), who describes his life and friends. The scene cuts to Jonathan and a cute young Latino woman in bed where the girl blows bubbles and Jonathan playfully punctures them with his lips, as the two engage in playful bubble gum sex.

Wassup Rockers stays on the surface as it depicts hostile relations with neighborhood African Americans, racist cops, and stereotypes of Beverly Hills denizens who they encounter in a day's skateboarding excursion to the up-scale Los Angles community. It's almost as if Clark's purpose was to exploit the bodies of young skateboarders and to show the Latino skaters getting it on with Beverley Hills chicks, rather than exploring their lives and social milieu.

Larry Clark emerges as a genuinely exploitative filmmaker. Just as the conventional genre of exploitation films exploit sex and violence for a profit, so does Clark exploit youth sexuality, drug subcultures, and a panorama of broken lives to make his "art films." Indeed, Clark's is an auteur cinema with a consistent style, vision, view of the world, and obsessive thematic explorations, enabling a French critic to exclaim that Larry Clark is "un artiste essential de la scène américaine."[15] A Larry Clark film guarantees orgies of teen sexuality with half or fully unclothed bodies, flaccid and erect penises, crotch and ass shots galore (Clark is an equal opportunity exploiter of guys and girls alike), and every imaginable form of raw sexuality (and some you might never have thought of). The main source of energy in Clark films is teen libido run amok; otherwise, his teens are empty and listless, vacant and mindless bodies for Clark to photograph in a style consistent from his first volumes of photography.

Hence, Clark is a prime exploiter of youth as objects of voyeurism and fetishism, portraying again and again youth involved in casual sex, heavy drug use, and committing petty and ultraviolent crime, including murder. Often the teens are drugged out through excessive substance abuse, although there are a few scenes with energetic skateboarding, seemingly the only expressive outlet of life energies that Clark allows in his epics of dissolution and hopelessness. For Clark, youth *are* a social problem with unruly bodies that refuse discipline, who waste away in casual sex and hard drugs, easily falling into a life of crime, and thus being a major menace to adults and to society. Clark's teens are completely asocial and nihilistic, where the only value advocated is having sex, surely a dirty old man's fantasy that teens are an ever-available and willing sexual object. Clark's lost and vacant teens have no role models, no nurturing parents, no inspiring school teachers, and no community to help them mature. In Clark's nihilistic Teen Wasteland, there are no possibilities, no hope, and no future.

Further, Clark takes no responsibility for providing any guidance or positive paths for his teens and instead leads them down the path of destruction as surely as Nazis led Jews to the death-camps. Clark's cinema is Thanatopic, governed by instincts of destruction and death, leading nowhere as his broken and wasted young lives proceed to their inevitable fall.

In addition to adults such as Clark and others who depict youth cultures negatively and exploit the lives of youth in cinematic form and narratives, since the 1960s there have been many young directors of variable genders, races, and social types who have attempted to present their own representations of youth, as I indicate earlier. While Clark's representations are utterly despicable and prejudicial, the youth films of Richard Linklater, by contrast, often mock and satirize the worlds of conventional middle-class life and bourgeois ideology, just as Kevin Smith's films mock the structures of alienated labor and in *Dogma* (1999) organized religion. Youth films by women, gays and lesbians, and people of culture explore subcultures and give voice to experiences often excluded from mainstream cinema. Thus, it is up to future generations of youth to overcome the limitations in the politics of representation of gender, race, class, sexuality, and age, and to provide more empowering representations and narratives to guide the youth of the future.

NOTES

1. For an overview of the war on youth in Hollywood film, see Henry Giroux *Breaking in to the movies*. Malden, Mass.: Blackwell, 2002.
2 On media culture and Hollywood film as contested terrains, see Douglas Kellner, *Media culture. Cultural studies, identity and politics between the modern and the postmodern*. London and New York: Routledge, 1995, and *Cinema wars: Hollywood film and politics in the Bush/Cheney era*. Malden, Mass. and UK: Blackwell, 2010.
3. See Karl Marx and Friedrich Engels, *The Marx-Engels reader*. New York: Norton, 1978.

4. On the exploitation film, see Brett Wood and Felicia Feaster, *Forbidden fruit: The golden age of the exploitation film*. New York: Midnight Marquee Press, 1999.

5. On the social construction of youth and stages and forms of contemporary youth culture, see Steven Best and Douglas Kellner, "Contemporary youth and the postmodern adventure," *The Review of Education/ Pedagogy/Cultural Studies*, Vol. 25, No. 2 (April–June 2003): 75–93.

6. On Hollywood and youth culture films, see Douglas Kellner and Michael Ryan, *Camera politica: The politics and ideology of contemporary Hollywood film*. Bloomington, Ind.: Indiana University Press, 1988, and Peter Biskind, *Easy rider, raging bulls*. New York: Simon and Schuster, 1998.

7. See Kellner and Ryan and Biskind, *op. cit.*

8. On the return of the Hollywood studio system and rise of blockbuster cinema, see Thomas Schatz, *The genius of the system*. Minneapolis, Minn.: University of Minnesota Press, 2010 (revised edition).

9. For discussions of many of these films, see Kellner, *Media culture*, op. cit.

10. See Giroux 2002.

11. Independent cinema is explored in Peter Biskind, *Down and dirty pictures*. New York: Simon and Schuster, 2004 and Yannis Tzioumakis, *American independent cinema: An introduction*. Rutgers, NJ: Rutgers University Press.

12. See the Internet Movie Database at http://www.imdb.com/name/ nm0164187/ (accessed December 25, 2009).

13. Information on the film is derived from the Internet Movie Database entries on *Ken Park* at http://www.imdb.com/title/tt0209077/ (accessed December 25, 2009).

14. See Matt Day, "Exclusive Interview with Larry Clark," December 17, 2008 at http://www.imdb.com/title/tt0209077/externalreviews (accessed December 25, 2009).

15. Yannic Vély, "Nos annees sauvage," at http://archive.filmdeculte.com/ film/film.php?id=644 (accessed December 25, 2009).

10

SIXTEEN AND PREGNANT: MEDIA MOMMY TRACKING AND HOLLYWOOD'S EXPLOITATION OF TEEN PREGNANCY

Caroline K. Kaltefleiter

Juno: I'm pregnant.
Leah: Honest to Blog? Maybe it's just a food baby.
Juno: This is no food baby Leah. I've taken like three pregnancy tests.
  And I'm forshizz up the spout!

Juno MacGuff, in Juno (2007)

The recent teenage baby boom in the United States has provided rich material for writers, producers, and directors in Hollywood. While teenage pregnancy is not a new issue, media preoccupation with teenage girls having babies has reached new heights in the last few years, thanks in part to media coverage of celebrity teen moms such as Jamie Lynn Spears and Bristol Palin, as well as the release of films such as *Knocked Up* (2007) and *Juno* (2007). The construction of teen pregnancy experiences on the big screen converts to a commodification of teen pregnancy on the small screen, one that often overlooks intersections of race and class and divisions of Otherness in making a choice to have baby. The reality television show *The Baby Borrowers* capitalizes on the experiences of five diverse teenage couples—ages 18 to 20, fast-tracking them to adulthood by having them set up a home and become parents—even for a short time. MTV's hit program *16 and Pregnant* is a "Real World" experience of teen pregnancy. The fictional/reality-based representation of teen parenthood is underscored with a statistical rise in the U.S. teen birthrate after fifteen years of decline.

The United States has the highest teen pregnancy rate in the industrialized world, and it rose considerably during George W. Bush's
presidency (McCreal, 2009). According to the Centers for Disease
Control in Atlanta, Georgia, one-third of girls in the United States
get pregnant before the age of twenty. The National Campaign to
Prevent Teen and Unplanned Pregnancy states there are "750,000
teen pregnancies annually. Eight in ten of these pregnancies are unintended and 81 percent are to unmarried teens" (Teenpregnancy.org,
2009). Across the country, stories of "Babies having babies is an issue
in the spotlight—especially in light of recent data showing that the
nation's teen birth rate has risen for the first time in 15 years" (Aasen,
2008). News of pregnancy pacts taking place at high schools across
the United States set off a media frenzy in the summer of 2008 when
it was reported that seventeen girls at Glouchester High School in
Massachusetts were expecting babies—more than four times the
number of pregnancies at the 1,200-student school from the previous
year (Kingsbury, 2008).

Dallas Morning News journalist Erik Aasen reports "Texas has the
highest birth rate in the nation" (2008: p. 1). The National Campaign
to Prevent Teen Pregnancy notes that the number of teen pregnancies for girls ages 15 to 19 in Texas is just over 80,000 cases, with a
profound number of girls of color pregnant between the ages of 15
and 19. Hispanic girls comprised nearly half of the teen pregnancies
at 43,000 cases (Teenpregnancy.org, 2009). While these numbers
may be startling to some, as I reflect on my experiences growing up
and attending high school in the city of Amarillo, Texas, the escalation of teen pregnancies in the Lone Star state comes as no surprise,
particularly in West Texas. The Texas Panhandle area has one of the
highest teenage pregnancy rates in the United States (Galvez-Myles
and Myles, 2005). The city of Amarillo lies in two counties and is
considered urban and has a population of over 185,000. Amarillo is
often described as a big small town, a glimmering rhinestone on the
infamous Bible Belt. Amarillo's claim to fame includes the Cadillac
Ranch, American Quarter Horse Association, and Pantex, the government facility known to be the final assembly point for nuclear
weapons in the United States. Amarillo is also known to have a significant migrant worker population, many of whom come from Mexico
and countries in Central America. Pregnancy rates for Hispanic and
Latina girls are among the highest in the entire state. Like many rural
towns or cities, young people in Amarillo rely on each other to keep
themselves occupied. My salvation from tumbleweeds, dust storms,
tornado warnings, and ethereal boredom was my high school debate

team. I spent most of my weekends traveling to speech tournaments across Texas and the southwestern United States. Traveling beyond the Amarillo city limits gave me a perspective that many of my peers did not have, that a young girl could have a life beyond graduating high school (or college), getting married, and having kids—or vice versa.

Twenty years after I left the Texas Panhandle, youth are still cruising the Sonic Drive-In and looking for random "hook-ups," real and now digital—a scene played out every weekend in many towns and cities across the United States. When they are not cruising old Route 66 and getting their kicks or gameboys/gamegirls off, they are watching shows like *My Super Sweet 16, Gossip Girl, The Hills,* and of course MTV's *16 and Pregnant.* Last summer, I went home for a visit and was struck by the number of pregnant teen girls I passed in parks, shopping malls, movie theaters, and even a western riding ring that I used to frequent as a teen. I was astonished by the ways in which these girls, many of whom were girls of color, prominently displayed their pregnancy. Traveling in groups, they sported cool maternity clothes, and one girl wore a t-shirt that read, "Pregnant and Proud." These girls represented a new girl clique— "it's cool to be pregnant."

Using cultural and textual analysis, this essay examines teen culture and the phenomenon of media-cultivated experiences of teen parenthood. This chapter incorporates the ongoing discussions of dissolving a feminist "wave" discourse in conjunction with recent debates in the academy over the divide between women's studies and girls' studies. Constructions of girlhood in popular culture and mass media, and the ways such representations affect young women in global contexts are central to understanding girls and their roles in contemporary society. Films such as *The Education of Shelby Knox* (2005) and *Juno* are examined in relation to the exploitation of teen sexuality and sexually transmitted diseases as well as teenage pregnancy. Attention will be given to deconstructing a dominant ideology of sex education and dismantling myths of teen motherhood while at the same time analyzing late capitalist interests in creating and sustaining a teen mom market articulated in television programs like *16 and Pregnant* and the *Baby Borrowers.*

SONIC YOUTH: SHELBY KNOX AND SEX EDUCATION IN TEXAS

If you want me I will be the one
That is always good.

And you'll love me too.
But you'll never know
What I feel inside.
That I am bad troubled little girl
Remember Mother?
We were very close,
Very, very close.

Troubled Little Girl, Sonic Youth,
Washing Machine, 1995, Geffen Records

Despite aggressive campaigns to curb teen pregnancy by the Texas Teen Prevention Coalition, statistics for the Texas Panhandle show a rise in the number of teen pregnancies over the last five years. The Texas Department of Health reported, "The teen pregnancy rate increased in 2007 for the second time in three years" (Pittman, 2009). Teen pregnancy rates include births, fetal deaths, and abortions for female residents of the county ages 13 to 17. "Potter County in Amarillo has one of the highest rates in the state with 41.9 per 1000 teenage girls getting pregnant each year (Ibid.).

Teen pregnancy isn't the only youth social issue gaining attention in the Texas Panhandle. In Lubbock, a city known for Texas Tech University, Buddy Holly, and Natalie Maines, the lead singer of the Dixie Chicks who publicly opposed the Iraq War, Maines's comments put the band in the national media spotlight as "activists" and subsequently jeopardized their music careers. In the midst of the Iraq War and celebrities and pop icons, a teenage girl named Shelby Knox emerged in the spotlight as a "sex ed" activist when she and members of the Lubbock Youth Commission spoke out against the "abstinence only" sexual education program in the Lubbock city schools. Knox and her peers decided to take on the abstinence-only sex education policy after it was reported that Lubbock had the highest rates of sexually transmitted infections (STIs) in the nation. (Knox, 2006: p. 75). Due to her activism, Knox became the target of discrimination at school. According to Knox, "My teachers received a letter with a warning about my disruptive activities and soon my hall pass privileges were revoked. Some teachers shunned me or made rude comments, while others offered quiet support and encouragement" (Knox, 2006: p. 77).

Knox and the Lubbock Youth Commission argued for a comprehensive sex education program that would be taught in all health classes. They wanted certified public health officials who would present diverse perspectives to all health education classes, and the establishment of an advisory board to guide the sex education program. The work of the Lubbock Youth Commission yielded a hearing before the

Lubbock City School Board that can only be summarized as a gesture of polite civility. Knox and her peers were accorded five minutes to present their entire proposal. As Knox put it,

> I presented our agenda to a sea of blank faces. I knew from the time I began speaking that they had already made up their minds. They listened politely and then dismissed the concerns of every student in the district. Two months later, the city cut the funding of the Lubbock Youth Commission, claiming it was not intended to be an activist group. (Knox, 2006: p. 77)

Through informal dialogues, the youth commission raised awareness about teen pregnancy and STIs, and garnered local and national media attention. Knox notes, "I never knew the extent of the misinformation floating around the halls of my high school until my efforts became fodder for the evening news" (Ibid.).

The Shelby Knox story not only drew headlines of network news programs, but also caught the attention of producers for MTV's *Fight for Your Rights Campaign*. MTV producers seized the moment of controversy in Lubbock, Texas, and turned its cameras on the struggle for comprehensive sex education, yielding high ratings and a profit for the network. As Knox notes, "Our partnership with MTV led to a large forum and a half-hour television special about the problems in Lubbock" (Knox, 2006: p. 76). The MTV *Fight for Your Rights Campaign* programs had become the equivalent of the ABC *After School* special of the 1970s. In both situations real social problems are taken out of context and glamorized by co-opting the real experiences of young men and women. The MTV *Fight for Your Rights Campaign* served as a foundation for a social marketing contest that also served as a promotional tool for the band *Good Charlotte*. In 2003, MTV announced the launch of "Protect Yourself with Good Charlotte, "a national sex ed contest designed to bring crucial sexual health information to a community in need and to educate and empower young people on their top issue of personal concern: sexual health.

The Lubbock sex education story also became the subject of a documentary film *The Education of Shelby Knox*, produced by Marion Lipschutz and Rose Rosenblatt. The film chronicles the journey of a teenage girl (Knox) and her pursuit of truth, freedom, and information about sex education for teens. While the filmmakers may be well intentioned in their coverage of teen pregnancy and abstinence-only programs, Knox's experience as a teenage activist is co-opted by the filmmakers, who ultimately chose to premiere their film at Sundance. No longer an alternative film festival, Sundance is known as one of the must-make festivals for both feature and documentary films. Unlike Slam Dance—a festival known for its anarchist tendencies organized by filmmakers for filmmakers or other independent festivals—Sundance courts media moguls, film entrepreneurs, agents, distributors, and of course celebrities. The focus of Sundance is less on the art, image, and issues of the films, but rather on the profitability of such texts and the commodification of personal narratives. In the case of Shelby Knox, the film leaves the realities and aftermath of experiences of teen pregnancy and sexually transmitted diseases in the dust of West Texas. The filmmakers arrange for Shelby to leave her hometown of Lubbock on a national tour to promote the film and to speak about sex education.

In 2008 at a conference in New Haven, Connecticut, I had a chance to hear Shelby Knox speak and to talk with her in a session on girls and sex education activism. In this session, she admitted to becoming a celebrity (e.g., the "sex-ed" girl") from the film. She acknowledged that the film's core issues—abstinence-only programs, STIs, and teen pregnancy—may have been eclipsed by her own struggles wherein Knox deals with devout Baptist parents and her Christian beliefs. In fact, the film depicts Shelby participating in a purity ceremony in which her parents place a purity ring on their daughter's finger. Knox and other participants pledge abstinence until marriage. The scene features Wayson Gerweig, founder of the Family Values Coalition. Shelby is seen throughout the film battling Gerweig and local politicians in her fight for a comprehensive sex education program. Such scenes create confusion and tension for viewers of the film as they attempt to decipher the real Shelby Knox.

Christian politics associated with the Shelby Knox story went beyond Lubbock, Texas—all the way to the halls of Congress. Funding for the film *The Education of Shelby Knox* (2005) became an issue when the Corporation for Public Broadcasting came under fire as part of a Republican investigation that reviewed a small post-production grant that the filmmakers (Lipschutz and Rosenblatt) got from the Playboy Foundation. The grant helped them complete and broadcast their film on the Public Broadcast System documentary show, *Point of View* (POV). On July 11, 2005, twenty-eight House conservatives sent a letter to Corporation for Public Broadcasting Chairman Kenneth Tomlinson, who resigned in November 2005, asking for detailed information regarding Playboy Foundation contributions to the PBS film, *The Education of Shelby Knox*. According to the letter, "The Playboy Foundation had funded a small number of film companies, including Cine Qua Non, which produced *The Education of Shelby Knox*." The letter goes on to state the conflict of interest inherent with PBS and sources of funding for the film. The film was funded in part by the taxpayers and by the Playboy Foundation. Members of the congressional committee wrote,

> It is obvious to us why the Playboy Foundation would have a financial interest to funding what amounts to "promiscuity propaganda," given that its founder has NOT made his millions promoting abstinence until marriage. What is less obvious is why PBS an organization that associates itself with "Big Bird and "Sesame Street" and recently represented itself to Congress as promoting family programming, would team up with the Playboy Foundation." (Letter to PBS, 2005)

In response, PBS and the Playboy Foundation defended *its* decision to fund filmmakers Lipschutz and Rosenblatt, noting that postproduction grants were given in the amounts of 5,000 to 10,000 dollars. They stressed such grants were used in the final rendering and editing process, not for the conceptualization, research, or narrative-gathering processes. The Playboy Foundation situated its interests in funding projects such as *The Education of Shelby Knox* within a framework of free speech and social change, endeavors articulated in their mission statement,

> "[T]o pursue, perpetuate and protect the principles of freedom and democracy." The Playboy Foundation seeks to foster social change by confining its grants and other support to projects of national impact and scope involved in fostering open communication about, and research into, human sexuality, reproductive health and rights; protecting and fostering civil rights and civil liberties in the United States for all people, including women, people affected and impacted by HIV/AIDS, gays and lesbians, racial minorities, the poor and the disadvantaged; and eliminating censorship and protecting freedom of expression. (Playboy Foundation, 2009)

In all, The *Shelby Knox* story represents a complex text of analysis wherein comprehensive sexual education programs are neither fully accepted nor rejected but rather used as a tool of exploitation by a number of parties. The Lubbock School Board squashed her proposal, but the information shared within the text of various media outlets pervaded the Lubbock community. Moreover, major television networks such as ABC, NBC, and MTV descended upon the West

Texas cattle town and created programming that capitalized on the statistical reality that Lubbock had the highest rate of sexually transmitted infections and teenage pregnancies in the nation. MTV took the whole phenomenon to a new level by incorporating the Lubbock epidemic into its *Fight for Your Rights Campaign*, which served as a means to promote both its own programming as well as artist representation and music sales of the band *Good Charlotte*. Meanwhile, elected officials in the Lubbock community got free media time and attention that allowed them to underscore issues they deemed important, not related to comprehensive sex education.

The Christian politics of the Lubbock School Board and members of the Republican Conservative Caucus sought to use the *Education of Shelby Knox* film as a means to attack the Corporation for Public Broadcasting and to eliminate CPB funding all together, based on the network's decision to include programming that caucus members deemed controversial and promoted "promiscuity." Meanwhile, the documentary filmmakers of *The Education of Shelby Knox* also cashed in on the STI and teen pregnancy epidemics in Lubbock. Taking their cues from MTV, their film uses "Real World"–style video and creates a cinema verite that glosses over the everyday life experiences of the teenagers whose lives are affected by abstinence-only sex education pr programs. The narratives of those teenagers affected by the realities of STIs and teen pregnancy are overshadowed by the camera's focus on the main subject, Shelby Knox, activist turned celebrity, whose experience and understanding of these issues remains at a distance, pushing those teens in need into blurred images and distorted realities.

THE JUNO EFFECT

Can't we just kick it old school. I could just put the baby in a basket and send it your way. You know like Moses and the reeds.

Juno MacGuff, *Juno* (2007)

Film critics and media theorists often refer to *Juno* as the little (girl) film that could and did deliver—controversies and profits.[1] *Juno* is a comedy-drama that follows the daily life of the title character who is an independent-minded teenage girl confronting the realities of an unplanned pregnancy and subsequent events that locate her in an existential sphere somewhere between girlhood and womanhood. The text situates sexual desire, biological possibilities, and social responses to girls' engagement in sexual intercourse, and allows for negotiated readings of sexuality choices confronting girls/women today. Jessica Willis (2008) points out that, "The cinematic production of *Juno* stirred a variety of social responses in relation to youth, sex, and sexuality" (p. 1). A number of studies and criticisms of *Juno* charge that the film is regressive for its disregard of teenage sexuality, minimal consideration of abortion, and its breezy handling of teenage pregnancy (Hoberman, 2008; Edelstein, 2008).

Prior cultural analyses and media reports of *Juno* have focused primarily on dominant cultural discourses of femininity associated with young women and their sexual subjectivity, (Hoberman 2008; Edelstein, 2008; Willis, 2008). The press even evoked the film in its 2008 coverage of the purported pregnancy pact of seventeen girls in Gloucester, Massachusetts, by referring to the "Juno Effect" as a means to explain the alarming rise in the number of unplanned pregnancies in that New England town (Kingsbury, 2008). *Juno* serves as an example of the ways in which adolescent female sexuality is conceptualized in Western popular culture. The film foregrounds girls' sexual agency within a new aesthetic of girlhood and integrates a politics of transgression wherein girls are agents of change and power.

The journey of Juno MacGuff is open to many interpretations and readings. Comments about the film vary from embracing the film to disavowing it. As one viewer comments, "I found the film's handling of the pregnancy deeply moving. Juno is not a victim. She is a fiercely intelligent girl who makes her decision based on her own values and ethics...(*New York Times* Reader Reviews, 12/27/2007). Meanwhile another viewer writes,

> There's a subtle suggestion here that getting pregnant is Juno's fault and her problem to fix it. Add to this the negative light shed on the possibility of abortion and you've got a pro-life movie masquerading as the newest cool thing. I'm not a bra-burning feminist, but am truly disgusted to havesat in a theatre packed full of people my age that weren't even parsing the messages that were being thrown at them. I know everyone's going to jump on me for saying it, but to me, "Juno" is not clever. It's not charming and politically incorrect; it's disempowering to women. (*New York Times* Reader Reviews 12/27/2007)

Such comments illustrate how the film offers competing readings in and out of the text, and calls to mind Stuart Hall's work on encoding and decoding texts. Hall (1980) emphasizes that texts through every moment in the process of communication, allow for active message composition (encoding) and message reception (decoding).

The message continuum, "from the original composition of the message/code (encoding) to the point at which it is read and understood (decoding), has its own determinants and conditions of existence" (1980, p. 129). Just as the construction of the message/code is an active, interpretive, and social event, so is the moment of reception. Hall identifies three primary positions of decoding messages and signs, including the dominant position or "preferred" reading, the "negotiated" position, and the "oppositional" position/reading.

In the case of *Juno*, the teenage pregnancy code becomes not only the main storyline, but also filters into a dominant reading of the film as one of pro-life. Readers/viewers whose social situations, particularly social class, align with dominant readings of the film are articulated in the vignettes documenting Juno's choices about her body, her baby, and her life, including one scene in which she is shown fleeing a neighborhood abortion clinic called *Women Now*. At the clinic, Juno runs into a classmate named Su-Chin who is a pro-life activist. Su-Chin, an Asian girl wearing square-framed glasses, is shown standing alone out front of the clinic, waving a placard that features an enlarged picture of an infant. The text on the sign reads: "NO BABIES LIKE MURDER!" Meanwhile, Su-Chin chants, "All babies just want to get borned (sic)!" The two girls exchange pleasantries and commiserate about finishing a paper for a teacher and then Su-Chin tells Juno, "Your baby probably has a beating heart, you know? It can feel pain, and it has fingernails." Juno replies, "Fingernails? Really?" (Halfron, L. Malkovich, J. Novick, M. et. al. Directors, *Juno, 2007*). Su-Chin's pro-life rant about fingernails, combined with a subsequent montage scene of girls tapping their nails in the clinic waiting room, serves to persuade Juno to abort her mission to terminate her pregnancy. The sequence ends with Juno rushing out of the clinic and past Su-Chin, who yells, "God appreciates your miracle" (Halfron, L. Malkovich, J. Novick, M. et. al. Directors, *Juno, 2007*). This sequence effectively silences further discussion and contemplation of abortion as a viable option for Juno, or for young girls period.

The obstacles and moral dilemmas that Juno encounters as a pregnant teen allow audiences to see a girl whose multilayered persona articulates a sense of new emerging formulations and negotiations of postmodern girlhood that is co-opted by the filmmakers so as to appeal to as many perspectives as possible. A. O. Scott (2007) notes that the film is neither pro-choice nor pro-life, but rather pro-adulthood. The existential experience of pregnancy becomes a location in which to tell a story about teenagers growing up too fast and adults who don't want to grow up at all. As Jessica Willis (2008) suggests, "Juno exists between childhood and adulthood, neither sexless nor parental, neither completely innocent nor entirely beyond redemption" (p. 242). Kimya Dawson, lead singer for the band *Moldy Peaches*, whose music is featured throughout the film comments,

> Regardless of the choice that is made by Juno, it is the fact that she has a choice that matters. Choice is still choice if the choice is [abort or adopt] or to keep the baby. I like that Juno is a strong girl, and the film is not so much about the social structure of high school, but her own sense of being of a girl. She reminds of my friends. (Arens, 2007)

Dawson articulates the fluidity of being a girl and negotiating life choices while director Jason Reitman capitalizes on the spaces between girlhood and adulthood, and exploits the essence of teen pregnancy by cloaking teen pregnancy in hip clothes, cool dialogue, and an alternative music track. Juno's dialogue hails from the digital landscape, a national teen-speak that has been enabled by Facebook, the Internet, texting, and blogging—language that authentically connects with today's youth. As one viewer put it, "Juno sounds just like so many of my 18 to 22 year children's friends who are a wonderful combination of smart and cynical, but deeply hopeful and idealistic under the too cool veneer (*New York Times* Reader Reviews, 12/28/2007). Such communication and participatory action demonstrates a state of postmodern girlhood wherein girls are engaged in changing cultural conceptions of "girls" and utilize aspects of performance to (re)envision gender roles in society. Juno's transient state of existence as a pregnant teen destabilizes both girlhood and motherhood, as is illustrated in the scene when her father, upon learning that she is pregnant, says, "Juno, I thought you were the kind of girl who knew how to say when." Juno replies, "I don't really know what kind of girl I am." (Halfron, L. Malkovich, J. Novick, M. et. al. Directors, *Juno, 2007*).

Ultimately *Juno is* an amalgamation of girl identities blended together for cultural consumption and (re)production in which teen pregnancy becomes cool, leading to the production of teen media, products, and accessories that capitalize on teen pregnancy, produced in a vacuum void of concrete issues and experiences related to teen pregnancy. Consider the "Pregnant and Proud" t-shirt I mentioned at the beginning of this article. The shirt was produced in a retro-seventies–style graphic with an intertextual reference to the "Hello Kitty" signature pink script produced by Sanrio. This shirt embodies the existential space between girlhood and adulthood by relegating teen pregnancy to a fashion accessory or fad, obscuring the adult realities of raising a child. According to Jane Brown, who runs the Teen Media Project at the University of North Carolina, "What's missing in the media's sexual script is what happens before and after. Why are these kids getting pregnant and what happens to them after?" (Kliff, 2008).

CANDY GIRL: SWEET SIXTEEN AND PREGNANT

While Jamie Lynn Spears, Juno, and now Bristol Palin are celebrated as media heroines, stories of real teen moms are being captured, marketed, and translated to the teen market on television shows like *The Secret Life of the American Teenager, Baby Borrowers*, and MTV's *16 and Pregnant*. According to research conducted by the National Campaign to Prevent Teen and Unwanted Pregnancy, " shows like *16 and Pregnant* and *Secret Life* are the kinds of shows that teens want to see: three quarters say they would like the media more about the consequences of sex" (Kliff, 2008: p. 1). Some media critics suggest that these topics can be risky for Hollywood producers and purveyors of celebrity magazines. "There's the entertainment value that may be at stake, lectures on condoms, don't exactly sell blockbuster films" (Kliff, 2008: p. 2). Some producers and writers want to avoid the controversy over abstinence-only programs or teen abortion storylines. Amidst the teen pregnancy media craze emerges a show like the *Baby Borrowers* on NBC whose slogan is "It's not TV; it's birth control." The *Baby Borrowers'* television experiment resembles a high school home economics project where young women and men are teamed up to care for an inanimate object such as an egg or a realist doll programmed to cry, urinate, and defecate just as a real baby would—only on reality television the doll is a real baby and there is no "easy bake" oven or easy answers to coping with this alternative reality. *Newsweek* magazine points out that the program attracted nearly 8 million viewers to its debut, or three times the viewership of *Secret Life* on the ABC network Family Channel (Kliff, 2008). The storyline throughout of all these shows equates to a hot plot device—teen gets pregnant, teen is horrified, and teen tells her family/boyfriend.

MTV's *16 and Pregnant* builds upon the pageantry of the network's hit programs *My Super Sweet Sixteen* and the video verite of the *Real World* coupled with stylistic borrowings from the box office smash hit film *Juno*. The indie-kid style of *Juno* incorporates a digital teen tech-speak that is juxtaposed against a backdrop of whimsical acoustic music to create a low-fi (fidelity) aesthetic to the film. The celluloid image blends into an animated representation of Juno and serves to articulate an existential presence between girlhood and womanhood. Meanwhile, the credits, handwritten with black marker that outlines bold primary colors with crayon strokes, create a sign system that connotes a childlike quality, one that resembles the layout and design of homemade zines, with cut-out images pasted on the page/screen.

The opening of *16 and Pregnant* resembles the title sequence of *Juno* and articulates an aesthetics of high school, reified in notebook doodles and zine layouts by teenage girls. Zines are crudely produced magazines, a mixture of cutout images and writing, arranged on a page by a computer or handwritten, photocopied, and stapled—actions that epitomize a do-it-yourself culture and form of communication. The free flow of expression and a do-it-yourself (DIY) sensibility is reified in the nonlinear layout, revision marks, and grammar contradictions. Black Sharpie marker pens are tools of choice in the bricolage of zine writing and production.[2] The pen is used to underscore words of importance and strike through original texts, while allowing the reader to see the original thought pattern and (r)evolution of one's ideas, or in the case of *16 and Pregnant* each girl's pregnancy. In each episode of *16 and Pregnant,* MTV's "Real World" signature style blends video of the pregnant teen girls into animated images outlined in black Magic Markers.

The first episode features a young woman named Maci. The opening sequence includes a close-up shot of a spiral notebook that features her name crudely drawn in thick black letters as well as other spontaneous drawings or doodles all over the front of the notebook. The episode progresses to include her boyfriend, Ryan, father of her soon-to-be-born son and the realities of living together before and after their son's birth. As David Zurawik notes, "the power of this documentary comes from MTV's commitment to having the filmmakers live with these kids 24/7—to show their world from the inside out—cinema verite style" (2009: p. 1).Viewers become voyeurs of the couple's lives. "We see and hear Maci alone in their apartment late at night while her boyfriend is out playing around with his friends. It is a devastating image of loneliness, fear and isolation" (Zurawik, 2009: p. 2). A sense of desolation is heightened when the celluloid image of Maci rocking the baby dissolves into an animated version of herself, one that charts the existential space between adulthood and girlhood.

The production technique of fading from video images to animated representations is used throughout each episode of MTV's *16 and Pregnant* to mark the end of each segment and to segue to a commercial break. Moreover, the whimsical marks on the two-dimensional notebook page/screen create a point of entry for MTV and its advertisers to connect with the teen demographic. Not surprising, brands are pouring money into TV campaigns, viral videos, social marketing, and Facebook ads to catch the attention of today's youth. Teen pregnancy is a hot issue that corporations such as Candies, the women's shoe company, are cashing in on under the guise of social marketing campaigns with high-profile ambassadors like Bristol Palin. The Candies Foundation was launched in 2001 with the mission "to educate America's youth about the devastating consequences of teen pregnancy" (Candies Foundation, 2009). The foundation's campaign includes celebrities such as Jenny McCarthy, Beyonce, and Ashlee Simpson in their public service announcements, media content, and social marketing. Their current Public Service Announcement (PSA) campaign "Wake Up America" premiered during the television show *Gossip Girl* and features former Playboy model Jenny McCarthy busting in on a teen couple about to "get it on" in the back seat of a car. A Candies Foundation spokesperson Neil Cole announces the tagline, "Just because you're wearing high-heeled sexy shoes doesn't mean you should have a baby." The emphasis is on "high heeled shoes." The ad contributes to a disingenuous form of communication with today's youth about teen pregnancy and privileges late capitalism in which teen pregnancy becomes an umbrella issue to incorporate globalized markets and mass consumption of Candies shoes for young women. The ad does little to offer support for pregnant teens or to promote self-protection. Most young women who viewed the PSA reacted negatively to the aesthetics, content, and overall message of the ad. As one online respondent put it,

> The ad doesn't choose sides in the abstinence versus contraceptive debate; it just presents pregnancy as consequence of sex. This tactic might scare teens, but the ad won't succeed without a viable solution to this fear. Candies needs to advocate a method of protection instead of preaching that if you have sex you'll get pregnant. (Issendorf, 2008)

Another young woman reacted to the irony of the Candies campaign. She writes,

> So Candies, a shoe manufacturer, now has Jenny McCarthy and Bristol Palin on board to denounce teenage pregnancy. Oh Thank God, the

moral fiber of our community has spoken out about what causes teenage pregnancy: sexy shoes. (Candies website 2009)

The Candies Foundation website also sends teen girls mixed messages about their bodies, sexuality, and teen pregnancy. As one young
woman writes about the website, "The first thing to catch my eye are
images of lovely Jamie Lynn, a poised Bristol with her then boyfriend
Levi, and four teenage girls, two with pregnant bellies, on a carefree
stroll" (Ibid.). The scene on the website bares a striking resemblance
to the group of girls I witnessed in Texas last summer—acting as
if being pregnant is no big deal—their front bump is another fashion accessory as is their "Pregnant and Proud" t-shirt or the Candies
shoes on their feet.

Conclusion

Research suggests that girls, especially girls of color, are reaching
puberty at earlier ages. (Shane, 2008). Hormones are kicking in well
before tween/teen girls have the emotional maturity, life experience,
or education to handle their sexuality and certainly a teen pregnancy.
The trend of marketing makeup, sexy lingerie, spa days, and dress-up
maternity clothes for pre-pubescent and teen girls is accentuated with
teen mom celebrities. Media brokers recognize the sexual insecurity
of girls today and capitalize on their experiences by sending mixed
messages about being a teen mom.

Sophisticated media production techniques demonstrated in films
like *Juno* and MTV's *16 and Pregnant* tap into the media psyche of
today's teens by using animated sequences to blur the lines between
childhood and adulthood. The digital flow in the animation process
combines elements of zine making and independent music making,
with layers of distortion and low-fidelity sound to advance the character
development of a teen mom. The fusion of celluloid images with hand-
drawn illustrations of pregnant teens constitutes an amalgamation of
girl identities that serves to break down codes of reality and give way to
a (post)modern girl. The produced image obscures (dissimulates) and
threatens to displace the authentic experience of teen pregnancy so as to
create interspatial representation of a girl-infused motherhood. As such,
pregnant teen girls are glamorized and are molded as a new marketing
niche to be capitalized on by not only maternity-related businesses,
but also companies eager to be seen as raising awareness about teen
pregnancy—with, of course, the hope of reaching this demographic
and selling their wares—such as the Candies shoe company.

Media companies such as Music Television, BET, and Hollywood film production companies are crucial to advancing this new teen girl identity. Producers and filmmakers repackage the teen pregnancy dilemma as a teen drama with a plotline that emphasizes the good girl/bad girl dichotomy with a new twist: Teens getting pregnant bad. Teens having babies good—equated as more profit and attention for media companies, advertisers, and celebrities. Bristol Palin is accorded celebrity status for her actions (getting pregnant) while at the same time she tells girls not to make the same mistake she made. Documentary films such as *The Education of Shelby Knox* or social marketing campaigns such as Candies "Wake Up America" give lip service to the issues of sexually transmitted infections or teen pregnancy without opening up a concerted dialogue about sexuality in American culture. In the end, the dismantling of myths associated with teen pregnancy requires us to not only acknowledge the media's role in the production of such representations, but also to create open communication about sexuality in our culture, to offer informative sex education classes, and to teach teens to be comfortable and confident with their sexuality while at the same time being in control of it.

NOTES

1. Juno originated as an independent film and went on to gain recognition among Hollywood movie elites as well as North American mainstream audiences and received four Oscar nominations. The film was budgeted for 6.5 million dollars and earned back its initial investment in twenty days and ultimately grossed nearly 150 million dollars in the United States and 230 million dollars worldwide (Box office, 2009).
2. For a detailed discussion of zine layout and design, see Alex Wrekk (2002) *Stolen Sharpie revolution*. Microcosm Publishing, Portland, Oregon.

REFERENCES

16 and Pregnant (2009). New York, NY: MTV Networks.

Aasen, E. (2008, January 26). Rising numbers, Hollywood put the spotlight on teen pregnancy. *Dallas Morning News* online edition. http://www.dallasnews.com/sharedcontent/dws/news/localnews/stories/012708dnmetteenmoms.a983de.html

Arens, D. (2007). Hollywood's unplanned baby boom: Waitress, Knocked Up, and Juno." *Works in Progress*

Baby Borrowers (2008). New York: NY: NBC television network.

Candies Foundation (2009). http://www.candiesfoundation.org/

Edelstein, D. (2008, January 22). Oscar nominations: A sad day indeed. *New Yorker*

Galvez-Myles R. & Myles, T. (2005). Teen pregnancy in the Texas Panhandle. *Journal of Rural Health.* Vol. 21. No. 3. 259–262.

Halfron, L. Malkovich, J. Novick, M. et. al. (Directors). (2008). *Juno [Video/ DVD].* California: 20th Century Fox Home Entertainment

Hall, S. (1980). "Encoding and decoding in the television discourse." In S. Hall, *Culture, media, language working papers in cultural studies.* London: Hutchinson.

Hoberman J. (2008, January 15). Gone baby gone: The heroines of 4 Months, 3 weeks and 2 days don't get to play indie-cute. *Village Voice*

Issendorf, L. (2008). Our side of the screen: Candies v. Trojan on preventing teen pregnancy. *Youth Marketing Channel.* Online edition.

Kingsbury, K. (2008, June 18). Pregnancy boom at Glouchester High. *Time.* com. http://www.time.com/time/world/article/0,8599,1815845,00.html

Kliff, S. (2008, July 23). Teen pregnancy Hollywood style. *Newsweek* online edition. http://www.newsweek.com/id/148437

Knox, S. (2006). Tales from the Bible Belt. In *We don't need another wave: dispatches from the next generation of feminists.* Seattle, WA: Seal Press http://www.ypulse.com/wordpress/wordpress/our-side-of-the-screen-candies-v-trojan-on-preventing-teen-pregnancy

Letter to PBS (2005, July 11). Republican Study Committee: Caucus of House Conservatives. http://hensarling.house.gov/RSC/mem_activity2005.shtml

McCreal, C. (2009, July 20). Teen pregnancy and disease rose sharply during Bush years agency finds. *Guardian.co.uk.* http://www.guardian.co.uk/world/2009/jul/20/bush-teen-pregnancy-cdc-report

New York Times Reader Reviews (2007). *New York Times* http://community.nytimes.com/rate review/movies.nytimes.com/movie/356873/Juno/

Pittman, D. (2009, January 16). Teen pregnancies up in Potter. *Amarillo Globe News* online edition. http://www.amarillo.com/stories/011609/new_12304900.shtml.

Playboy Foundation, (2009). http://www.playboyenterprises.com/home/content.

Secret Life of the American Teenager (2008). New York: NY: ABC Family Network.

Scott, A. O. (2007, December 5). "Seek Mr. and Mrs. Right for a baby on the way. *New York Times*

Shane, S. (2008, July 1). Reaching puberty early: environmental factors are putting black girls at risk. *Colorlines Magazine.* Online edition. http://www.encyclopedia.com/doc/1G1-181434546.html

Sonic Youth (1995). Troubled little girl. *Washing Machine.* Geffen Records.

Teenpregnancy.org (2009). http://www.thenationalcampaign.org

Willis, J. (2008). Sexual subjectivity: A semiotic analysis of girlhood, sex, and sexuality in the film Juno. *Sexuality and Culture:* 12 240–256.

Wrekk, A. (2002). *Black Sharpie revolution*. Portland, OR: Microcosm
    Publishing.
Zurawick, D. (2009, June 11). MTV shows harsh world of being 16 and
    pregnant. *Baltimore Sun* online edition. http://weblogs.baltimoresun.
    com/entertainment/zontv/documentaries/

11

ABOUT SCHMIDT AND ABOUT
THE HOLLYWOOD IMAGE
OF AN AGING ACTOR

Karen E. Riggs

Jack Nicholson has become widely known for "playing Jack Nicholson" in Hollywood films, so when he starred in Alexander Payne's 2002 *About Schmidt*, his performance attracted a different sort of critical attention. It is the intent of this chapter, through a close reading of almost 600 message board posts on the IMDB.com fan forum, to show how fans have been communicating online about Nicholson's role in this film over the past several years. Henry Jenkins describes fan message boards as one mode of participatory culture, which he envisions as a function of individuals interacting with each other in a now-convergent media culture according to a set of rules and outcomes that are not completely known to those in the community.[1]

That is certainly the case among the heavily used message boards on the IMDB.com website, where fans create postings that most often do not cite the points of others on the board but seem to serve as a consumer's mode of self-expression. In most cases, fans give little explicit information about their identities, but their rhetoric often creates occasion for inferences about such characteristics as life stage. This chapter aims to show how *About Schmidt* is viewed as a novel representation of aging in film and how Nicholson's performance and his character have remained an occupation of his fans through the seven years since the movie's theatrical release. A brief description of the film's storyline precedes the message board discussion.

The film, based loosely on a novel by Louis Begley, is set in director Payne's hometown, Omaha, Nebraska, itself depicted as a symbolic doppelganger of a bland Midwestern United States.[2] Nicholson plays Warren R. Schmidt, who retires from a bureaucratic job as a life insurance actuary at age 66. At his pro forma retirement dinner, he is so miserable that he leaves the party room and heads for the restaurant bar for a solo drink. Later in the week, his newly minted MBA replacement blows off Warren's attempt to feel that he can still contribute. His one-dimensional wife, Helen, whose very existence irritates him, drops dead soon afterward, and his only child, Jeannie, arrives from Denver for the funeral with her intended husband, Randall, a schemer/loser. Soon, Warren concludes that his life is purposeless and that, according to his actuarial charts, he is destined to die at age 74 with apparently nothing to show for it.

In the midst of all this, Warren sits, rudderless, aimlessly cruising through television channels with his remote control until his attention is captured by the voice of Angela Lansbury hailing him to view pictures of poverty-stricken children in the developing world.[3] Warren gets out his checkbook and his pen. Upon learning that his "adoptive child" is a six-year-old Tanzanian boy named Ndugu, he begins a series of spleen-venting letters, irrationally trying to communicate to this young child his adult feelings and impressions about his new life and the questionable accomplishments in his accrued past. The letters become a plot device as Nicholson narrates them in Warren's voice.

Warren pads dully about a house now filled with empty pizza boxes and other daily detritus. He is unshaven, gray whiskered, and haggard. Finally, missing Helen, he immerses himself in her personal belongings, down to smothering his face in her cold cream in a pitiable attempt to reconnect to her absent self. He stumbles upon a shoebox filled with yellowed love letters that reveal an affair between Helen and his best friend. Devastated, he jumps into the Winnebago that Helen had insisted on buying for their retirement years. He drives toward Denver to surprise Jeannie and, he hopes, stop her from marrying "beneath her." Warren surprises her with a phone call saying he will arrive soon. She demurs, saying that he should arrive only a day or two before the wedding, not a week ahead.

He undertakes a road trip down a flat memory lane, one highlight of which is discovering that his childhood house has been replaced by a tire store. Ultimately, Warren arrives at his future in-laws' house in Denver. Randall's mother, played by Kathy Bates, is a wild New Age woman who makes the repressed Warren uncomfortable with her sexual openness. The most talked-about scene in the movie, by critics as well as the posters in the forum described in this chapter, is when the middle-aged, plump Bates is shown in a brief, nude, full-frontal shot slipping into a candle-ringed hot tub with her reticent guest.

Warren goes on to try to talk Jeannie out of marrying Randall, but, failing, he gives a dutiful father-of-the-bride toast at the reception. It is apparent that the toast disappoints both Jeannie and himself, because they both know that his blessing is contrived.

ABOUT SCHMIDT MESSAGE BOARD THEMES

As expected, posters were motivated to express strong views. Message board posters across fandom express strong approval or disapproval of popular culture and the people who produce it. In many online venues where popular culture is discussed, postings are tempered with qualifications acknowledging that although the writer mostly likes or doesn't like the subject, factors in the other direction exist. On the message boards of the International Movie Database site, IMDB.com, such qualifications are common.

Frequently, messages on the *About Schmidt* board state fans' perceptions of a mixed bag of quality, even as they speak strongly about Nicholson's acting. In almost all cases in which posters express dislike for the film, they note that Nicholson's performance was excellent, although in a few cases, critics upbraid Nicholson as "boring" or "doddering" and the like. Fans tend to state that Nicholson is, for example, "brilliant" in the part.

The themes that emerge from a close reading of the postings on this message board are concentrated into these categories: approval or disapproval of the slow speed of the film, along with Nicholson's out-of-character performance; approval or disapproval of the film's mislabeling or lack of clarity of genre; and approval or disapproval of the film's portrayal of aging. Positive and negative reactions to both the depiction of aging and the realities of aging abound throughout the board, but usually are linked to or extend from mention of the other major themes. The quotations used in this chapter are typical of the commentary on the themes found among the board postings.

ABOUT SCHMIDT'S DETRACTORS

Most of the film's detractors express boredom with what they see as the plodding slowness in storytelling, disappointed that the lively Nicholson would submit himself to such a nonvehicle of a film. They express disappointment that Nicholson did not rely on the high-concept styling that made him *The Shining*'s Jack Torrance, *Batman*'s Joker, and Melvin Udall in *As Good As It Gets*. In other words, they would have preferred to see Nicholson play Nicholson.

Although posters tend not to identify themselves by age, both
the language used and comments related to generation suggest that
About Schmidt disappointed many younger viewers because its genre
is difficult to pin down. Many of these posters seem almost angry that
the film's promotion depicts it as a comedy when it is actually a darkly
comedic drama, which appears to them to move so lugubriously that
they could not maintain interest. Some writers report that they walked
out of the theater, unhappy that they had spent "good money" on the
cinematic release of what they consider "junk." Others talk about
starting and stopping the DVD until they had dragged themselves
through a tedious experience. This poster registers an angry critique
of the film's slow speed:

BOOOOOOOORING, 1 July 2003 Author: Zoopansick from Ohio

This movie is so boooooring and so overrated. Nothing happens, don't
waste your time like I did and expect something funny or entertaining. There was a TON of positive buzz on this movie and I thought it
was gonna be Jack being funny or something. Boy was I misinformed.
I sat there waiting for something to happen but it never did. Now
maybe Jack was good, but seriously think for a moment. Seriously....
Are you really entertained by a "subtle understated performance" with
virtually no action? If you are then see it, otherwise don't.

A substantial minority of these posters, whose language suggests
that they might be far younger than the characters, express disgust
at the film's depiction of aging, especially as it is embodied through
supporting actress Kathy Bates. Their disparaging remarks about
Bates focus on what they perceive as the grotesqueness of her naked
body, captured in two brief frontal shots: "Pish," writes J-Mclean
from England: "Where to start, I think the Genre on IMDB About
Schmidt is classed as a Comedy/Drama. The closest Genre classifica-
tion I would think of would have to be horror as I am still having
nightmares brought on by the full frontal shot of the character played
by Kathy Bates." A similar post came on January 5, 2003:

movie sucks, its boring, long, and depressing. and kathy bates gets
naked :(,

                                         Author: soe219 from texas

Save your money, this movie is boring, bland, and utterly depressing. The comedy in it is sparse, and the drama is overdone. Also, fair
warning, Kathy Bates bares her breasts in a scary hot tub scene. Not
for the squeamish.

Then, another post:

> Yeaaah, 11 April 2003 Author: Mysterio1337 from Enschede, The Netherlands
>
> Maybe the worse movie i have ever seen. It all starts boring and there is still hope that it will get better cause Jack is playing in it ,but NO!! Its so boring its about the life of a retired guy damn how boring. The only good thing about this movie is that i fell asleep so i did get a nice night rest. There's not more to say about this one. GreetZ

ABOUT SCHMIDT FANS

About two-thirds of these IMDB posters commend the film in one way or another. Among these fans, people compliment the story, Payne's direction, and Nicholson's talent, in addition to other factors. Many of these fans praised the pacing of the movie and how it matches Nicholson's Warren Schmidt:

> Alienated from life, 5 November 2006 Author: Ford-kp from Vienna, Austria
>
> It is hard to recommend About Schmidt to anyone, without actually knowing that person. Not only does the story seem unconventionally uneventful to most of modern audiences, but it also moves with an unhurried patience that will let many viewers shift in their seats. It really depends on whether one can develop an interest to the film and its subject matter, which shows a retired man suddenly facing the void and meaninglessness of his existence. About Schmidt moves slowly, but it moves with grace. The film's success is deeply in debt to Jack Nicholson, subordinating his personality to the character of Warren Schmidt. It must have been difficult for somebody like Nicholson to display the role's required lack of passion without letting Schmidt lose his human touch. Yet, his portrayal is excellent in its understatement, and his numerable supporting actors do not disappoint either. Fans of Nicholson will be assured in their belief, that their favourite is not only one of the best, but also one if the most versatile actors still working today.

A substantial amount of the discussion has to do with Nicholson playing against, if not type, then "being Nicholson." Applause for Nicholson's atypical character portrayal is common among such postings as this one:

> An atypical Nicholson, spanning the emotional spectrum, 7 April 2006 Author: auralgiant from United Kingdom

The actor is known for having forged roles as the stubborn and self-made, shrewd man with an obvious taste for peril, to the downright psychopathic maniacal individual with the devilish eyebrow. But the frailty and 'want-of-love' in Warren Schmidt cannot do anything but open up the heart of the strictest and most cynical viewer, portraying a myriad of emotions with one single glance or old-age crease.... Overall not to be missed, the comical moments are not lacking and in my eye, a new, better understanding Nicholson emerging.

Disapproval by apparently younger fans is by no means universal on the board. Some express delight in the quiet movement of a film that displays a new side of Nicholson, whom they consider a Hollywood landmark. A few tell about watching the film with their parents or other older family members. They remark that the film had awakened new appreciation in them for what these relatives were going through in the aging of a life, or perhaps a signal in what lies ahead for theirs. Here is one example:

> simply beautiful, 24 November 2004 Author: f-main from UK
>
> I was dubious when my 65 year old father picked this DVD up from the shelf at Blockbuster. "Great choice dad!" secretly wondering why I let him pick 2 films out of the 3 in the special offer they had going. You see, my father has a penchant for Woody Allen and anybody who has a rather dry sense of humour, this includes Nicholson. We sat down tonight, and the first thing that hit me was the way that the film was shot. It is shot using rather blue and green hues, so the film is rather subdued. Secondly, the music stands out. Instead of using a typical 'boohoo' orchestra, the film uses beautiful wandering piano and marimba sounds. The characters, I could easily relate to. Helen, the faithful wife who is excited about getting to spend a new chapter of her life with her husband. The husband, who obeys his wife but secretly resents it. A sudden change which causes a rethink in everything he has done up until that point. At first, this appeared to be a comedy, but it was soon revealed to be a beautifully poignant film. Throughout, it questions mortality, what you can achieve in life, and how to cope with loss, or change. I don't think I have ever cried as much in 2 hours as I did during this film, and yet at the same time laughed so hard that my sides were splitting. I would thoroughly recommend anybody to watch this film. It will stay with you for a long time.

Just as the negative posters tend to deride the film's treatment of aging, many of the pro-*Schmidt* fans applaud it. Payne, Nicholson, and Bates, they conclude as a group, demonstrated the dignity, poignancy, and elegance of aging, or at least its potential:

> a tear jerker, 30 March 2006 Author: ofelia from Canada

I loved this movie because anyone can relate to what Jack Nicholson's character goes through. No matter what your age, we all go through periods in our lives where we experience the same type of distress and sorrow and so this movie made me realize something that I already knew but it was basically confirmed. Age is just a number which tells us how long we have been on this earth. It is not an indication of how much knowledge we have or if we are superior or inferior to others. We should not be defined by our ages whether you are considered to be "older," "old," "younger," and/or "young." Tragically, this is not something that the average person may see when viewing this film, they may just see it as a film about an "old guy who goes through life's ups and downs"!!!!

About Schmidt certainly has not been the only American film in the past decade to put a sympathetic spin on aging without growing maudlin. Examples include *The Banger Sisters* (2002),*Calendar Girls* (2003), *The Swimming Pool* (2003), *Revolutionary Road* (2008), and *Julie and Julia* (2009). In a celebrated 2003 role role in something's Gotta Give, Nicholson plays Harry Sanborn, a late middle-aged bachelor with a taste for younger women. Opposite Diane Keaton, Nicholson's character vies with that of Keanu Reeves for the female lead's affections and, of course, wins her over in the end, despite the Reeves character's sincere charm and manners, respectful adulation, and obvious youth. Nicholson's rowdy playboy achieves a state of adulthood as a result of the Keaton character's caregiving following his heart attack. The most referenced bit of physical comedy in the movie comes just following that attack, with Reeves's doctor character questioning the victim in the emergency room about whether he was using Viagra at the time. After a prideful Harry says no, probably because his love interest and her mother (Keaton) are in attendance, Reeves says that's a good thing, since the erectile dysfunction drug could interact negatively with the drug he was receiving for his heart attack treatment. Nicholson quickly jerks the IV needle from his arm, displaying the apparent sexual obsession of an aging man who is facing his own mortality. This intersection of physical vigor and aging is a quirky one as popular culture continues to refigure what it means to become post-young.

What is perhaps most intriguing on the IMDB.com message board, then, is that the majority of remarks about Nicholson's acting and his role in *About Schmidt* suggest that the character is elderly at sixty-six years old. In reality, as Baby Boomers in America rapidly reach that age and beyond at about one every eight seconds,[4] the cultural doorstep of old age is being pushed further to the margins. A mass of people whose identity has been so notoriously linked to youth over more than sixty years is gaining fame as a mass of people who will refuse to get old. The pacing of *About Schmidt*, along with Nicholson's tamped-down, run-down character, belie this tacit cultural expansion of middle age.

The singular thing regarding *About Schmidt* as opposed to some of the films mentioned earlier is that it demonstrates, as many of the posters on the message board write, the strengths and limits not merely of age but of humanity. That can be said of earlier films that probe aging, such as *Driving Miss Daisy* (1989) and *Cocoon* (1985). The distinction for the fans whose posts are found on the *About Schmidt* IMDB.com message board is the singularity of the linkage of aging with Nicholson's outrageous persona. Here is a sample of the remarks made along this line:

> A film you will remember for the rest of your life
>
> 13 August 2005   Author: lulubagley from United States
>
> This would have been an innocuous film had anyone save Jack Nicholson starred in it....This movie is built upon subtleties that not only relate to men approaching the autumn years of life, but to all males in general; at least, I would hope so. Although pretty much a rather low-keyed movie, the final scene bears a poignancy that causes me to give this film 5 out of 5 stars.

Some of the posters express hope that *About Schmidt* and a few other films they name might signal a move from Hollywood away from both disparagement of aging and the invisibility of aging actors in positive roles. In expressing such hope, some blur Nicholson's identity with his role. This is not an unusual leap, to be sure, but in this film is a special case: The singular Nicholson, whom fans repeatedly describe as an actor who plays his own persona in movies, is this time shown in a departure from that persona. That departure has led some of the posters to see Nicholson himself, then, as elderly. For example, AlexDroog71, United States, wrote on May 16, 2009: "[M]an did I love this film! I cried along with Jack, and he knows maybe now that he is an old man and the picture somehow broke him up."

With Nicholson now a septuagenarian, whether he is old is a debatable matter. What is important is that many viewers of the film, perhaps quite young themselves, *see* him as old.

AGING, CULTURE, AND NICHOLSON

Jack Nicholson, sixty-five when he played the sixty-six-year-old Schmidt, embodies a Hollywood audience that spans more than forty years. Ardent film fans, despite their ages, have familiarized themselves with a range of the star's movies that have been classified across genres. Audiences have responded to him as a headlining vehicle when he has appeared in these diverse films. He has represented youthful rebellion, wanton excess, and exaggerated humor. Despite his films' range, however, it became obvious in my analysis of the IMDB.com posters that people have seen Nicholson as largely consistent in his portrayals of dozens of leading-man characters. During the course of my research on this paper, one of my students echoed the comments of many fans: "When I saw Jack Nicholson in Batman, I thought: This is Jack Nicholson playing the Joker playing Jack Nicholson." As so many posters on the IMDB.com forum note, Nicholson performing as Schmidt is a slippery phenomenon. Some fans express strong discomfort with Nicholson "playing against type": that is, reigning in the excess for which he is known. It is worth asking whether many people simply have become uncomfortable witnessing the increasingly apparent mortality of a giant symbol of Hollywood glamour, grinning machismo, and enviable power.

Results of this research cannot stand in for the opinions expressed by *About Schmidt* viewers as an entirety, and their revelations about the posters are limited to the posts themselves. Both those avenues are worth investigation. On the whole, however, it became clear that the majority of the young film fans who post on this board about this movie—perhaps late teens through their thirties, and that is an inference that I consider to be strong—have been disappointed in the commanding star's decision to participate in what they consider a passive role. At the same time, a large proportion of posters whose words suggest that that they are older—perhaps Baby Boomers and beyond—seem comfortable, even gratified, by Nicholson's candid expression of what they themselves might be facing—the threat of erasure of a life.

These observations suggest that life stage identification informs the reception of popular culture, not merely in the sense of what people choose to watch or listen to or how people interpret texts through the filter of their ages. What comes through as especially salient is that popular culture consumers who are growing older in American society might deliberately connect their worries, anxieties, and even their optimism about their future with such themes, subtle or strong, in their representations. This seems especially true when those representations come in the form of a cast of characters that is led by the remarkable and celebrated Jack Nicholson.

A chief question that is raised by the totality of the postings concerns the question of *What is old age?* Several of the posters write of Schmidt as a middle-aged character, but many more noted that he is "old" or approaching or experiencing "old age." A few posters refer to him as "elderly." Most of those who say that Warren is old do not describe Nicholson in the same way. They tend to describe Nicholson as "playing an old man" or "playing an aging man." Again, it's impossible from examination of the postings to conclude whether these distinctions appear along generational lines. I infer from some of the colloquially expressed incendiary attacks on the film ("B-O-O-O-O-O-R-I-N-G!!!!) that are often linked with descriptions of Schmidt as "old" likely come from younger posters, although I am not suggesting that younger posters in general conclude that the character—or star—is "old." Some posters, who appear to range across age lines, suggest that Schmidt is "middle-aged," but it is unclear what these posters intend by these brief mentions, especially as distinguishable from "old age."

The dilemma for me here is whether people (Westerners, as the posters generally are) see sixty-six as middle or old aged. Of course, Western cultures have varying ideal types of ages and generations, but, generally, as increasing proportions of people aged sixty and older are permeating the West, ideas about aging are in flux. In the United States and most of Western Europe, for example, populations are experiencing what cultural scholars of aging have come to agree is an elongated middle age and a late, brief, old age.

About Schmidt arguably positions its main character, and Nicholson portrays him accordingly, as *old*. The story tells of a sudden retiree's realization that his life has meant nothing, and he finds redemption in his connection with a young boy. The conclusion of the film is ambiguous: Does Warren go on to exercise this newfound meaning in his life? Or does he satisfy himself with this redemption as a concluding bookend of that life? Early in the film, Warren's wife, Helen, surprises him in their new RV with breakfast. "This is the beginning of a whole new chapter," she says. That turns out not to be quite so. But it isn't the end, either.

Nicholson delivers what many of the IMDB.com posters decide is a poignant concluding scene. After little expression throughout the story, Warren reads a letter from the nun who has been caring for Ndugu. She has enclosed a stick-figured picture that the boy has colored, depicting himself and Warren holding hands under a young child's typically scrawled sunshine. Schmidt lets loose a cathartic stream of tears when he learns how much he means to the Tanzanian boy. At this concluding point, Schmidt's life stage remains open for debate. And, as some posters note, so does Nicholson's.

Male leads such as Nicholson, among the seemingly larger-than-life Clint Eastwood and Morgan Freeman, for example, will continue to get starring roles despite their extended years (in part because powerful figures such as Eastwood produce and direct their own films, whether appearing in them or not). Whether like-aged female stars will do so is another debate with a preceding scholarly discussion. However, it is worth noting that female actors such as Helen Mirren, at age sixty-five, and Meryl Streep, sixty, are active on screen, even as they remain generally younger than the men they play alongside.

The fine point is how Hollywood will portray these aging actors as the Baby Boomers—a population of 80 million born from 1946 to 1964 in the United States—continue their march into their seventies, and notions of "old age" continue to be moving targets. Moviegoers have in past decades generally witnessed artists in their thirties as prime-aged stars. Kate Winslet, Johnny Depp, and Halle Berry have been three such examples. But some of Hollywood's most talented actors are "getting some age on them." Several, such as Sally Field and Glenn Close, have gone to television and achieved high numbers of regular viewers. Others remain in feature films, and still others have virtually disappeared.

But what of such stalwart Boomers as Bates? It is more likely, I contend, that they will continue to be "bankable" leads into their seventies than most actors who are their elders. Baby Boomers have more disposable income than their own elders, and they spend it. Unlike their parents, the Boomers also grew up on high-volume consumption of media culture. Older male stars such as Nicholson and his brethren aren't Baby Boomers, but that generation has grown up and matured watching their films, such as *Easy Rider* (1969) and *Butch Cassidy and the Sundance Kid* (1969). Nicholson's star cohorts, even including the late Paul Newman, whose roles were popular as he was almost 80, have practically come to be *honorary* Boomers. And Nicholson is one star who attracts moviegoers ahead of the Boomer generation to attend and rent movies.

Much of the criticism on the IMDB.com board is that *About Schmidt* is out of step with Nicholson's screen persona and his celebrity. Such commentary also has been paid as a compliment to his performance in the role. As Nicholson and other celebrated movie stars extend their careers toward and beyond the half-century mark, it is encouraging that young directors such as Payne can choreograph such "out-of-step" performances and keep these actors alive in Hollywood.

Representations of aging in Hollywood film are mixed in their celebration and denigration, so it is easy to argue what truths persist in being told and what new truths are supplanting them. Storytelling and culture have a dialectical relationship, and our stories about getting old come from experience, myth, and the creative process. As a greater percentage of the American population—and, presumably, the feature film audience—moves into the categories of "middle" and "old" age, it will be significant to analyze how the Hollywood film adjusts to this. Especially interesting will be analysis of stars of true "Baby Boomer" age when older actors such as Nicholson recede in visibility. The stakes of representation might lean increasingly toward celebration and away from denigration. Of course, just the opposite could occur, as film slips more firmly into the hands of younger producers and directors and is consumed by post-Boomer generations.

NOTES

1. Henry Jenkins, *Convergence Culture: Where Old and New Media Collide*, New York: New York University Press, 2006.
2. Payne was forty-one at the time of the film's release.
3. Lansbury's voice is ironically disembodied. She has been among the Hollywood stars to rail against what she has identified as an ageist Hollywood production system. It is doubly ironic that Lansbury's performance in *About Schmidt* is uncredited.
4. www.aarp.org.

4

HOLLYWOOD BEYOND THE HUMAN

12

ECOLOGICAL CONNECTIONS AND CONTRADICTIONS: PENGUINS, ROBOTS, AND HUMANS IN HOLLYWOOD'S "NATURE" FILMS

Salma Monani and Andrew Hageman

As Raymond Williams has noted, "nature" is probably the most complex word in the English language with a rich and varied history of meanings (Williams, 1976). In the American context, popular understandings of nature are firmly embedded in the continent's colonial history of European contact with a region purportedly "wild" and open for control (Braudy, 1998; Nash, 2001; Marx, 2005; Sturgeon, 2008). Puritan, Enlightenment, and Romantic ideas weave together to create a polysemic sense of nature as the biophysical world that is both God's creation and Satan's domain, revered and reviled, ultimately exceptional and mythic—both a material resource base and a source for metaphysical challenges and rejuvenation. And yet, these varied and often contradictory views of nature often function through a consistent, dominant idea of nature; what one might call the "received idea of nature." In this received idea, "nature" is invariably imagined as geographic landscape and biophysical place populated with wild animals, and it is frequently perceived as radically other. In particular, environmental rhetoric of "nature at risk" suggests an oppositional tension between nature and humanity, which is often exacerbated by the sense of an ideal-ized nature, or Nature capitalized (see, for example, Cronon, 1996; Buell, 2005; Morton, 2007). Unlike an allegedly corrupt human culture, "Nature" is often imagined as an ahistoric realm, unsullied by human touch.

As myriad scholars have suggested, however, such an idea of Nature as ahistorical, other, distinct, and dichotomous from human culture is paradoxical and problematic. For example, William Cronon writes, "far from inhabiting a realm that stands completely apart from humanity, the objects, and creatures, and landscapes we label as 'natural' are in fact deeply entangled in the words and images and ideas we use to describe them" (1996, p. 20). Enmeshed in systems of human representation, nature is always sociocultural and political. And, within Euro-American ideological worldviews, Nature is often inextricably interwoven with exploitative ideas of race, class, gender, humanity, and animality, all of which have been detrimental to sustaining compatible relationships among humans and between humans and the biophysical world (see, for example, Haraway, 1989; Callicott and Nelson, 1998; Adamson, 2001).

Rather than simply subscribe to the problematic received idea of Nature we seek to disturb the discourse that has become so familiar to Americans and others across the globe via Euro-American sociopolitical hegemonies, including the Hollywood film industry. Cinematic discourse exerts astonishing power, and Hollywood cinema in particular exerts this power ubiquitously in America and transnationally. However, while many films inside Hollywood and out operate through registers of Nature, many, when examined closely, also involve complex structural and systemic aspects that can be recognized as disrupting these registers. In this chapter we examine two recent Hollywood box office hits, *March of the Penguins* (2005) and *Wall·E* (2008) to consider how even those Hollywood films that appear to reinforce traditional conceptions of "Nature" contain contradictions capable of disrupting this ideal. As Pierre Macherey has claimed, "No ideology is sufficiently consistent to survive the test of figuration" (2006, p. 218), and the ideology of "Nature" in Hollywood films is no exception.

At a basic level, a comparative analysis of these films serves to highlight similarities and differences between two popular Hollywood environmental film genres—the documentary wildlife film and the fictional eco-film. Analysis of the representations of nonhuman animal, machine, and human in each film serves to emphasize how these generic films are useful illustrations of what many Hollywood films offer as prescriptive environmental pedagogy. By also paying attention to systems of production, distribution, and reception, we underscore the sociohistorical capacities and limits of each film's pedagogical potential. Ultimately, analysis of these films is critical for understanding the roles Hollywood films play in building, sustaining, and challenging attitudes and practices that engender exploitation, whether the exploited be animal, vegetable, mineral, human, or machine.

MARCH OF THE PENGUINS

La Marche de L'Empereur, directed and co-written by Luc Jacquet, a French biologist-turned-filmmaker, premiered at the Sundance Film Festival on 21 January 21, 2005. Presented as a story about Antarctica's emperor penguins, the French version included voice actors who spoke for the penguins on screen. This version of the film had limited success in its home country, though it did attract the attention of film studios at Sundance who then revamped the film to generate an American blockbuster. *March of the Penguins* is the second most profitable documentary in American history after Michael Moore's *Fahrenheit 9/11*. Its box office success encouraged Disney to launch its first new production label in sixty years, Disneynature. Buying into a potential viewing market, Disneynature capitalizes on a genre that Disney first popularized in the 1940s to 1950s through its *True Life Adventures*. Classified as "blue-chip," these wildlife films provided images of distant wildernesses and animal subjects characteristically hard to photograph in stunningly aesthetic and purportedly educational contexts, suggesting filmic techniques of exceptionally high quality.

In the tradition of *True Life Adventures*, *March of the Penguins* replaces the talking animals of the French version with the baritone, measured voice-over of actor Morgan Freeman and substitutes Emilie Simon's quirky electronic score with Alex Wurman's more soothing symphonic tones. The result, marketed by Warner Independent Films and the National Geographic Society, was a finished product praised as an exemplary blue-chip wildlife film in its focus on the annual migration of penguins from ocean to inland Antarctica and back. Tagged as a story of love and survival—"even in the harshest place on Earth, love finds a way"—the film sold itself as an apolitical story about the breeding and familial habits of penguins. Responding to the controversy generated by the American conservative right suggesting that the penguins were a "natural" symbol for traditional heteronormative love and family values, Laura Kim, a vice president of Warner Independent stated, "You know what? They're just birds" (Miller, 2005). Primarily, *March of the Penguins* was praised as a feel-good movie, portraying a spectacular representation of the received idea of nature—ahistorical, apolitical, and stunningly sublime. Allison

Benedikt of the *Chicago Times* wrote: "It's an incredible tale of ritual and perseverance, both for the emperor penguin and the untouched land, sparkling white, aqua, pristine and brutal" (2007).

However, there is nothing apolitical or ahistorical about the world depicted by *March of the Penguins*. Instead, Benedikt's response is useful to highlight the paradox of the received idea of nature as portrayed in this film. On the one hand, the visuals depict a sublime landscape devoid of people yet inhabited by nonhuman animals, thus suggesting an "untouched land," or Nature. On the other hand, narrated as a tale of familial love and survival, the film overlays this "untouched" world with human cultural constructs that elicit comments such as those of the American conservative right. More specifically, the binary established between Nature (distant, "untouched" Antarctica and its nonhuman inhabitants) and culture (humans) is both blurred by the obvious anthropomorphism of the penguins and paradoxically also reinforced. For example, Morgan describes the penguins as "not that different from us, really. They pout, they bellow, they strut, and occasionally they engage in contact sports" as the camera and soundtrack underscore the comedy of what appear to be rotund, genial, waddling humanlike creatures confronting their social and material world. Throughout the film penguins are made to resemble humans—in the way they make love, in their familial obligations, and in their stoic resilience against the hardships of their material environment (which, in turn, is personified, for example, as "the mother of all blizzards" and the "wind's rage"). However, even as the penguins are made humanlike, the film reinforces the binary of Nature/culture in ways that Jennifer Ladino astutely points out appear all too reminiscent of Euro-American frontier narratives (2009). Freeman's opening words juxtaposed with panoramic and aerial sweeps of Antarctica's vast expanse, state "there are few places as hard to get to in this world, but there are even fewer places that are as hard to live in." When we are finally introduced to the penguins, via an extreme long shot of indistinct, small, yet upright creatures, they are described as a "tribe," "stubborn," and "stalwart souls" against the backdrop of the humanly inhospitable Antarctic terrain. The film pits the material environment against penguin in much the same way frontier narratives pit it against humans. While penguins might symbolically stand in for humans, Nature, as the material environment, still exists as a dichotomous realm.

Also, despite cultural overlays that bring penguin and human into the same sphere, the binary of Nature/culture is nonetheless maintained through a sense of animal-otherness. Specifically, the voice-of-god narrator of the wildlife genre suggests a purportedly objective examination of the animal-other. Accompanying the first in-focus shot we have of a penguin leaping out of the water and shaking itself off on the ice, Freeman conversationally provides some seemingly scientific details: "[T]he emperor penguin is technically a bird, though one that makes his home in the sea. So, if you are wondering what he's doing on the ice, well, that's part of our story." Such factual, "scientific" details enforce a distance between viewer and animal—the penguin is an object of curiosity with which its audience members are obviously unfamiliar.

Essentially, Nature in *March of the Penguins* is multilayered and paradoxical. The combination of factual representation of a species in its environment coupled with the humanlike qualities it is then endowed with suggests that Nature (both animal and its habitat) is distant and other; Nature is also antagonist (the material environment) and yet exemplary as an ideal for humans to strive towards (penguin "perseverance" and "love" are "natural" endowments to mimic).

Environmentally, such representations become problematic when they encourage erroneous information about a species and its ecosystem in ways that can adversely affect both (Mitman, 1999; Bousè; 2000; Chris, 2006). In the case of *March of the Penguins*, the feel-good experience of reveling in Nature might raise issues of individual and familial mortality (as it did with the American conservative right) and it might even spark appreciation toward the nonhuman animal and its environment. However, when coupled with elisions of sociopolitical and historical contexts, such representations may in fact contribute to adverse ecological impacts in Antarctica. For example, encouraged by the seemingly "untouched" Nature on screen, individuals such as Linda Garrison travel to Antarctica to experience firsthand this imagined distant, exceptional, other world. Writing on About.com, Garrison states:

> Penguins rank high in most everyone's vote for the cutest animals on earth. Penguin lives have been chronicled in movies such the *March of the Penguins* and *Happy Feet*. The best way to get a true appreciation of penguins is to take a cruise to Antarctica. (2007)

Yet critics warn that tourist appreciation may be harming the species' survival. In particular, luxury cruise ships such as the one Garrison traveled on are culprits of environmental pollution. Ship accidents are particularly dangerous to fragile marine ecosystems, and maintaining and operating such ships is also potentially harmful (Helvarg, 2003; Copeland, 2006; Goldstein, 2008). Often termed "floating cities," cruise ships create huge amounts of waste; in addition, their diesel engines contribute to greenhouse gas emissions (Copeland, 2006). As evidence for human-induced climate change mounts, scientists and the public are realizing that the Antarctic is one of the most vulnerable environments on Earth (Intergovernmental Panel on Climate Change, 2007).

In addition to cruise-ship tourism, one cannot ignore the effects of the broader consumerist culture bolstered by Hollywood films such as *March of the Penguins*, as viewers are encouraged to express their love for Nature by buying merchandise that leverages and reinforces images of "cute" penguins. Approximately 25 to 35 percent of all revenue for toys sold is tied to licensed or entertainment property, with studios getting a 10 to 15 percent cut from wholesale receipts (Szalai, 2009). Most toys sold in the United States are manufactured in other countries such as China, Mexico, Taiwan, and Hong Kong (U.S. Department of Commerce, 2006), and thus raise additional questions of ecological sustainability and social justice as resource extraction, transport, antipollution, and labor laws all become pertinent concerns.

As one begins to interlace on-screen Nature representations with the networks of off-screen material and sociopolitical contexts in which cinema is embedded, it becomes difficult to endorse Hollywood's prescriptive environmental pedagogy, which in wildlife films is to swoon over purportedly "untouched" Nature without providing any sense of the multilayered contexts that frame it. For example, Alexander Wilson writes that literally projected audiovisually, the virtual world of films "can't bridge the cultural and philosophical abyss between us and what in recent years we have come to call the environment" (1992, p. 122). *March of the Penguins*, with its explicit absence of sociopolitical context and its edited portrayal of penguin life, suggests an especially troubling abyss generated by wildlife films. Its story, beginning "at the beginning"—the coupling of animals to procreate—and ending "at the beginning too, with words like new life, rebirth, hope" (Wilson, 1992: p. 118), can lull its viewers into a sense of comfortable "natural" continuity. Nature, such narratives suggest, is indestructible; it "perseveres" against all odds. If the world is indestructible, then what need for environmental concern? Not only is environmental concern for the nonhuman animal negated, but the allegorical stand-in of the nonhuman animal for human beings similarly distorts concerns for other humans, at its harshest feeding into discourses of social Darwinism, where arguments for the "survival of the fittest" justify social injustices.

Despite these troubling dimensions, one can be cautiously optimistic of Hollywood's eco-pedagogical potential because wildlife films do invite us to consider the nonhuman world and human relationships with it. Depending on the agency of the viewer, such considerations can be surprisingly subversive in their recoding of the hegemonic binaries Nature/culture, Animal/human, and Us/Other. For example, Ladino argues that in *March of the Penguins* scenes of a penguin mourning its dead chick "open up unexpected lines of empathy between viewers and this animal" that, she continues, allow for "species autonomy by permitting nonhuman animals to participate in 'our' [human] affective domain" (2009, p. 68). In effect, traditional hierarchies of what constitutes animality and humanity are challenged even when Nature is touted, and may, in turn, engender more equitable relationships with the nonhuman world. More generally defending Nature images on screen, Sean Cubitt argues, "if we cannot know, we cannot care" (2005, p. 58).

Ultimately, the pedagogical power of wildlife films is their ability to inform human viewers of something they often cannot know otherwise—Antarctica with its penguins is a world geographically distant from that of the average viewer. The cinematic machine brings it figuratively closer, albeit by disassembling, manipulating, and reassembling it into something that *must* be acknowledged for what it is—a representation framed by ideological, sociopolitical, and material interests. Acknowledging the contexts of such documentary mediations exposes the fallacy of Nature and allows an astute viewer to ask probing questions about how Hollywood, itself a production always based on an interlocking negotiation between various components of the world (humans, machines, and in the case of wildlife films, nonhuman animals), might represent the blurring of traditional Nature/culture binaries in ways that might engender sustainable relationships.

To further explore this question, we turn now to *Wall·E*, a fully animated fictional eco-film. While *March of the Penguins* might be thought of as recording the material world into the machine, the diegetic world in *Wall·E* is a digital production rendered through computer graphics. Furthermore, *Wall·E* is set in the future and its narrative focuses on sentient robot protagonists. We focus on this narratives of machines and ecological apocalypse to describe how *Wall·E* provokes readings that recode traditional dichotomies established by the received idea of nature. At the same time we suggest that its commercial imperative to appeal to a mass audience, much like that of *March of the Penguins*, defines its prescriptive environmental pedagogy as inherently paradoxical.

Wall·E

Although director Andrew Stanton has claimed that he didn't have "a political bent or ecological message to push" (Vulture, 2008), *Wall·E* has been widely received as an eco-film. As a story that traces the adventures of the last functioning trash compactor, Wall·E, who is left to clean up a polluted, ecologically devastated Earth, the film participates in a subgenre of postapocalypse narrative, specifically "ecopocalypse." Cinema, from Hollywood to independent, is rife with images of the world's end (see Murray and Heumann, 2009 and Brereton, 2005). From Roland Emmerich's *The Day After Tomorrow* (2004) and *2012* (2009) to the green-remake of *The Day the Earth Stood Still* (2008), the rage against the machines of Shane Acker's animated *9* (2009), and the adaptation of Cormac McCarthy's bleak novel, *The Road* (2009), Hollywood studios are speculatively banking on ecopocalypse translating into big box office returns while fulfilling Fredric Jameson's claim that, "It seems to be easier for us today to imagine the thoroughgoing deterioration of the earth and of nature than the breakdown of late capitalism; perhaps that is due to some weakness in our imaginations" (1994, p. xii).

Wall·E is provocative within this subgenre for the way it reconfigures the ecopocalypse to present a dire message, not simply as a precautionary tale about humans disregarding the effects of our consumer-driven actions, but also as unmistakably cute. Not only does *Wall·E* make cuteness integral to its rendition of ecopocalypse, but it also conjures this cuteness through two figures conventionally coded as repulsive: a machine and a cockroach. Through its prolonged opening of the film before any humans appear, *Wall·E* draws the viewer into the lives of these two embodiments of the nonhuman other such that one might perceive visions of a postecopocalyptic world through these other, anamorphic subject-positions. This technique refreshingly challenges the usual mode of ecopocalypse visions in which the audience observes the world through a single surviving human (*I Am Legend,* 2007) and/or objective camerawork (*Life After People,* 2008/9), both of which generate a privileged fantasy of humans somehow remaining and enjoying a world devoid of any other humans. In other words, *Wall·E* provides subjective presence and points of view after the ecopocalypse but only of nonhuman varieties.

Wall·E's recoding of machines is striking because it comments on a long history of negative representations of machines in their relationships to humans and the received idea of Nature. While Romantic critiques of the Industrial Revolution have, for example, often depicted machines as unnatural, *Wall·E*'s portrayal of its machine protagonists is not of objects that destroy our world but of sentient creatures facilitating connections. Much as *March of the Penguins* imbues penguins with humanlike qualities, *Wall·E* presents its machine protagonists as having emotions beyond their programming. For example, following the opening introduction to the character, Wall·E, with all his quirky interests and habits, Eve, another sentient machine, arrives on Earth. She is violent and driven solely by her "Directive"—the word she utters forcefully at several points in the film. As such, Eve stands in, at least initially, as the standard coding of the machine as something that, even if sentient, is determined by its programming and as such is not human—she does not possess independent will. Ultimately, Wall·E is able to pique Eve's interest in more than her program-determined mission. As a result, caring and contact overcome her machinic parameters in a narrative development of love overcoming the most mechanistic of existences that resonates with the power of love articulated in the *March of the Penguins* tagline: "Even in the harshest place on Earth, love finds a way."

Eve's conversion from violent unfeeling machine to caring sentient machine complements Wall·E's characterization in coding machines as more familiar to humans. These familiarizations of the machines in *Wall·E* reveal fractures in the ways machines are typically depicted in film and conceptualized in the popular social imaginary. The machine can, at turns, be a malevolent force that separates human beings from some purportedly authentic Nature and version of being human, and a utopian force that resolves ecological woes to ensure our survival and enable human beings to reach our species' potential. *Wall·E*'s capacity for revealing these fractures is underscored by *Wall·E*–inspired Internet mash-ups, such as a popular one posted on YouTube that dubbed the audio of a trailer for the original *Terminator* film with the video trailer for *Wall·E* ("wall-e-nator"). The effect of this synthesis is superficially ridiculous yet ultimately unsettling because despite Wall·E's differences from the T-800 Series Terminator, the adjectives about the terminator's implacable pursuit of his programmed mission resonate with the figure of any machine.

That *Wall·E* alerts us to cultural conceptualizations of machines within the ecological context is particularly crucial within the framework of public environmental discourse. At present, governmental and other organizations worldwide are prescribing new green machines as the solution to ecological crises. Thomas Friedman, for example, promotes a green industrial revolution agenda (though with the primary intention of the United States retaining a position atop the globalization hierarchy) in *Hot, Flat, and Crowded: Why We Need a Green Revolution—And How It Can Renew America* (2008). The paradoxical notion that machines may be both a curse and cure for humanity has persistence across such seminal texts as Karl Marx's *Capital* (1867) and Donna Haraway's "A Cyborg Manifesto" (in *Simians, Cyborgs and Women: The Reinvention of Nature*, 1991) to name but two, and *Wall·E* brings this vital issue and its nuances to the forefront of public attention as decisions are being made about how machines may be called upon, as in *Wall·E*, to dig humanity out of our ecological hole.

To explore the sociopolitical relationships mentioned earlier, the figuration of machines in *Wall·E* must be linked with analysis of what the movie has to say about who is to blame for the ecopocalypse and the direction humanity is taking into the future at film's end. By the time humans appear in the film, the viewer has been saturated with the decimated landscape of Earth that humans produced and from which they fled. This narrative casts the ecological issue in *Wall·E* not as a debate about whether or not ecological crisis is possible or imminent, but as a consideration of how and why the crisis already happened. When humans finally appear on screen, the viewer may consider their allegorical potential by contemplating the potential lessons they illustrate linking this fictional world with the world we inhabit.

From their first appearance in the film, the humans seem to invite allegorical reception. The people living in space, far from the polluted, deserted Earth, are represented as obese, lazy, and totally fixated on the personal screens they watch passively. As the humans hover around the ship, consuming massive beverages and audiovisual media, there is in the background an eye-catching sign that reads "Welcome to Economy" with the word "Economy" pulsing subtly. As the setting is the interior of the *Axiom*, the spaceship where the humans have lived for the past 700 years after abandoning Earth, "Welcome to Economy" appears to distinguish between different classes on board the ship, as in the First, Business, and Economy classes, which are part of modern-day travel on airplanes and other vehicles. What is unusual about this association, however, is that the ship does not appear to have any distinctly separate class spaces, at least none explicitly shown on screen. The passengers move apparently unrestricted throughout the ship. But if there are no separate travel class areas on the *Axiom*, what purpose does the "Welcome to Economy" sign serve?

Because it raises issues of socioeconomic class in relation to the style of travel, the sign serves as a subtle prompt for the viewer to inquire about precisely who got on board this ship and how and why that was the case. After all, the passengers all seem to be predominantly Euro-American. In addition, the *Axiom* appears to be the only ship in space, which provides us with a potentially traumatic and significant elision in *Wall·E*. Were those who did not make it into space simply left behind eventually to perish in a *Blade Runner*-esque deteriorating world, or were there only Euro-Americans left alive at the historical moment of the departure? What we find so useful about *Wall·E* is the way its nuances raise such crucial troubling questions without providing tidy answers.

For example, the "Welcome to Economy" sign could also be read as a metanarrative cue informing the viewer that the images on screen are symbolic of how a capitalist consumer-based economy works. As with the travel interpretation, though, this reading is incomplete because the film does little to demystify the mechanisms of an ecologically devastating system; it contains only a few oblique references to economic production and distribution. One of these occurs when the captain checks the ship's status report and the computer announces the regenerative food buffet status is unchanged. A thoughtful viewer is left to ponder why humans were able to design a self-sustaining eco-spaceship capable of functioning for hundreds of years in space but were unable to design sustainable technological societies and remain on Earth in the first place. Furthermore, while the ship is labeled frequently as a Buy N' Large product/service complete with its constant barrage of BNL advertising, there appears to be no labor or employment of any kind other than that performed by the machines; nor is there any corporate competition, thus making the ubiquitous ads superfluous: In other words, economy remains mystified.

As with *March of the Penguins*, the lack of visible sociopolitical contexts problematizes the prescriptive environmental pedagogy of *Wall·E*. For example, its silence regarding how the Earth was made uninhabitable makes it hard to understand who might be to blame— was the ecopocalypse produced by the corporation BNL, everyone who consumed via BNL, a combination of these, or something else altogether? There is no obvious eco-villian. Instead, the film runs the risk David Ingram describes as an "attribution of blame to a nameless and inaccessible 'they,'" which not only suggests a "depoliticization of environmental issues in Hollywood film" (2000, p. 3) but also undermines the film's allegorical potency. Furthermore, the casual inclusion of the phrase "Operation Re-Colonize" as the move to re-inhabit Earth suggests that the humans' actions are still saturated in the Euro-American capitalist ideology that was in place when Earth was initially ruined. There is little reason to imagine that *Axiom*'s humans, despite their fulfillment of the Nietzschean dictum of forgetting, will be any better positioned to manage the curve of history this time around.

Essentially, *Wall-E*, like *March of the Penguins*, provides a polysemic and oftentimes constrained sense of ecological relationships that tends to deflect its audiences from focused attention to sustainability and the problematic dimensions of the received idea of Nature. The conclusion of *Wall-E* is a good example of this deflection as it retreats from the recoded focus on robots to highlight the *human re-colonization* of Earth. Even though the closing credits do not dismiss robots entirely, the sequence provides the viewer with a final paradox. The still images accompanying the credits depict human history basically repeating itself. In this repeated historical trajectory, though, machines coexist with humans from the beginning and the art-history trajectory that begins with a cave painting suggestively stops just prior to the Industrial Revolution in England. In an interview about the closing credits, Pixar animator Alex Woo remarked, "We didn't want earth 2.0 to follow the same destructive path that forced the humans to leave the planet in the first place. We ultimately decided that we would stop our depiction of the re-civilization process somewhere before the industrial revolution" (*The Art of the Title*, 2009). The Van Gogh-esque image of Wall-E and Eve in a garden setting suggests a harmonious world of humans, machines, and animals coexisting, but ironically without allowing the history that enabled these machines to exist in the first place. As such, *Wall-E* contains openings for recoding the nonhuman other that would blur the conventional Nature/human/machine distinctions of the received idea of Nature, yet these openings remain coupled with the hegemonic system of Nature tropes against which they seem to be working.

HOLLYWOOD ECOPEDAGOGIES

The similarity in our analyses of *March of the Penguins* and *Wall-E* suggest that they are representative of how Hollywood productions engage with ecological issues. The concluding position of this chapter is an effort neither to exculpate Hollywood by attending to its complexities and recodings, nor is it to cast Hollywood as a moustache-twirling eco-villain of the film industry. Rather, our position is grounded in the complex notion that all films, Hollywood and otherwise, are determined in significant ways by the economic modes of production, distribution, and consumption that shape not only how we live in the world but also how we narrate it. In other words, to understand how cinema is capable of constructing, reinforcing, and also deconstructing ideological representations of something like Nature, we must analyze the narratives on screen as well as modes of production, distribution, and reception. One need only think of the expansive attention paid to the technological production of James Cameron's *Avatar* (2009) to see that narration and production are fully interconnected and that audiences were fascinated by these connections. And yet, this fascination often appears deeply unreflective about the relationships between the machines, techniques, and the film industry in general in relation to matters of economic and ecological sustainability, despite *Avatar* being a story precisely about unsustainable practices driving these future humans to intergalactic mining expeditions. In this light, we have suggested through our analyses of *March of the Penguins* and *Wall·E* a methodology of ecocinema critique that works to make apparent the less visible elements of cinema when the subject is ecological.

As we show through our discussions of *March of the Penguins* and *Wall·E*, first, this methodology includes analysis of films' influence on public discourse. While it is practically *de rigueur* for high-level Hollywood professionals to claim that their films are apolitical, as evinced by Laura Kim's and Andrew Stanton's remarks earlier, public responses to these films suggest that they do affect social discussion of ecological issues. Whether it is *March of the Penguins* used as "natural" evidence for family values or the Intelligent Design concept, or *Wall·E* being leveraged by "crunchy con" blogs in favor of their socioenvironmental agendas (Dreher, 2008), these films become embroiled in contests over claims to *the* correct interpretation of their messages. Because Hollywood films do indeed play a role in shaping public discussions about ecology, an ecocinema critique must attend to the evidence of any film's discursive impacts.

Second, this methodology includes analysis of films' influence on public behavior. As noted earlier, *March of the Penguins* and *Wall·E*, like other Hollywood productions, drive massive quantities of merchandise consumption, from DVDs and plush toys to tourism (so-called "eco-tourism" and otherwise). In addition to consumption are the ecological impacts of film production itself, an issue that entered mainstream public discussion when global news agencies reported on Thai environmental activists protesting the use of Maya Bay in the making of Danny Boyle's *The Beach* (2000). In that instance, Hollywood's popular status was leveraged to increase the profile of environmental issues, and likely this instance is what has led to popular claims of carbon-neutral film production, as outstandingly illustrated in the DVD extras for the eco-remake of *The Day the Earth Stood Still* and the romantic dramedy *Away We Go* (2009). Furthermore, films can initiate habits like recycling, joining conservation organizations, and seeking further education on sustainability. And it is crucial to note that the behaviors linked with films range along a continuum of sustainability so that rarely can a single film be critiqued as thoroughly ecologically favorable or detrimental.

The final element of this proposed methodology is analysis of the contradictions in films' messages. *Wall-E*'s problematic "Welcome to Economy" and recoding of the machine, as well as the complex and often paradoxical figurations of the Nature/culture binary in *March of the Penguins* are revealing examples of how Hollywood films contain both ecologically progressive as well as regressive elements. What such contradictions reveal are precisely the ideological blind -spots that prevent even the ecologically concerned from fully escaping the social, economic, narrative, and other structures that contribute to our ecological crises. In focusing on the incompleteness of films' messages about the world we inhabit, we can begin to work through any desires for the production of the perfect eco-film that will finally get the ecological vision and accompanying prescriptive remedy exactly right. Instead, we can approach all films for their pedagogical capacity to help us limn the frontiers of our own ability to think and imagine our relationships with the complex ecological structures of the world of which we and our films are part.

REFERENCES

Adamson, J. (2001). *American Indian literature, environmental justice, and ecocriticism: The middle place.* Tucson, AZ: The University of Arizona Press.

Avatar. Cameron, J. (Director). (2009). Twentieth Century-Fox Film Corporation. [Film]

Away we go. Mendes, S. (Director). (2009). Big Beach Films. [Video/DVD]

Benedikt, A. (2007). Movie review: 'March of the Penguins.' *The Chicago Times.* Retrieved September 10, 2009, from http://chicago.metromix. com/movies/review/movie-review-march-of/159561/content.

Bousé, D. (2000). *Wildlife films.* Philadelphia, PA: University of Pennsylvania Press.

Braudy, L. (1998). The genre of nature: Ceremonies of innocence. In N. Browne (Ed.) *Refiguring American film genres* (pp. 278–310). Berkeley and Los Angeles: University of California Press.

Brereton, P. (2005). *Hollywood utopia: Ecology in contemporary American cinema.* Portland, OR: Intellect, Ltd.

Buell, L. (2005). *The future of environmental criticism: Environmental crisis and literary imagination.* Malden, MA: Blackwell Publishing, Ltd.

Callicott, B., & Nelson, M., P. (Eds.). (1998). *The great new wilderness debate.* Athens and London: The University of Georgia Press.

Chris, C. (2006). *Watching wildlife.* Minneapolis, MN: University of Minnesota.

Copeland, C. (2006). *Cruise ship pollution: Background, laws and regulation, and key issues; congressional research service report.* Retrieved September 10, 2009, from http://www.ncseonline.org/NLE/CRS/abstract. cfm?NLEid=153.

Cronon, W. (Ed.). (1996). *Uncommon ground: Rethinking the human place in nature.* New York and London: W.W. Norton & Company.

Cubitt, S. (2005). *Ecomedia.* Amsterdam and New York: Rodopi.

Dreher, R. (2008). Wall-E: Aristotelian, crunchy con. *Beliefnet.* Retrieved September 10, 2009, from http://blog.beliefnet.com/ crunchycon/2008/07/walle-aristotelian-crunchy-con.html.

Garrison, L. (2007). *Ten favorite pictures of Antarctica cruise—Penguins in Antarctica.* Retrieved August 2, 2009, from http://cruises.about.com/ od/antarcticacruises/ss/penguin_photos.htm.

Goldstein, J. (2008). Antarctica tourism: What's in it for the penguins? *National Public Radio.* Retrieved August 2, 2009, from http://www. eturbonews.com/1874/antarcticas-march-tourists.

Haraway, D. (1989). *Primate visions: Gender, race, and nature in the world of modern science.* New York: Routledge Press.

Helvarg, D. (Updated 2003). *Is rise in tourism helping Antarctica or hurting it?* Retrieved August 2, 2009, from http://news.nationalgeographic. com/news/2003/08/0822_030822_antarctictours.html.

Ingram, D. (2000). *Group rights: Reconciling equality and difference. Kansas*: University of Kansas Press.

Intergovernmental Panel on Climate Change. (2007). *Fourth assessment report: Climate change 2007.* Retrieved August 2, 2009 from http:// www.ipcc.ch/?wa=MUSZ0909.

Jameson, F. (1994). *The seeds of time.* New York, NY: Columbia University Press.

Ladino, J. (2009). For the love of nature: Documenting life, death, and animality in Grizzly Man and March of the Penguins. *Interdisciplinary Studies in Literature and Environment,* 16(1), 53–90.

Macherey, P. (2006). *A theory of literary production* (G. Wall, Trans.). New York: Routledge Classics. (Original work published 1966.)

March of the penguins. Jacquet, L. (Director). (2005). National Geographic Feature Films and Warner Bros. [Video/DVD]

Miller, J. (2005). March of the conservatives: Penguin film as political fodder. *New York Times*. Retrieved August 2, 2009 from http://www.nytimes. com/2005/09/13/science/13peng.html?ei=5088&en=36effea48de3fa2 2&ex=1284264000&partner=rssnyt&emc=rss&pagewanted=print.

Mitman, G. (1999). *Reel nature: America's romance with wildlife on film*. Cambridge, MA: Harvard University Press.

Morton, T. (2007). *Ecology without nature: Rethinking environmental aesthetics*. Cambridge, MA: Harvard University Press.

Murray, R., & Heumann, J. (2009). *Ecology and popular film: Cinema on the edge*. Albany, NY: State University of New York.

Nash, R., F. (2001). *Wilderness and the American mind* (fourth ed.). New Haven and London: Yale University Press.

Wall·E. (2008). Stanton, A. (Director). Pixar Animated and Walt Disney Pictures. [Video/DVD]

Sturgeon, N. (2008). *Environmentalism in popular culture: Gender, race, sexuality, and the politics of the natural*. Tucson, AZ: University of Arizona Press.

Szalia, G. (2009, February 12). Hollywood eyes more play dates with toy industry. *Reuters*. Retrieved August 2, 2009, from http://www.reuters. com/article/televisionNews/idUSTRE51C0YS20090213.

The Art of the Title Sequence. (2009). *Wall·E* (+Jim Capobianco & Alex Woo interview). Retrieved September 10, 2009, from http://www.artofthetitle.com/2009/06/22/wall-e/.

U.S. Department of Commerce. (2006). *Industry outlook: Dolls, toys, games, and children's vehicles NAICS code 33993*. International Trade Association. Retrieved August 2, 2009, from http://www.ita.doc.gov/td/ocg/outlook06_toys.pdf.

Vulture. (2008). *Pixar on Wall·E: Environmental themes? What environmental themes?* Retrieved August 14, 2009, from http://nymag.com/daily/entertainment/2008/06/pixar_on_walle_environmental_t.html.

Wetsprocket. (2008). *wall-e-nator*. YouTube online video. Retrieved September 10, 2009, from http://www.youtube.com/watch?v=GP7vZ7GwzLA.

Wilson, A. (1992). *The nature of culture: Northern American landscape from Disney to Exxon Valdez*. Malden, MA: Blackwell Publishing, Ltd.

13

HOLLYWOOD AND NONHUMAN ANIMALS: PROBLEMATIC ETHICS OF CORPORATE CINEMA

Tony Kashani

A Robin redbreast in a cage
Puts all heaven in a rage.

William Blake, Auguries of Innocence

In the first act of the highly popular and successful Hollywood film *Tombstone* (1993), director George Cosmatos introduces the main protagonist, Wyatt Earp, played by bona fide Hollywood star Kurt Russell, arriving in a train. In an attempt to establish Earp's character as a man of justice, Cosmatos employs a horse in his mise-en-scene (the technique of deliberate arrangements of visuals within the scene to create an intended meaning).

First we see Earp stepping out of a passenger wagon, dressed in an Armani-designed suit. The camera tilts up, guiding the audience to project and identify (Kashani, 2009) and embrace a cinematic fact about our hero: He is handsome and confident. Next, Earp notices a beautiful horse (his) in a wagon and an unidentified laborer trying to get the horse off the wagon. The man has a heavy piece of rope in his hand, repeatedly slapping the horse hard across the head to try and get him to step off the wagon. Wyatt Earp walks up to the man, swiftly grabs the rope from his hand, and in an "eye for an eye" fashion slaps him over the head with it, saying, "It hurts, don't it?" After a pause to make sure the point has sunk into the man's consciousness, he tells him, "Let go of that stud and go on about your business."

At this powerful cinematic moment we, as audiences, have moral empathy for the horse. Moreover, the moral status of the horse, a nonhuman animal, is greater than the man, a human animal, who abuses him. The protagonist has certainly assumed as much. To be sure, the horse, a sentient being, has the capacity to feel physical pain and pleasure. The narrative suggests that Wyatt Earp, a cinematic archetype, given his virtuous character, intuitively understands what nineteenth-century utilitarian philosopher Jeremy Bentham, considering humanity's moral obligation toward nonhuman animals wrote, "The question is not, Can they reason? Can they talk? But, Can they suffer?" (1976, p. 130).

In what follows I will offer an examination of Hollywood's role in the representation of nonhuman animals' moral standing and rights. In an interdisciplinary attempt I will appropriate pertinent theories, examine a number of films, and argue for the necessity of a cinema that goes against anthropocentrism (the assumption that human interests are superior to all things on this planet). The cinema I argue for produces potentially transformative ecocentric (moral consideration for the entire ecosystem as a whole, including humans and nonhuman animals) stories humanity can learn from and apply its lessons to everyday living. Moreover, my argument will rest on a tradition that academics have been calling critical theory. It is important to note that this tradition, whether coming from the Frankfurt School or a contemporary independent thinker like Henry Giroux or Jurgen Habermas, is not monolithic. The method of critical theory is interdisciplinary, and its inquiry looks into the morality of the subject. To be sure, there are many critical theories. What sets them apart from the ubiquitous descriptive theories is their objective. A critical theory is primarily concerned with gauging a society's condition and generating thoughts and ideas that can be applied for purposes of social justice. In that spirit, I will attempt to integrate cinema studies with moral philosophy in this concise treatment. Ultimately, I will present an argument that is grounded in moral philosophy and speaks about the ethics of cinema.

MORALITY OF HOLLYWOOD

Taking a cue from Bentham, the prominent ethicist Peter Singer (1975) wrote a pioneering book, aptly titled *Animal Liberation,* in which he established a normative theory, assigning direct duty to human animals to abstain from inflicting needless suffering on nonhuman animals. Given the pedagogical strength of Hollywood and its counterpart corporate cinemas in other nations, I should like to consider the following questions: Does Hollywood practice speciesism (a failure, in attitude or practice, to accord any nonhuman being equal consideration and respect (Dunayer, 2004))? To what extent is Hollywood, with its influential films, providing a speciesist representation of nonhuman animals? And are there examples of Hollywood cinema offering a critical narrative in support of nonhuman animals? The fact that our planet is in need of a transformation is what critical theorist Herbert Marcuse would have called a "given." The human species has been tinkering with the ecosystem, plundering the earth's resources, exploiting nonhuman animals, and inventing weapons of mass destruction. Humankind is essentially responsible for the perilous conditions the whole world and its living creatures are finding themselves in. That is a given. We have also created a value system that is predicated on an economic theory of value. This kind of value system started permeating every facet of our existence once the practice of neoliberalism, more commonly known as a deregulated free market economy, was ushered in by powerful neoconservative agents like Ronald Reagan and Margaret Thatcher. If we apply the logic of neoliberalism (i.e., the logic of the marketplace) to everything, including our moral value system, we simply end up with a condition where nothing has any value. Notions like truth, justice, fairness, beauty, kindness, courage, and compassion are rendered meaningless with this way of thinking.

Has Hollywood played a role in accelerating this paradigm? The short answer, of course, is an emphatic yes. But things like this do not happen in a vacuum, and our tendencies are generated as a result of a complex history. Given that my inquiry in this paper is about the representation of nonhuman animals in Hollywood, I will examine the various dimensions of its anthropocentric paradigm concerning the moral standing and rights of nonhuman animals. Examining speciesism twenty-five years ago, moral philosopher and animal rights advocate Tom Regan (1984) asked a profound question, "Is it possible that species themselves have a kind of value that is not reducible to the degree to which they serve human interest?" (p. 9). As correctly put by Regan, "Most people would deny this." Four centuries ago, the discoverer of analytical geometry and inventor of the thesis "I think, therefore I exist," Rene Descartes (1596–1650) called nonhuman animals "nature's machines," incapable of feeling pain, pleasure, and actually being without consciousness. In a Cartesian paradigm a dog has no consciousness and the noises he may make if a person steps on his tail are mechanical. For so long this was the orthodoxy, dictating that nonhuman animals could not feel or even think, given that they do not have a language—like ours. This thinking is nonsensical.

Speak to any person who has lived with a dog and he or she will tell you about his or her companion's feelings, loyalty, experiences of pleasure, pain, and depression. We now know that nonhuman animals have the capacity to suffer and therefore have moral standing, which ought to yield possession of certain rights.

To be sure, granting nonhuman animals "rights" is the stuff of nonanthropocentric thinking. A significant portion of human beings, on a global scale, accept anthropocentrism uncritically. This begs the question, where does Hollywood, generally speaking, fit in this morally dubious condition? Given the pedagogical strength of Hollywood cinema, influencing its audiences to the extent of consciousness building (Giroux, 2002), it behooves us to look at its ideological films through a critical lens and inquire about the ways in which we may be able to extract alternative readings. As Giroux points out, "Film [cinema] has become prevalent in popular culture as a medium through which people communicate to each other" (2002, p. 6). The power and reach of corporate cinema (i.e., Hollywood), which is intertwined with other entities of globalization, should not be underestimated. Hollywood cinema has the ability to shape or shift paradigms on a global scale. But Hollywood is multifaceted, and although its hegemonic agenda is to create a monoculture for the planet, its filmmakers are human beings with all the complexities of the human condition, which entails potential for radical transformation. I argue that to understand better the complexity of corporate global cinema, which I also interchangeably refer to as "Hollywood cinema," given the industry's interconnection with gigantic conglomerates, we must view it as a system. Moreover, to clarify the ways in which this system works one ought to apply what moral philosophers call "conceptual analysis." So, let us conduct a brief conceptual analysis. Does the system exploit animals? Yes, quite frequently. Conversely, does the system also produce films that can be interpreted as advocates of nonhuman animals' moral standing and rights? Yes, but infrequently. Is the system capable of wielding its pedagogical power towards an integration of ecocentric ethics into our lives? Indeed, it is. Let us explore some examples.

Anthropomorphizing of Nonhuman Animals

There is a great body of evidence to support the claim that Hollywood exploits nonhuman animals. Yet this is a question-begging notion. We might be inclined to ask how does Hollywood do this and, what is more, why? Part of the answer to the first part of this question is anthropomorphism (the attribution of human characteristics to non-human beings). Hollywood cinema has had a long tradition of anthropomorphism, which is deeply ingrained in its culture of narrative construction. As for the why, we can look at the system as an industry looking to make profit derived from "happy" consumers exercising their learned consumerist habits. A system that follows the logic of capitalism looks to exploit all available resources to benefit the capitalists. Who then started the tradition of anthropomorphism? One name that immediately comes to mind is Walt Disney, the founder of the Disney empire. Today, it would be short-sighted to think of the Disney Corporation as merely a business looking out for the interests of its shareholders. Disney is also a behemoth of the culture industry, an enormous ideological institution, enjoying the hegemonic status of America's—and by extension much of the world's—supplier of "moral lessons." It suffices to say that Disney has also achieved the mythical status of protector of "family values," and is beloved by many a conservative human animal.

Ever since Mickey Mouse made his debut in 1928 in the world's first completely synchronized sound cartoon, *Steamboat Willie*, Disney gave birth to what Giroux (1999) calls "animated pedagogy." Walt Disney anthropomorphed a mouse to enable its cultural machinery in teaching kids the consumerist ways of being. When thinking about mice vivisection, for example, those who look at the world through an anthropocentric lens do not see Mickey Mouse injected with deadly bacteria, tortured, and killed. In what ought to be a morally unacceptable speciesist act of cruelty, they simply see "useful" instruments as means to an end that "serves" the interest of humans. In the animal experimentation field there is a common test known as the LD-50. The LD-50 test (LD stands for "lethal dose" and 50 stands for 50 percent) is in essence an oral toxicity experiment whereby 50 percent of nonhuman animals used are killed to determine the toxicity level of a cosmetic product. Typically a cosmetic company will use mice by force-feeding every single mouse the product under test and awaiting the results. This kind of test can last anywhere from two weeks to six months (Rowlands, 2002), yielding data for the "scientists" to consider. All the while 50 percent of the mice die, as expected, depending on the amount of toxic material they digest.

During the LD-50 test these mice, presumably Mickey Mouse's cousins, suffer a great deal. The symptoms are a plenty, to be sure. They can range from vomiting to diarrhea to internal bleeding and so on. At the end of a typical LD-50 test, once 50 percent of the mice are dead and the results are achieved, the other 50 percent are simply killed by the "scientists" performing the tests. To be sure, this sort of experiment ought to be morally unacceptable, even for strong anthropocentrists, because the test has no significance when applied to humans (Winston Miller, 1996). Would Mickey Mouse agree to an LD-50 test? I think not. For many ordinary people Mickey Mouse is the transcendental mammal who is like their best friend, except more cuddly and cute. This is, of course, the logic used by white racists who love their black athletes and entertainers. In their eyes Michael Jordan is not really black. He is perhaps an uber-black?

Similarly, do people who love Bugs Bunny, the anthropomorphed animated rabbit named "the greatest cartoon character of all time" by TV Guide of America (CNN, 2002), question the morality of commercial product-testing on rabbits? Several cosmetic companies conduct a test known as the Draize test, which is named after the American toxicologist John H. Draize, credited for developing it (Lin, 2009). The test entails dripping concentrated chemical solutions into the eyes of rabbits. Rabbits are used for this test because of the low amount of tears produced by rabbits' eyes, allowing the substance to remain in the eye instead of being washed out. Perhaps this is why we never see Bugs Bunny cry in his films. Moral philosopher Mark Rowlands (2002) explains this process in detail,

> You are most likely to fall victim to the Draize test if you are a rabbit or, increasingly, a dog. If so, you can expect to be placed in a holding device, from which only your head protrudes (to prevent you from scratching at your eyes). Then one of your lower eyelids is pulled outwards, and a test substance (shampoo, ink, bleach, oven cleaner, etc.) is placed in the resulting gap. Your eye is then held closed. Perhaps the application will be repeated. Then, you will be observed for eye swelling, ulceration, infection, bleeding, and the like. The study can last up to three weeks. The best you can hope for is to spend the next few weeks in various degrees of discomfort, with an irritated eye that you are prevented from scratching, but it is quite probable that you will spend those weeks in agony. In some cases, you might suffer total loss of vision due to serious injury to your cornea. Then, of course, the obvious denouement: you are killed. (p. 127)

In *Looney Tunes* films (1977–1996) directed by Chuck Jones, Bugs Bunny is the kind of protagonist who is intelligent, self-reliant, and peace loving. But when bullied or threatened, Bugs, the reluctant hero, fights back and always wins. This is indeed a hero formula utilized by the system for many a feature film (Kashani, 2009). Would Bugs Bunny put up with the Draize test? Would Bugs Bunny allow humans to use him as a means to an end? The answer is, of course, obvious, but to what extent is the average American citizen who loves to put Bugs Bunny's picture on his or her national stamp (in 1997, Bugs appeared on a U.S. postage stamp, an achievement that has eluded Mickey Mouse, thus far) concerned about the treatment of rabbits in cosmetic companies' laboratories? It seems, then, that Bugs Bunny's job is to pass down an anthropocentric moral vision to his audiences, and in turn, teach them to make moral mistakes in not considering the vicious speciesist activities by these cosmetic companies under a moral rubric.

It is important to note that due to heavy pressure and much agitation by the animal liberation movement several cosmetic companies have abandoned the practice of the Draize test. In fact, they now have available to them other methods of testing that do not involve using nonhuman animals (Singer, 1997). This is a great victory for the animal liberation movement; however, Hollywood, in adhering to the system's convention of stereotyping activists, often depicts animal rights activists as misguided loonies. Case in point is the immensely popular *Twelve Monkeys* (1995) in which director Terry Gilliam decides to represent animal rights activists as irresponsible and dangerous. It is also important to note that many companies continue this morally reprehensible practice, citing cost-effectiveness and yielding lower prices to their loyal customers.

What if Hollywood decides to make a few fiction films where the protagonists are members of the animal liberation movement and in a melodramatic fashion are able to free not just a token lovable monkey or bird, but a great many species of nonhuman animals? Indeed, what if Brad Pitt played the role of the president of the United States and fought against factory farming and eliminated the industry altogether? In addition, what if such a film was supported by the powerful public relations machinery of Hollywood and released worldwide?

Corporate cinema can and should drink from the creativity well that cinema of the Other offers. South Korean auteur filmmaker Ki-duk Kim's *Spring, Summer, Fall, Winter...and Spring* (2003) is one, for example. Ki-duk Kim's cinema, while anchored in Zen Buddhism, teaches some profound universal lessons about our place in the universe. One particularly poignant sequence teaches about the moral standing of nonhuman animals. In the context of mentor and mentee we see a monk and a young boy as his student. They live in a small house on a raft, which is always floating on a small lake. The boy goes ashore from time to time to learn about nature, sometimes alone, and sometimes under the supervision of the master. One day, while playing in the little ponds, the boy decides to amuse himself with some animals. He ties a string around a fish and a small stone to the other end of the string to make it hard for the fish to swim. Ignorant to the fish's suffering, he enjoys this immensely. Then he does the same thing to a frog and a snake. All the while the master observes the boy quietly and inconspicuously. The boy, of course, does not know that the master is watching him. That night when the boy is sleeping, the master ties a heavy stone to the boy's back. The next morning the master orders the boy to return to shore and free the fish, the frog, and the snake. In a most profound moment of cinematic pedagogy the master tells the boy, "If one of them has died, you will always carry that stone in your heart." The boy is able to free the fish and the frog but finds the snake crushed and killed. This causes tremendous suffering for the boy, who cries uncontrollably for a long time, shown via a vivid montage. This is not just a simple lesson about the injustice of animal cruelty; it is also about the moral equality of all sentient beings.

MARCH OF THE PENGUINS

One of the most internationally beloved films featuring nonhuman animals as protagonists is the French documentary *March of the Penguins* (2005). With a $77 million budget, multiple language narration options, well-known voices such as Hollywood's Morgan Freeman, and global distributorship, including Warner Brothers, *March of the Penguins* fits under the category of corporate cinema. Shot in Antarctica, French director Luc Jacquet's film is a tale about the emperor penguins' breeding cycle. Folks who marvel at the technological evolution of cinema will certainly call this cinematic achievement "marvelous." The film, to be sure, is documentation of an amazing evolutionary event in which these magnificent birds negotiate the cruelties of nature in order to propagate. The emperor penguins can indeed teach us a great deal about our own place in natural selection's evolutionary realm. Like them, we, too, are members of a mysterious ecosystem. In a publicity note on the film's website (through Warner Brothers), Jacquet discusses the environment of the film:

> There are no living cells in Antarctica, and in this white desert, the emperor is the sentinel, the last living element on the planet—assuming we are still on the same planet. Although Antarctica is not yet space, it is almost no longer earth! We are on the border between

reality and fantasy. Emperor penguins, desert nomads...nature creates mirages. All our references are gone, or simply reversed[;] even the seasons are reversed. If you haven't experienced freezing 100-mile-an-hour (162 kph) winds, it is hard to imagine what it is like. (Warner Brothers, 2009)

This is a visual magnum opus and a celebration of the emperor penguins' strength and perseverance. The birds are not harmed by the film crew, and people around the world loved the fact that these penguins are not extinct. So what is wrong with this picture? We have to remember that the medium of cinema is polyvalent and the ways in which we encounter this film determine the power of such cinema. As culture critic Stuart Hall points out:

It is not that the image has a meaning. It is, as it were, in the relations of looking at the image, which the image constructs for us that that meaning is completed. And I'd say the image has a whole range of potential meanings. But the meaning that you as a spectator take depends on that engagement—psychic, imaginary engagement—through the look with an investment in the image or involvement in what the image is saying or doing. (Jhally, 1997: p. 15)

In the most Hollywood version of the film where Morgan Freeman's voice, in the tradition of early documentaries, acts as the "voice of God" (Kashani, 2009), *March of the Penguins* exploits the unknowing penguins to construct a love story much like any other love story told in romantic comedies, TV sitcoms, Hallmark films, and other moralistic tales about monogamy and "family values."

The film opens with bird's-eye-view shots of the continent's majestic landscape. Freeman's voice narrates a brief history of the region, which is concise and informative. Next we see a long shot of the only inhabitants of Antarctica, and Freeman (the voice of God) informs us, "...In some ways this is a story of survival, a tale of life over death, but it's more than that really." At this point the audience ought to be intrigued and curious about these mysterious nonhuman animals and their evolutionary story; however, the corporate filmmakers deliberately take a turn toward artificiality. Freeman continues, "This is a story about love." After a fade-in of the title, superimposed over an image of the glaciers and lighting up in angelic manner, we see the penguins again. To reinforce the superimposed love story, Freeman announces, "Like most love stories it begins with an act of foolishness." The film continues this trajectory, and given the subjectivity and intentionality of the medium, and judging from the film's financial success, we can see that suspension of disbelief is in full force throughout the film. The documentary transforms into a romantic comedy. Penguins effectively become stand-ins for the likes of Matthew McConaughey and Kate Hudson. Although it may be very helpful to see nonhuman animals like us have moral empathy for other members of the ecosystem, this type of cinema is intended to serve as metaphoric rendition of our false consciousness.

One strategy we can adopt for a negotiated reading of this film is to see it without its narration—in any language. One question we can come away with is how can we have moral empathy for the penguins or any other nonhuman animals?

In respect to moral empathy, philosophers George Lakoff and Mark Johnson (1999) offer a conceptual analysis, vis-à-vis the Golden Rule of Christianity (Do unto others as you would have them do unto you). They write,

> The morality of empathy is not merely that of the Golden Rule, because others may not share your values. Moral empathy requires, instead, that you make their values your values. This constitutes a much stronger principle, namely, "Do unto others as they would have you do unto them. (p. 309)

Cinema is capable of generating moral empathy, to be sure. Following Lakoff and Johnson's logic, which I tend to agree with, I argue that if a film superimposes human values on some nonhuman animals, this will only generate moral empathy for human animals who want to believe in the proverbial premise of "love conquers all," rendering nonhuman animals instruments to achieve a human end. We see this kind of phenomenon with the so-called "dog lovers" who participate in the practice of dog breeding, dog designing, and dog owning, where they dictate the terms for "their" dog's existence. One is inclined to conclude that these people are not dog lovers at all, but they love themselves to the extent where they are willing to exploit dogs for their own pleasure. The flip side of this is the condition in which some people go to animal shelters and rescue unwanted dogs, saving their lives. They also provide an environment for the rescued dogs to roam freely and have a peaceful and natural existence.

CINEMA FOR ANIMAL RIGHTS ADVOCACY

It may seem paradoxical, but every now and then Hollywood manages to make films that advocate for nonhuman beings liberation from egoist human authorities. This is usually done with easy-to-digest formulas of bonding a morally upstanding, but misunderstood, human with the nonhuman being that needs to be liberated. A famous example is *Free Willy* (1993), a narrative about a twelve-year-old boy, modeled after François Truffaut's child protagonist Antoine Doinel in *400 Blows* (1959), bonding with a 7,000-pound Orca whale living in captivity at an adventure park. The boy and the whale are two misfits who yearn for true freedom. If read with a biocentric lens, the film can offer a transformative lesson about the principle of equality and the moral obligation of humans to respect the right of nonhuman animals to be free from human tyranny. The success of *Free Willy* generated *Free Willy 2: The Adventure Home* (1995) in which an oil spill and danger of massive ecocide are front and center. And *Free Willy 3: The Rescue* (1997) confronts the immoral act of whale poaching.

In this age of militarism and egocentric thinking, prevalent here and elsewhere on the planet, one relatively obscure film from the 1980s offers possibilities of alternative reading towards antimilitarism and a healthy advocacy for animal rights. The film is aptly titled *Project X* and it is directed by Jonathan Kaplan, who is best known for *The Accused* (1988), a factual feature film about a rape victim's relentless quest for justice, which garnered Jodie Foster her first Academy Award. *Project X* (1987) features Mathew Broderick, who in some ways embodies the "other" kind of Hollywood star. There is nothing ambiguous about *Project X*, and its thesis is clear: Nonhuman animals that are used as instruments to achieve evil ends must be freed from human tyranny, because it is the morally right thing to do. While Broderick is the human protagonist of the film, Virgil, played by Willie (a monkey actor), shares hero duties with him. What *Project X* can do for its audiences, perhaps inadvertently, is to create awareness about the ways in which Americans' tax dollars are spent for military purposes.

If we consider (moral) equality of nonhuman animals, we will be compelled to recognize the "interests" of these sentient beings. I posit all nonhuman animals have vital interests, regardless of their species. They can be humans, monkeys, birds, or horses. It makes no difference—they all have moral standing and interests. The uncritically accepted notion that animal experiments help save human lives resides in the moral mistake category. What is implicit in *Project X* is an ethical statement about military testing of nonhuman animals. There is absolutely no moral justification for exploiting monkeys to test the limits of nuclear explosion tolerance. Although clearly communicating the message of great suffering induced, *Project X* does not show the torturous training of monkeys in great detail, adhering to sanitizing conventions of Hollywood. At this point I should like to fill in the gap to some extent.

Before a monkey can learn to operate a flight simulator he or she undergoes a systematic electric shock treatment designed to compel the monkey to balance the so-called "primate equilibrium platform." The way this works is by giving a monkey close to 100 electric shocks a day to make him or her conform. This torture can go on for days or weeks, depending on cognitive ability and willpower of any given monkey. Once the monkey is well trained and able to pull the sticks, push the right buttons, and steer the flight simulator, he or she is ready to be given a dose of radiation. The training continues with electric shocks and what the Air Force calls irradiation (this part of the experiment is depicted in the film unambiguously). The objective of the experiment is obvious: to obtain data to see if human pilots can endure a nuclear attack enough to be able to strike back at an enemy. To what avail, one is compelled to ask. What humanitarian cause does this experiment serve? The Matthew Broderick character asks the same question, and with the help of Virgil's former scientist friend, played by Helen Hunt, who has taught Virgil sign language, assists Virgil and his fellow primates to fly in a real airplane to freedom.

Twenty-two years has gone by since *Project X* was released. The U.S. military budget is a bloated $713 billion, which is more than the rest of the world's budget combined (Shah, 2009) and the U.S. Air Force continues to use monkeys, dogs, and rabbits in its "scientific" experiments. To be sure, Hollywood, an agent of ideology, practices dubious ethics by rejecting screenplays that advocate for animal liberation. There is an unwritten code in Hollywood that says to its players to exploit resources and do not confront the powers that be, and if you do, do it in a toothless manner, so not to harm the status quo. This is aptly illustrated in Robert Altman's *The Player* (1992) during a historical eight-minute tracking shot (i.e., homage to maverick filmmakers Orson Wells and Bernardo Bertolucci) where Griffin Mill, a movie executive (a player) played by Tim Robbins, listens to a movie pitch by an (unnamed) established screenwriter. The dialogue goes as follows:

> *Writer*: Does political scare you?
> *Griffin*: Political doesn't scare me. Radical political scares me.
>   Political-political scares me.

Writer: It's lightly politically radical, but...
Griffin: Is it funny?
Writer: It's funny.
Griffin: It's a funny political...
Writer: It's a thriller too and it's all at once.
Griffin: So what's the story?
Writer: I want Bruce Willis. I think I can talk to him. It's a story about
a senator, a bad guy senator at first. And he is travelling around the
country and the country is dying.
Griffin: So, it's sort of a cynical political thriller comedy.
Writer: Yeah, but it's got a heart...in the right spot. And, anyway, he
has an accident and he becomes clairvoyant; like a psychic.
Griffin: Oh I see...So, it's kind of a psychic political thriller comedy
with a heart.
Writer: With a heart, not unlike *Ghost* meets *Manchurian Candidate*.

That is indeed modus operandi for much of Hollywood.

CONCLUSION

There is no question that *Homo sapiens* is the dominant species on the
planet. I argue that with this dominance comes a moral responsibility.
In formulating his famous "categorical imperative," the grandfather
of modern nonconsequential duty-ethics Immanuel Kant (1724–
1804) proclaimed, "Act as to treat humanity, whether in thine own
person or in that of any other, in every case as an end withal, never
as a means only." It suffices to say that according to Kant, morality
requires recognition of inherent dignity in human beings; therefore,
it is our moral duty to treat others as ends, and not as means. To be
sure, Kant did not consider the dignity of nonhuman animals. But
Kant was a product of his history (to borrow a thesis from Friedrich
Hegel (1770–1831)). Had he lived today, I hazard a guess, he would
extend his system of morality to include the moral standing and rights
of nonhuman animals. In any event, we ought to appropriate Kant's
moral imperative and treat nonhuman animals as ends and not instruments we can exploit for our own interest.

We have to accept the fact that we, too, are animals and many
things that we do are determined by our biology. As many studies have shown we share close to 99 percent of our DNA with the
bonobo chimpanzee (Wrangham & Peterson, 1996). In many ways
the apes are our close relatives, given the shared genetics. We share our
biology with nonhuman animals. Why not share our morality with
them too? I argue that we have a moral obligation toward our animal

brothers and sisters. What role can cinema play in making this thesis a widespread acceptable norm? Documentary cinema is one form
that can jolt people out of their ignorant comfort zone and compel
them to conduct self-inquiry in respect to their complicity as well as
direct involvement in nonhuman animal exploitation. Two excellent
examples of this type of cinema are *Earthlings* (2003) and *The Cove*
(2009). *Earthlings* (2006) employs Oscar-nominated Hollywood star
Joaquin Phoenix as narrator to tell the story of nonhuman exploitation against a visual background of gruesome imagery. It is prolific
and intense. Ric O'Barry, former dolphin trainer (he was the dolphin
trainer for the 1960s *Flipper* TV series) turned Marin activist, is the
star of *The Cove* (2009), which is edited in montage sequences to play
like a thriller. Associated Press recently reported,

> The Japanese town [Taiji] chronicled in the award-winning film "The
> Cove" for its annual dolphin hunt that turns coastal waters red with
> blood has suspended killing the animals—at least for this week's
> catch—following an international outcry. (2009)

Following the logic of the Soviet master Sergei Eistenstein's collision montage (Kashani, 2009), the makers of *The Cove* collide carefully edit images of dolphins gracefully dancing underwater with the
same dolphins getting speared in a cove by the less intelligent human
Japanese fishermen. The lasting image, which should reside in audience's psyche, is the water in the cove turning red with the dolphins'
blood.

While the power of documentary cinema should not be underestimated, and its presence on our social map is necessary, I argue that
we need fiction cinema to assume the lion's share of ethical responsibility in doing the right thing. A cinema that utilizes the enormous
power of fiction narrative to create a paradigm-shifting consciousness
is a cinema that accepts the moral responsibility it ought to embrace.
Although free-marketers deny this, reality is asserting itself in the
twenty-first century. Changes of enormous ecological significance are
occurring, and our species is solely responsible for them. It is time
for all of humanity to understand that we, humans and nonhuman
living entities, are all in this thing together. Humans have evolved in
the context of biodiversity. In the audiovisual age, considering the
gargantuan pedagogical power of electronic storytelling, we need
cinematic stories that remind us of this fact. Humanity is in desperate
need of a transformation. Cinema is the perfect vehicle to usher in
such transformation. Cinema with stories of egalitarian biodiversity

can help to reduce speciesism, emancipating nonhuman animals. I have asked whether Hollywood respects the moral status and rights of nonhuman animals and if humankind has a moral obligation toward them. Given that the neoliberal paradigm is the dominant paradigm of today, it stands to reason to ask whether Hollywood can go through a paradigm shift and work for the good guys. Only time will tell.

REFERENCES

Altman, R. (Director). (1992). *The player* [Motion Picture]. United States.
Bentham, J. (1976). A utilitarian view. In T. Regan & P. Singer (Eds.), *In animal rights and human obligations* (pp. 130) Englewood Cliffs, NJ: Prentice Hall.
Blake, W. (1783). *Auguries of innocence* . Retrieved October 2, 2009, from,http://www.blakearchive.org/blake/.
CNN. (2002). Bugs Bunny tops greatest cartoon characters list. Retrieved October 1, 2009, from http://archives.cnn.com/2002/SHOWBIZ/TV/07/30/cartoon.characters/index.html.
Cosmatos, G. (Director). (1993). *Tombstone* [Motion picture]. United States.
Disney, W. (Director). (1928). *Steamboat Willie* [Motion Picture]. United States.
Dunayer, J. (2004). *Speciesism.* Derwood, MD: Ryce Publishing.
Gilliam, T. (Director). (1995). *Twelve monkeys* [Motion Picture]. Unites States.
Giroux, H.A. (1999). *The mouse that roared: Disney and the end of innocence.* New York: Rowman and Littlefield Press.
Giroux, H. A. (2002). *Breaking in to the movies: Film and the culture of politics.* New York: Blackwell.
Jacquet, L. (2005). *March of the penguins* [Motion picture]. France.
Jhally, S. (Director). (1997). *Stuart Hall: Representation & media* [Motion picture]. United States.
Kaplan, J. (Director). (1987). *Project x* [Motion Picture]. United States.
Kaplan, J. (Director). (1987). *The accused* [Motion Picture]. United States.
Kashani, T. (2009). *Deconstructing the mystique: An interdisciplinary introduction to cinema.* Dubuque, IA: Kendall/Hunt.
Kim, K. (Director). (2003). *Spring, summer, fall, winter…and spring* [Motion Picture]. South Korea.
Lakoff, G. & Johnson, M. (1999). *Philosophy in the flesh.* New York: Basic Books.
Lin, D. (2009). *What is the Drazie test.* Retrieved October 9, 2009, from http://animalrights.about.com/od/vivisection/f/DraizeTest.htm.
Little, D. (Director). (1995) *Free Willy 2: The adventure home* [Motion picture]. United States.
Monson, S. (Director). (2006). *Earthlings* [Motion Picture]. United States.
Pillsbury, S. (Director). (1997). *Free Willy 3: The rescue* [Motion picture]. United States.

Psihoyos, L. (Director). (2009). *The cove* [Motion Picture]. United States.

Regan, T. (Ed.). (1984). *Earthbound: New introductory essays in environmental ethics.* NY: Random House.

Rowlands, M. (2002). *Animals like us.* New York: Verso.

Shah, A. (2009). World Military Spending. Retrieved October 15, 2009, from http://www.globalissues.org/article/75/world-military-spending.

Singer, P. (1975). *Animal liberation.* New York: Random House.

Singer, P. (1997). *Practical ethics.* New York: Cambridge University Press.

Truffaut, F. (Director). (1959). *400 blows* [Motion picture]. France.

Warner Brothers. March of penguins/Publicity. Retrieved October 1, 2009, from http://marchofpenguinsthemovie.warnerbros.com/.

Winston Miller, D.L. (1996). *The LD50 test: A failure of Extreme, but Measurable, proportions.* Retrieved October 9, 2009, from http://zunny.com.

Winser, S. (director). (1993). *Free Willy* [Motion picture]. United States.

Wrangham, R.W. & Peterson, D. (1996). *Demonic males: Apes and the origins of human violence.* Boston, MA: Houghton Mifflin.

CONTRIBUTORS

Carl Boggs is the author of numerous books in the fields of contemporary social and political theory, European politics, American politics, U.S. foreign and military policy, and film studies, including *The Impasse of European Communism* (1982), *The Two Revolutions: Gramsci and the Dilemmas of Western Marxism* (1984), *Social Movements and Political Power* (1986), *Intellectuals and the Crisis of Modernity* (1993), *The Socialist Tradition* (1996), and *The End of Politics: Corporate Power and the Decline of the Public Sphere* (Guilford, 2000). With Tom Pollard, he authored *A World in Chaos: Social Crisis and the Rise of Postmodern Cinema*, published by Rowman and Littlefield in 2003. He edited an anthology, *Masters of War: Militarism and Blowback in an Era of American Empire* (Routledge, 2003). He is the author of *Imperial Delusions: American Militarism and Endless War* (Rowman and Littlefield, 2005). A new book, *The Hollywood War Machine: Militarism and American Popular Culture* (co-authored with Tom Pollard), was released by Paradigm Publishers in 2006. He is currently finishing a book titled *Crimes of Empire: How U.S. Outlawry Is Destroying the World*. He is on the editorial board of several journals, including *Theory and Society* (where he is book-review editor) and *New Political Science*. For two years (1999–2000) he was Chair of the Caucus for New Political Science, a section within the American Political Science Association. In 2007 he was recipient of the Charles McCoy Career Achievement Award from the American Political Science Association. He has written more than 200 articles, along with scores of book and film reviews, has had three radio programs at KPFK in Los Angeles, and was a political columnist for the *L.A. Village View* during the 1990s. After receiving his PhD in political science at University of California, Berkeley, he taught at Washington University in St. Louis, UCLA, USC, UC, Irvine, and Carleton University in Ottawa. For the past twenty years he has been professor of social sciences at National University in Los Angeles, and more recently has been an adjunct professor at Antioch University in Los Angeles.

Benjamin Frymer is assistant professor of sociology in the Hutchins School of Liberal Studies, Sonoma State University, co-director of the Modern Media Project and organizer of the Modern Media Dialogue Series at Sonoma State University. He works in the areas of critical theory, youth, education, media, and cultural studies focusing on contemporary alienation. His publications include co-editing the book *Cultural Studies, Education, and Youth: Beyond Schools* (forthcoming, Lexington Books), an analysis of the Frankfurt School's contributions to the study of modern education, and several pieces on the Columbine High School shootings.

David Gumaro García is an assistant professor at the University of California, Los Angeles Graduate School of Education and Information Studies. His research and teaching examines the interconnectivity of history and education, focusing on local educational histories of Mexican Americans, the pedagogy of Hollywood's urban school genre, and Chicana/o *teatro* (theater) as public revisionist history. García's research is published in journals and books such as *Qualitative Inquiry, Handbook of Latinos and Education*, and *Radical History Review.*

Lawrence Grossberg is the Morris Davis Distinguished Professor of Communication Studies and Cultural Studies, adjunct distinguished professor of anthropology, and the director of the University Program in Cultural Studies at the University of North Carolina at Chapel Hill. He has won numerous awards from the National Communication Association and the International Communication Association, as well as the University of North Carolina Distinguished Teaching Award (for post-baccalaureate teaching). He has been the co-editor of the international journal *Cultural Studies* for over fifteen years. He has written extensively about the philosophy and theory of culture and communication, and the interdisciplinary practice of cultural studies. His research focused for many years on American popular music and youth culture, but his recent work has turned to the contemporary U.S. political culture and the global struggle over the possible ways of being modern. His work has been translated into a dozen languages. His most recent books include *Caught in the Crossfire: Kids, Politics and America's Future* (Paradigm, 2005), *New Keywords: A Revised Vocabulary of Culture and Society* (with Tony Bennett and Meaghan Morris, Blackwells, 2005), and *Media Making: Mass Media in a Popular Culture* (with Ellen Wartella, D. Charles Whitnemy and MacGregor Wise, Sage, 2005). He has also recently published essays on the state and futures of cultural studies, Richard Hoggart,

James Carey, Stuart Hall, theory at the CCCS, and the possibility of other "modernities." His current projects include a critical examination of how cultural studies can respond to the present contexts (*Bad Stories Make Bad Politics: Cultural Studies and the Challenge of the Contemporary*), including an interrogation of the concepts of modernities, economies, and the popular.

Andrew Hageman is a doctoral candidate in the English Department at the University of California, Davis. His research focuses on intersections of machines, ecology, and ideology in literature, cinema, and critical theory. He has published ecocritical film analyses of David Lynch's *Mulholland Drive* in the journal *Scope* and Lou Ye's *Suzhou River* in the edited volume *Chinese Ecocinema*, as well as the essay "When Nature Calls: Or, Why Ecological Criticism Needs Althusserian Ideology" in the journal *Polygraph*.

Caroline K. Kaltefleiter is coordinator of women's studies and associate professor of communication studies at the State University of New York College at Cortland. She has over twenty years of broadcast activism experience as a news anchor and producer for public and community radio stations in Texas, Georgia, Ohio, and New York. She served as producer and director of the documentary "Burn Out in the Heartland," a 60-minute piece that investigates the crystal methamphetamine culture among teens in Iowa and Nebraska. She continues to work on radio documentaries for National Public Radio and anchors a radio program titled *The Digital Divide* on public radio station *WSUC-FM*. She received her PhD from Ohio University in communication and women's studies. She holds an MA from Miami University and participated in the Center for Cultural Studies, where she began her research on youth subcultures and activism, including work on youth culture capitalism, post-feminism, and popular culture. Her forthcoming text (Garland Press) *Revolution Girl Style Now: Trebled Reflexivity and the Riot Grrrl Network*, examines the girl feminist movement and its use of alternative media forums such as 'zines, websites, and MP3 musical recordings. Her current research project articulates cyberfeminism within a discourse of new media studies. The project examines the construction, manipulation, and redefinition of women's lives within contemporary technoscientific cultures.

Tony Kashani is faculty in the Ph.D. program in Interdisciplinary Studies at Union Institute & University. He is co-director of the Modern Media Project at Sonoma State University.and a scholar member of GSA (Global Studies Association). Aside from many scholarly articles, Dr. Kashani is the author of two editions of *Deconstructing the Mystique: An Interdisciplinary Introduction to Cinema* (Kendall/ Hunt Press), and has recently completed his latest book manuscript, *Cinema for Social Change: The Logic and Politics of Cinema in the Planetary Age* (forthcoming, Edwin Mellen Press). Presently he is co-editing *Lost in Media: Ethics of Everyday Life* (Peter Lang Press, forthcoming). He has collaborated with the world-renowned theorist of pedagogy Henry A. Giroux and the long-time Native American feminist scholar/activist Annette Jaimes-Guerrero in projects regarding media pedagogy and representation of Native American women in the media. A trilingual interdisciplinary thinker whose work is anchored in critical theory, Tony Kashani is an Iranian American. He believes in appropriating theory for practice toward achieving social justice. On a personal level, an accomplished athlete, he is committed to achieving a balance within the "mind-body-spirit" complex. He lives with his family in San Francisco. His website is www. tonykashani.com.

Douglas Kellner is George Kneller Chair in the Philosophy of Education at UCLA and author of a large collection of books and articles on social theory, politics, history, and culture, including *Media Culture* and *Media Spectacle*; a trilogy of books on postmodern theory with Steve Best; the editor of a series of Herbert Marcuse's work; and a trilogy of books on the Bush administration, including *Grand Theft 2000, From 9/11 to Terror War,* and his latest text, *Media Spectacle and the Crisis of Democracy*. He lectures and presents at conferences across the United States and throughout the world, and is considered one of the leading critical theorists in the country today. His website is http://www.gseis.ucla.edu/faculty/kellner.

Toby Miller is chair of the Department of Media and Cultural Studies at University of California, Riverside. His research interests include film and TV, radio, new media, class, gender, race, sport, cultural theory, citizenship, social theory, cultural studies, political theory, cultural labor, and cultural policy. He is editor of *Television & New Media* and *Social Identities*, editor of the book series *Popular Culture and Everyday Life* (Lang); he has also been chair of the International Communication Association Philosophy of Communication Division; editor of *Journal of Sport & Social Issues*; and co-editor of *Social Text*, the *Blackwell Cultural Theory Resource Centre*, and the book series *Sport and Culture* (Minnesota) *Film Guidebooks* (Routledge) and *Cultural Politics* (Minnesota). Miller is the author of numerous books, including *The Well-Tempered Self: Citizenship, Culture, and*

*the Postmodern Subject, Technologies of Truth: Cultural Citizenship
and the Popular Media, SportSex,* and his latest, *Cultural Citizenship.*
Miller has taught media and cultural studies across the humanities
and social sciences at the following schools: University of New South
Wales, Griffith University, Murdoch University, and NYU.

Salma Monani, PhD, is a new assistant professor at Gettysburg
College. A graduate of the University of Minnesota, her dissertation
was entitled *Nature Films and the Challenge of Just Sustainability.*
She has authored a number of articles examining the ways in which
film's visual and scripted rhetoric work to advance or undermine ethics of environmental justice and sustainability. She currently serves as
film review editor for the journal *Green Theory & Praxis: The Journal
of Ecopedagogy.*

Anthony J. Nocella II is completing his doctoral work at Syracuse
University and is a professor in sociology and criminology at SUNY
Cortland and Le Moyne College. He is also a life skills teacher at
Hillbrook Youth Detention Facility, where he is the editor of a poetry
book series "Poetry Behind the Walls," which can be found at the
online journal *Social Advocacy and Systems Change.* His areas of inter-
est include disability studies, critical animal studies, critical/green
criminology, critical/eco-pedagogy, and anarchist studies. He is a co-
founder of more than fifteen active political organizations, including
Institute for Critical Animal Studies (ICAS), Outdoor Empowerment
(OE), Save the Kids (STK), and Sacco and Vanzetti Foundation, and
four scholarly journals, which include *Green Theory & Praxis, Peace
Studies Journal, Journal on Critical Animal Studies,* and *Journal on
Terrorism and Security.* He is a board member of the American Friends
Service Committee (AFSC) and has published more than twenty-five
scholarly articles, and is working on his eleventh book, co-edited with
Richard Kahn, *Greening the Academy: Environmental Studies in the
Liberal Arts* (forthcoming, Syracuse University Press). His other books
include *Contemporary Anarchist Studies: An Introductory Anthology
of Anarchy in the Academy* (Routledge, 2009), *Academic Repression:
Reflections from the Academic Industrial Complex* (AK Press, 2010),
A Peacemaker's Guide for Building Peace with a Revolutionary Group
(PARC, 2004), co-editor with Steve Best, *Terrorists or Freedom
Fighters? Reflections on the Liberation of Animals* (Lantern Books,
2004), and, with Steve Best, *Igniting a Revolution: Voices in Defense
of the Earth* (AK Press, 2006). His site is www.anthonynocella.org.

Karen E. Riggs is a professor in the School of Media Arts and Studies
at Ohio University. She teaches undergraduate courses in media

studies and graduate courses in cultural studies, qualitative methods, and the Digital Divide. Her research focuses on media and age. She has published two books: *Granny @ Work: Age and Technology on the Job in America* (Routledge, 2004) and *Mature Audiences: Television in the Lives of Elders* (Rutgers University Press, 1998). She is also the author of several refereed journal articles, book chapters, and conference papers. Riggs's current project is a third book, *Groovin': Baby Boomers, Identity, and Marketing*. This book will explore the Baby Boomers' influence on the changing confluence of marketing practices and cultural definitions of aging. It treats such topics as Botox, Viagra, classic rock, packaged nostalgia, and revolutionary practices of the American funeral industry. The project analyzes how the marketing industry is "selling Boomers to themselves" through techniques including the use of nostalgic touchstones intended for the purpose of Boomers' vicarious consumption through their children, such as hula hoops, Nick at Nite reruns, and Bruce Springsteen downloads. Riggs is former director of the School of Media Arts and Studies, and was founding director of the Game Research and Immersive Design (GRID) Lab.

Michael A. Raffanti has a varied professional background in education and social justice. A California native, he completed his bachelor of arts in history and philosophy at the University of Portland, and his juris doctor at Boston College Law School. He also holds a master in teaching degree from The Evergreen State College, where he focused on multicultural education. He earned his doctor of education degree from Fielding Graduate University. Michael became interested in an educational career while practicing poverty law in San Francisco. His involvement in developing a law academy at an urban high school precipitated Michael's movement from law to education. While earning his teaching license, he directed the education department of an AIDS service organization and developed HIV prevention programs for adolescents, gay and bisexual men, and communities of color. Michael has taught third grade in urban settings and served in a variety of educational leadership roles. He also taught at-risk high school students in a weekend community college program. A scholar-practitioner, Michael's research interests are interdisciplinary, with particular emphases on diversity, systems change, and multicultural education. Michael lives in the Pacific Northwest with his partner, and is an avid tennis player, world traveler, and animal rescuer.

Shoba Sharad Rajgopal is the director of the Women's Studies Program at Westfield State College in the Department of Ethnic and

Gender Studies, where she teaches courses pertaining to gender, race, and representation. Her PhD is in media studies from the University of Colorado's School of Journalism and Mass Communication. She has an interdisciplinary graduate certificate in women's studies as well as two master's degrees, and speaks five languages. Prior to her arrival in the United States, she worked for seven years as a broadcast journalist for the Indian TV networks based in Bombay (Mumbai), India, and has also done in-depth news reports for CNN International. Her journalistic work focused on the struggles of women and indigenous peoples in the postcolonial nation-state. Her academic research areas are cultural studies, feminist postcolonial and transnational theory, grassroots movements for social justice, Asian diasporic identities, South Asian cinema, globalization, and international ethnic studies.

Shirley R. Steinberg is associate professor at McGill University in the Department of Integrated Studies in Education. She is the author and editor of many books and articles in cultural studies, including *Media Literacy: A Reader* (2007), *Teen Life in Europe* (2005), *Contemporary Youth Culture: An International Encyclopedia* (2005), *Kinderculture: The Corporate Construction of Childhood* (2004), *The Miseducation of the West: How Schools and the Media Distort Our Understanding of the Islamic World* (2004), and *Adolescent Culture, Knowledge, and Gender in Contemporary Film and Music* (2004). A former theatre director, Shirley is a contributor to *The Globe and Mail* and the *Montreal Gazette* as a cultural critic. She holds a PhD in cultural studies from Pennsylvania State University.

Richard Van Heertum is visiting assistant professor of education at CUNY/College of Staten Island, teaching classes in the Education and History Departments. He recently completed his PhD in education and cultural studies at the University of California, Los Angeles, where his dissertation focused on cynicism and democracy. He previously earned a master's in economics from San Diego State University. He has published over twenty academic essays, including works in *Policy Futures in Education, Interactions, McGill Journal of Education*, and a number of anthologies, and has presented his research at numerous conferences and public lectures. He has also published extensively in the popular press, with over 120 articles on music, movies, the arts, and politics (*The San Diego Union Tribune, San Diego Reader, Slamm Magazine* (ex-staff writer), *Asbury Bay Press, Style Weekly*, and *LA Weekly*). He served as program officer of the Paulo Freire Institute at UCLA, and as one of the primary editors for a book on the politics of aging by noted UCLA public policy professor Fernando Torres-Gil. He is co-editing a book series with Bentham *Educating the Global Citizen*.

Tara J. Yosso is an associate professor in the Department of Chicana and Chicano Studies at the University of California, Santa Barbara. Her teaching and research examine educational access and equity through a critical race theory framework, emphasizing the community cultural wealth Students of Color bring to schools. In addition to her book, *Critical Race Counterstories along the Chicana/Chicano Educational Pipeline*, (Routledge, 2006), Yosso's research is published in journals such as *Race Ethnicity and Education*, *Harvard Educational Review*, and *Journal of Popular Film and Television*.

INDEX

#

7th Heaven, 55–56
16 and Pregnant, 171, 173,
    182–185
300, 111, 125

A

Aasen, Erik, 172
ableism, 106–107, 111–112
abortion, 180, 182
About Schmidt, 189–191, 196, 198
    negative responses, 191–193
    positive responses, 193–196
Aldama, Arturo, 116
animal abuse, 225–226, 230
Another Day in Paradise, 161–162
anthropocentricism, 220, 222,
    224–225
anthropomorphism, 206, 222–226,
    219–220, 223, 227–228
anti-war cinema, 21
Anzaldua, Gloria, 119
Attali, Jacques, xviii
Avatar, 215

B

The Baby Borrowers, 171, 173, 182
Benedikt, Allison, 206
Bentham, Jeremy, 220
Berg, Peter, 17
Bjork, 75
Blake, William, 219
The Blind Side, 62–63
Boggs, Carl, 5, 13–28, 120,
    127, 235
Brokeback Mountain, 131, 135–137

backlash, 137–139
Bruno, 142–144
Bully, 162–163

C

Campbell, Richards, 121
Candies Foundation, 184–186
capital punishment, 66–67,
    70–72, 76
Chaplin, Charlie, 1
Charlie Wilson's War, 22
Chomsky, Noam, 120
Christonormatized, 45–46, 54
    Christotainment, 52–63
    see also Left Behind, Revelations
Clark, Larry, 158, 167–168
    *see also Ken Park, Kids, Teenage
    Caveman, Wassup Rockers*
Clover, Carol, 68, 70–71
Cohen, Sacha, 121
colonial gaze, 116–119, 121–123,
    125–127
counter-hegemony, 3
    independent films, 134–135
    youth films, 156–157, 168
The Cove, 232
Crash, 123
Cronon, William, 203–204
The Cross and the Switchblade,
    59–60
Cubitt, Sean, 209

D

Dangerous Minds, 88–92
Dead Man Walking, 72–78
dependencia theory, xvi

Descartes, Rene, 221
Disney, 14, 223
    Disneynature, 205
Dittmars, Linda, 30, 43
Draize test, 224–225
Dyer, Richard, 116

E
ecocentric, 220, 231–232
ecopedagogy, 204, 208, 210,
    213–216, 232–233
ecopocalypse, 210–213
Eisenstein, Zillah, 117
Euro-American ideology, 204, 206,
    213–214
Eurocentrism, xv, 115–116

F
Facing the Giants, 61
Fernandes, Deepa, 119
*Fight for Your Rights
    Campaign*, 175, 178
Flywheel, 60–61
Frankfurt School, 2, 4, 120, 220
Franklin, Bruce, 24
Freedom Writers, 92–97
Frymer, Ben, 1–10, 236

G
García, David
    Gumaro, 6, 85–103, 236
General Electric, 14
Giroux, Henry A., i, 2, 4, 73,
    117–118, 157
Giroux, Susan S., i
Gone Baby Gone, 36–39
Good Will Hunting, 39–42
Gramsci, Antonio, 15, 133
Grossberg, Lawrence, xiii–xiv, 2,
    236–237

H
Habermas, Jurgen, 220
Hageman,
    Andrew, 8, 203–218, 237
Hall, Stuart, 179–180, 227

hegemony, xvi
    colonial discourse, 117
    cultural, 2–3, 14–16,
        30–31, 43, 132–135,
        144–146, 222
    see also ableism,
        Christonormatized,
        masculinity, racial
        microaggressions
    compare counter-hegemony
Highway to Heaven, 54
A History of Violence, 70
Hollywood, xiii–xiv, xviii, 1
    aging films, 190–192, 195,
        199–200
    animal activists, 225
    animal advocacy, 229
    crime films, 68
    cultural influence, 1–2
    juvenile delinquency, 153–155
    minority representation, 116–118,
        121–123, 125–127
    portrayal of queer
        culture, 136–138
    pro-military, 17–20, 26–28
    propaganda distributor, 26
    urban school genre, 87–88
    working class
        representation, 29, 30–42
    see also Indiewood
Home of the Brave, 17
Hometown Legend, 60

I
*I Now Pronounce You Chuck and
    Larry*, 139–140
independent films, 134–135
*Indiana Jones and the Temple of
    Doom*, 118–119
Indiewood, 132, 134–135, 137,
    141, 145
Ingram, David, 213
The Internet, 4
    International Movie Database,
        189, 191–197
    You-tube, xviii

J
Jacquet, Luc, 226–227
Jameson, Fredrick, 3, 210
Jarecki, Eugene, 27–28
Joan of Arcadia, 56–57
Johnson, Mark, 228
Juno, 171, 173, 178–183, 185

K
Kaltefleiter, Caroline, 171–188, 237
Kant, Immanuel, 231
Kashani, Tony, 1–10, 105–114,
    126, 219–234, 237–238
Kellner, Douglas, 7, 16, 43, 66,
    153–169, 238
Ken Park, 165–166
Kids, 158–160
Kim, Laura, 205, 215
Kissinger, Henry, xviii
Knight, Charles, xv
Knox, Shelby, 174–178
    The Education of Shelby Knox,
    173, 175–177, 186

L
Ladino, Jennifer, 206, 209
Lakoff, George, 228
LD-50 test, 223–224
Left Behind, 47–49, 52–53

M
MacDonald, Dwight, 29
Macherey, Pierre, 204
Maira, Sunaina, 119–120
Manifest Destiny, 14
*March of the
    Penguins*, 204–210, 226
Marcuse, Herbert, 3, 132–133, 221
masculinity, 135–136
McChesney, Robert, 120
McClintock, Anne, 119
media culture, 2, 15
Melville, Herman, xv
mestizaje, 119
militarism, 13–15, 17–20, 22–28
    military-industrial complex, xvi

Milk, 140–142
Miller, Toby, xv–xix, 238–239
Monani, Salma, 8, 203–218, 239
Monomyth, 36, 70–71
My Super Sweet Sixteen, 182
Mystic River, 33–36, 70

N
Nature/culture binary, 203–216
neoliberalism, xvi, 1, 9, 110,
    113, 221
    see also hegemony
New World Information and
    Communication Order
    (NWICO), xvi–xvii
News Corporation, 14
Nicholson, Jack, 189, 193, 195–197
Nocella II, Anthony, 1–10,
    105–114, 239
Not Without My Daughter, 125–126

O
old age, 197–200
Olson, Kay, 110

P
Palin, Bristol, 171, 182, 184–186
pedagogy, xiii, 220
    public, 2, 4–5, 232
    see also ecopedagogy
Playboy Foundation, 176–177
Pollard, Tom, 13, 120, 127
Pretty In Pink, 32–33
prison-industrial complex, 65
Project X, 229–230

R
racial microaggressions, 85–86,
    89–98
    *see also Dangerous Minds,
    Freedom Writers*
racism, 119–120
Raffanti, Michael, 7, 131–149, 240
Rain Man, 108
Rajgopal, Shoba, 115–129,
    240–241

Rambo movies, 18–21, 23–25
Reeves, Jimmy, 121
Regan, Tom, 221
Revelations, 49–53
revenge justice, 68–71
Riggs, Karen, 7, 189–200, 239–240
Robb, David, 26–27
Ross, Steven, 29
Rowlands, Mark, 224

S
Said, Edward, 119, 121, 125
Schwarzenegger, Arnold, 70–71
Scott, A.O., 20, 35, 180
sex education, 173–178, 185–186
Share, Jeff, 43
Shockley, William, xv
Shohat, Ella, 115
Singer, Peter, 220
Smith, Sydney, xv
Spears, Jamie Lynn, 171, 182, 185
speciesism, 221, 223
Spring, Summer, Fall, Winter...and Spring, 225–226
Steinberg, Shirley, 5–6, 45–64, 241
Syriana, 124–125

T
teen
   parenthood, 171, 173, 181, 185
   pregnancy, 171, 174–176, 178, 181–182, 184–186
   sexuality, 173, 177, 179, 185, 185–186
Teenage Caveman, 163–164
Texas
   Amarillo, 172–174
   Lubbock, 174–178
   Panhandle, 172–174

Time-Warner, 14
Tiptoes, 109
Tombstone, 219–220
Touched by an Angel, 54–55
Tropic Thunder, 108–109

U
United States
   early media, xv
   international media influence, xvi–xviii
   TV drama sales, xvii

V
Van Heertum, Richard, 1–10, 29–44, 65–81, 241–242
vanguardism, xiii
Viacom, 14
Vietnam Syndrome, 18, 24
The Visitor, 123–124

W
Wall·E, 204, 209–216
Wassup Rockers, 167
Williams, Raymond, 203
Willis, Jessica, 179, 181
Wilson, Alexander, 208
World Trade Center, 62

X
X-Men, 110–111

Y
Yosso, Tara, 6, 85–103, 242
youth films, 156–157, 168

Z
Zavarzadeh, Mas'ud, 30
Zurawick, David, 183